Knowing Silence

How Children
Talk about
Knowing Silence
Immigration
Status in School

Ariana Mangual Figueroa

University of Minnesota Press
Minneapolis
London

The University of Minnesota Press gratefully acknowledges support for the open-access edition of this book from The Graduate Center of the City University of New York.

Interlude images were edited by Drew Martin.

Portions of chapter 3 were previously published in "Speech or Silence: Undocumented Students' Decisions to Disclose or Disguise Their Citizenship Status in School," *American Educational Research Journal* 54, no. 3 (2017): 485–523.

Published by the University of Minnesota Press
111 Third Avenue South, Suite 290
Minneapolis, MN 55401-2520
http://www.upress.umn.edu

Available as a Manifold edition at manifold.umn.edu.

ISBN 978-1-5179-1044-0 (hc)
ISBN 978-1-5179-1045-7 (pb)

Library of Congress record available at https://lccn.loc.gov/2024000297.

Printed on acid-free paper

The University of Minnesota is an equal-opportunity educator and employer.

How Children
Talk about
Knowing Silence
Immigration
Status in School

Ariana Mangual Figueroa

University of Minnesota Press
Minneapolis
London

The University of Minnesota Press gratefully acknowledges support for the open-access edition of this book from The Graduate Center of the City University of New York.

Interlude images were edited by Drew Martin.

Portions of chapter 3 were previously published in "Speech or Silence: Undocumented Students' Decisions to Disclose or Disguise Their Citizenship Status in School," *American Educational Research Journal* 54, no. 3 (2017): 485–523.

Published by the University of Minnesota Press
111 Third Avenue South, Suite 290
Minneapolis, MN 55401-2520
http://www.upress.umn.edu

Available as a Manifold edition at manifold.umn.edu.

ISBN 978-1-5179-1044-0 (hc)
ISBN 978-1-5179-1045-7 (pb)

Library of Congress record available at https://lccn.loc.gov/2024000297.

Printed on acid-free paper

The University of Minnesota is an equal-opportunity educator and employer.

para Lucía y Marcela

Contents

Preface and Acknowledgments
How I Enter

When I began the study that forms the basis for this book, I was thrilled at the idea of going back to school. This would be the first time since I'd left classroom teaching to pursue a doctorate degree that I would spend most of my work week inside a public elementary school. I was returning to a familiar school system (I'd been a student and a teacher in New York City public schools), but I now had a different role as a professor entering the classroom to conduct ethnographic research.

In the eight years since I'd left public school teaching, I had been studying the relationship between citizenship and childhood in a wide variety of contexts. I had worked with immigrant families in California, Pennsylvania, and New Jersey, spending time in their homes and learning from the ways in which they sought opportunities within and beyond school settings. I had spent years preparing teachers to meet the needs of English language learners and students from immigrant families against the backdrop of rising anti-immigrant sentiment. All of my experiences as a teacher, graduate student, and scholar were united by a desire to better understand the relationship between citizenship status and public schooling. I was hopeful that this new project would deepen my knowledge and allow me to help others in the field grasp how immigration status shapes the educational experiences of children and families living in the United States.

I'm drawn to this work for a variety of reasons, but certain aspects of my own childhood are relevant to how I enter the field. I grew up in a bilingual Puerto Rican household in upper Manhattan. My father, like all of my grandparents, was born on the island, and my mother was the first in her family to be born on the mainland. Unlike the families at the center of this study, everyone in

my family was a U.S. citizen; however, this fact was not uncompli-
cated. My parents taught me that Puerto Ricans had been granted
birthright citizenship shortly after the United States established
colonial rule over the island. I also learned that Puerto Rican citizenship was two tiered: those of us born on the mainland had full
birthright citizenship, while our Puerto Rican family members
born and residing on the island had a form of statutory citizenship. They were granted many of the privileges of U.S. citizens but
were barred from full participation in the nation's democracy. For
example, they were limited to voting in primaries (not general
elections) and were unable to vote for their congressional representatives. From a young age, then, I learned that citizenship was
uneven and unstable—as well as inextricable from larger questions
of politics and place.

I attended elementary school in El Barrio at a time when nearly
50 percent of the Latin American population in New York City
was Puerto Rican.[1] Before every school assembly, we sang three
anthems ("The Star Spangled Banner," "La Borinqueña," and "Lift
Every Voice and Sing") that shaped my burgeoning sense of the
historical complexity and racial plurality of this nation-state.[2]
After graduating elementary school with a scholarship to attend a
private middle and high school, I made weekend trips to El Centro
to read issues of *Pa'lante* and study Puerto Rican history missing
from my course textbooks.[3] I left New York for college and returned
to work as an English as a Second Language (ESL) and Spanish
teacher, first in a South Bronx high school, then in an elementary
and middle school in East New York, Brooklyn.[4] While the Puerto
Rican population citywide had declined by more than 15 percent
during this ten-year period, the neighborhoods where I taught remained majority Puerto Rican.[5] In the months after September 11,
2001—my first year of teaching—a group of public school teachers
and I founded the New York Collective of Radical Educators in an
effort to stop a broad set of policies from hurting our students.[6]
Our early campaigns included working to end military recruit-
ment in schools and calling for an end to high-stakes testing.

When I returned in 2013 to launch this ethnographic project in
one New York City classroom, I was no stranger to the school system or issues facing immigrant families. These experiences helped
me build important relationships with administrators, teachers,

and community organizers at the school I'll call P.S. 432. One of the first challenges in establishing this study was figuring out how to connect with immigrant families that included undocumented students when public schools do not (for reasons that I will discuss below) collect or report demographic information on students' and families' citizenship status. After months of talking with P.S. 432's teachers and learning about their students in the most general terms, I finally obtained the specific information I needed by meeting with the school's ESL teacher.

P.S. 432's ESL teacher barely spoke during my visit to her office. Instead, she handed me a document titled "Report by Place of Birth" (RPOB) and left me to read it on my own. The RPOB is a schoolwide roster of all registered students labeled by language ability. The roster also includes additional demographic information for each student: birthplace and date, year the student entered the public school system, and current grade. This ESL teacher had been charged—like many ESL teachers in New York City—with helping families who live and learn in languages other than English to enroll in school. In order to complete a family's registration, she was required to administer a Home Language Survey (HLS) that included questions about which language or languages the family spoke at home. She used these data to decide whether to recommend that the child take a grade-specific language assessment called the New York State English as a Second Language Achievement Test (NYSESLAT). These two procedures— administering the HLS and NYSESLAT—are used to determine students' eligibility for ESL and bilingual programs. As ESL teachers enroll, assess, and assign classes to their newest students, they also contribute to the administrative work of creating and updating their school's RPOB.

Looking over the roster, I remembered that I'd been handed a similar document during my first year of teaching. Back in 2001, when the principal of a small South Bronx high school gave me our school's RPOB, most of our students hailed from the Spanish-speaking Caribbean. They were Puerto Rican students with U.S. citizenship, or they were students from the Dominican Republic who had, by and large, obtained family-sponsored visas before entering the United States.[7] I remembered that the NYSESLAT— like so many other standardized tests that I was responsible for administering—made it harder, rather than easier, for me to ascertain who my students were and what they knew. In some cases, bilingual students scored poorly because the test measured their fluency in middle-class cultural norms more than their proficiency in English. In other cases, students were made to take the test because the previous ESL teacher had assumed their Spanish surnames meant they did not speak English. In both instances, children were miscategorized as low performing or in need of remediation.[8] In those early years of teaching, I directed my energy toward advocating for language learners and working against deficit views of them; I wasn't yet thinking much about the connections between language proficiency and immigration status.

Twelve years later, when I returned to New York City as an ethnographer, I had learned to read between the lines. I had come to understand that basic demographic information used to assemble a portrait of a student's schooling trajectory and primary language—their birthplace, year of enrollment, and age—could also tell a story about their immigration experiences. The student data remained the same but had taken on new meaning for me. After a decade of living and working alongside Latin American families with different immigration statuses, I had learned to attend to what is explicitly stated, but also to what is implied, by the demographic labels we use in schools. P.S. 432's RPOB included five students—all ten- and eleven-year-old girls assigned to one fifth-grade classroom—who were born outside the United States. These five girls were Catalina and Aurora, who were born in Mexico and came to the United States as toddlers; Pita, who was born in El Salvador and migrated to New York City in early childhood; and Jenni and Tere, from the Dominican Republic, who had just moved to New York City that summer. I got to know these five students, along with a sixth, Hazel, who was born in the United States to parents from El Salvador. Soon after these initial conversations, all six students and their families agreed to participate in this study.

The RPOB contained specific demographic information about Catalina, Aurora, Jenni, Tere, Pita, and Hazel that also mirrored larger trends in U.S. immigration. At that time, the border between the United States and Mexico had become so highly militarized that families migrating north were staying in the United States on arrival rather than coming and going as they once had.[9]

The RPOB bore this out: there were only a handful of children in the upper elementary grades born in Mexico or Central America, they had enrolled in school before 2010, and they were now in fifth grade. In other words, nearly all the students at P.S. 432—a public school in one of Brooklyn's primary immigrant neighborhoods—were born in the United States. This was because fewer and fewer families were crossing into the United States at the southern border with small children in tow; instead, younger children were born in the United States to immigrant parents who were doing their best to stay put. It was a coincidence that all of P.S. 432's fifth graders born in Latin America were girls. While in this book I foreground immigration status over gender, a particular kind of closeness developed among us that has helped to sustain this project over many years.[10]

Reading between the lines helped me to see an argument that I've been making for some time: that immigration and educational policies are interrelated and shape the experiences of students attending public schools.[11] In 1982, the Supreme Court held in *Plyler v. Doe* that Texas had violated the Equal Protection Clause of the Constitution's Fourteenth Amendment when it restricted free public schooling to citizens of the United States or "legally admitted aliens." Although the Court affirmed prior case law holding that public education is not a right guaranteed by the Constitution, the majority in *Plyler* did emphasize the unique nature of public schooling. "Both the importance of education in maintaining our basic institutions and the lasting impact of its deprivation on the life of the child" distinguish it from other social welfare "benefits," Justice Brennan wrote for the majority.[12] In guaranteeing equal protection of the law, the Fourteenth Amendment precluded Texas from denying children access to free public education based on their or their guardian's citizenship status.

In the decades since *Plyler,* federal and state education departments have worked to ensure that the law in action accords with the law on the books. In an effort to prevent inquiries that might have chilling effects on parents and children who are legally entitled to public education, various levels of government have mandated staff and teachers not ask for proof of immigration status when determining residency in the school district for purposes of enrollment.[13] The implementation of these mandates has been far from uniform. On a local level, educators have—sometimes unwittingly, sometimes purposefully—violated these mandates by asking for forms of documentation that require parents and guardians to reveal their undocumented status.[14] These unlawful violations can instill fear in immigrant families and result in the exclusionary practices that the *Plyler* ruling meant to guard against.

As a researcher and as a professor, it can be hard to speak openly with teachers about the connections between immigration status and schooling. Because educational policymakers at the federal, state, and school district levels typically require school staff to uphold *Plyler* by not inquiring about students' status, educators have had little opportunity to talk openly about the relationship between students' citizenship status and their educational experiences. The policies instituted since the *Plyler* ruling have been taken up as a "don't ask, don't tell" mandate where talk about students' immigration status in school is discouraged. This silence is reinforced by federal regulations detailed in the Family Educational Rights and Privacy Act (FERPA), which, among other things, protects students' privacy by prohibiting educators from sharing identifiable information about their students without parental consent. Where the mandates issuing from *Plyler* establish the "don't ask" principle, FERPA strengthens the "don't tell" part of the equation.[15] The result is that educators protect educational access by establishing an institutional culture of "status quo silences" surrounding undocumented students.[16]

In the absence of professional conversations about students' immigration status, educators rely on an existing lexicon of educational labels that can misconstrue students' lived experiences. I often hear teachers refer to their immigrant students as English learners when in fact the vast majority of students designated as language learners are U.S.-born citizens.[17] Educators and school leaders often assume that they should consult their school's ESL teacher with questions about how to best serve their immigrant students, even when there is rarely anything in their training that prepares ESL teachers to take on the role of advocate.[18] In this context, children's privacy may be protected, but misnomers and false assumptions can make it hard for educators to serve them well.[19]

The labels that we educators use to refer to our students shape how we perceive them. At the same time, our inability to talk openly about the connections between immigration and education can render important dimensions of our students' experiences invisible to us. This can lead to professional ignorance regarding citizenship's significance—an ignorance we can project onto our young students if we assume that they are unaware of the realities associated with their immigration status. Working alongside immigrant families, I have wondered how we can teach our students well when we know so little about their lives. This question has only grown more urgent in light of research indicating the need for educators to develop pedagogy that draws on students' experiences and knowledge to support new learning.[20] My goal in this book is to broaden our shared understanding of just how much children know about citizenship so that we can also imagine new possibilities for supporting them through teaching, research, and advocacy.

In light of the preceding discussion regarding the ways in which demographic labels used in education illuminate or obscure important aspects of students' lives, I'll take a moment to define some of the key terms used throughout this book.[21] Birthright U.S. citizenship is obtained on the principle known as jus soli—from the Latin word for soil—which confers citizenship to those born on U.S. territory.[22] The ways in which this principle has been applied or denied to groups of people on the bases of race, gender, and other criteria have changed over time as politicians and lawmakers determine whom to welcome in, whom to keep out, and on what terms.[23] A noncitizen person can become a U.S. citizen through a process called naturalization that leads first to obtaining lawful permanent resident (or green card) status and then to full citizenship. I use the terms "birthright citizenship" and "juridical citizenship" interchangeably. Both underscore that the rules regarding citizenship today are bound by laws that were first spelled out in the Fourteenth Amendment of the U.S. Constitution. However, I avoid using the term "legal citizenship" except when quoting other sources so as not to reify the legal/illegal binary prevalent in mainstream discourse that has shaped the national conversation on immigration in harmful and dehumanizing ways.[24]

The children and families at the center of this study often refer to being a U.S. citizen as "having papers" (*papeles* in Spanish), and I will frequently join them in using this expression. This suggests a binary formulation that is not entirely accurate because there is in fact a broader range of immigration statuses, but the emphasis on papers—on material documents—will be important as the book develops. I won't define all of the possible U.S. immigration statuses here, and these categories change over time, but I will use the following terms to refer to four status types represented in this project: undocumented, lawful permanent resident, family-sponsored visa, and U.S. born.

The first of these terms—"undocumented"—merits elaboration. Mae Ngai explains that to be undocumented is "a historically specific condition that is possible only when documents (most commonly a visa) are required for lawful admission, a requirement that was born under the modern regime of immigration restriction."[25] Although there are many different ways to refer to this group, I follow the example set by organizations like the New York State Youth Leadership Council (NYSYLC, YLC for short), the first undocumented youth-led nonprofit in New York, who refuse the language of illegality and, along with other immigrants living without papers, proclaim that they are "undocumented, unapologetic, and unafraid."[26]

Beyond references to an individual's immigration status, I will consistently use the term "mixed status" to refer to the families at the heart of this book. A mixed-status family is one kind of immigrant family that "may be made up of any combination of legal immigrants, undocumented immigrants, and naturalized citizens. Their composition also changes frequently, as undocumented family members legalize their status and legal immigrants naturalize."[27] At many points in this book, we will encounter mixed-status families, classrooms, and peer groups; we will track both the differing levels of vulnerability and possibilities for solidarity that arise within these contexts.

"Juridical citizenship" is not the only category of belonging within a nation-state. Studies of "cultural citizenship" examine bids for inclusion made by negotiating access to the everyday social, economic, and democratic life of a community through active expressions of belonging despite lacking legal rights.[28] This may include, for example, adults speaking out publicly about health care rights, delivering performances representing community-wide concerns, and organizing protests decrying deportation.[29] This kind of civic participation is not dependent on juridical citizenship; in fact, these examples call attention to the many ways in which undocumented and noncitizen community members actively work to access rights and resources while also being denied access to birthright citizenship and naturalization procedures. Moreover, this "nonjuridical concept of membership suggests the production of collectivities that are not national but transnational, sited in borderlands or in diaspora."[30] We will attend closely to the specific impact of juridical status on childhood and schooling while also becoming attuned to the wide variety of meanings activated by the term "citizenship."

Public schools play an important role in socializing students to ideas about citizenship by teaching certain forms of participation in the country's political system; these can range from pledging allegiance to the U.S. flag to voting in local and national elections.[31] Educators often use the term "citizenship" metaphorically to mean good behavior or belonging: some districts issue report cards that provide a citizenship grade for attendance and homework completion, while others display bulletin boards that read "citizens of the world" in their school hallways.[32] This book explores examples like these in much greater detail, but from the perspective of students and their families. I use the broad term "educator" to refer to school leaders and classroom teachers as well as other adults working in schools, such as guidance counselors, parent coordinators, and office staff.

This book focuses on what citizenship means to children and how they communicate their understanding in the course of their everyday lives. In the coming pages, I share what I have learned from and about Catalina, Aurora, Jenni, Tere, Pita, and Hazel throughout the past decade. Each has taught me valuable lessons about the ways citizenship matters; each has shown me that she is not limited by the labels assigned to her. Across the length of this project, they have reiterated through their words and their actions that they want the adults in their lives to hear their voices and understand their stories. I hope that this book helps to amplify their perspectives so that educators can recognize just how much children know and bring to school each day.

Le doy gracias al grupo de niñas y a sus queridas familias, quienes confiaron en mí a lo largo de estos años. A Spencer Foundation/ National Academy of Education postdoctoral fellowship offered crucial support for data collection from 2013–14. I'm grateful to the real Ms. Daniela for welcoming me into her classroom as an ethnographer and for remaining my friend once I'd left. Teachers Janet and Claudia helped to deepen the intergenerational dimension of this project. My editor, Pieter Martin, was committed to this book at every stage. My thanks also to Rachel Moeller and Terence Smyre for their expert guidance in seeing the book through to its print and Manifold versions. Thank you to my students (many of them also teachers) who worked closely with me on data analysis: Daiana, Gabriella, Julianne, Meredith, Rosa, Sindy, and Viviana at Rutgers and Carmín, Julissa, Lucy, Rachel, Rocío, and Wendy at CUNY. I finished writing this book at The Graduate Center and counted on the support of many colleagues, in particular Wendy Luttrell in the PhD program in Urban Education and José del Valle in the PhD program in Latin American, Iberian, and Latino Cultures. My work with Tatyana Kleyn at CUNY-IIE and Rebecca Lowenhaupt on PIECE—along with our project collaborators—has deepened my thinking about education and immigration. Thank you to Kate Vieira for reading and rereading drafts and to Marjorie Faulstich Orellana for her brilliant feedback. Dear friends and colleagues commented on sections along the way: Cristina Mendez, Cynthia Carvajal, Daniela Alulema, Dave Stovall, Edwin Mayorga, Erica Turner, Fabienne Doucet, Jenna Queenan, and Maddy Fox. A special thanks goes to Liliana Garces and Lisa Kelly for their helpful guidance on the sections regarding *Plyler*'s significance. My family—near and far, pasado y presente—have supported me and my work at every turn. Mami, Papi, Eli: los quiero. Time and again, the women I call my sisters have given me ánimo. Ben, my closest and most caring reader, believed in this book before I ever started writing it and has read every word I've put down since. This book, this life, are better for the love he's brought to it.

Transcription Conventions

Symbol	Significance
> <	Speeding up speech
< >	Slowing down speech
?	Strong rise in intonation and can be, but is not necessarily, an interrogative
↑	Raised intonation
↓	Falling intonation
.	Falling or final intonation contour
CAPS	Raised voice, usually shouting
_	Stress or emphasis
o	Words spoken quietly or softly
oo	Whispering
::	Prolongation of the preceding sound
-	Cut off prior word or sound
(( ))	Authors' comments

These conversational analysis transcription conventions are adapted from Emanuel A. Schegloff, *Sequence Organization in Interaction: A Primer in Conversation Analysis* (Cambridge: Cambridge University Press, 2012), https://doi.org/10.1017/CBO9780511791208. I use this notation system when transcribing turns of talk (or dialogue) to represent the linguistic and paralinguistic resources speakers use in conversation; however, for increased legibility, I do not apply these conventions to block quotes presented without surrounding talk. Spanish punctuation—for example, a question mark or exclamation point—is displayed differently depending on the text: in the transcripts it represents intonation (and is not inverted at the start of a sentence), while in the block quotes it follows orthographic conventions in Spanish (and is inverted at the beginning of a phrase).

Introduction
Children as Knowing

How and when do children show us what they know? How do children growing up in mixed-status immigrant families express their understanding of ideas that circulate widely in their communities—concepts like "citizenship," "birthright," and "documentation"—that are legitimated by nation-states, encoded in policies, and reinterpreted by parents and guardians? When do children choose to speak or remain silent about their and their loved ones' experiences of coming to and living in the United States? This book seeks to answer these questions in children's own words.

The predominant view in the field of education—as well as in the scholarly disciplines and mainstream discourses that shape this field—maintains that children remain largely unaware of the realities associated with having or not having papers until they enter adolescence and young adulthood. This book will demonstrate that elementary school-age children are, in fact, actively learning about and making sense of the ways in which citizenship affects their everyday lives. My goal in presenting this multiyear, multi-sited study of listening to children—to both their speech and their significant silences—is to render visible the sociopolitical context of contemporary childhood so that teachers and researchers can critically reflect on their relationships with and responsibilities to students growing up in mixed-status communities. The ethnographic account presented in these pages is a testament to how much children do indeed know, and how they make considered decisions about when and where to share their knowledge with the rest of us.

Mixed-Status Families

The children in this study—Catalina, Aurora, Pita, Hazel, Tere, and Jenni—are all members of mixed-status families. Mixed-status families include members with different immigration statuses. According to 2021 estimates, more than 16.7 million people live in mixed-status households that include at least one undocumented member.[1] Approximately 6 million of the people in these households are younger than 18 years of age.[2] Most of the children growing up in these families are U.S.-born citizens like Hazel, while others are undocumented minors like Catalina and Aurora. Still others arrive in the United States without authorization or in possession of temporary travel visas, then begin the process of applying for more permanent resident status, as in the cases of Pita, Tere, and Jenni. A decade ago when I began this project, the mixed-status families in P.S. 432's school community resembled national trends in that younger children were U.S.-born citizens while their older siblings and parents were undocumented.[3]

As this book will show, children growing up in mixed-status families learn about how state-defined categories—like "citizen" and "noncitizen," in the parlance of the United States Citizenship and Immigration Services—organize their lives starting at a young age.[4] These early lessons inform children's beliefs about their own belonging and affect their participation in public institutions like schools. In the coming pages, we learn from children in two kinds of mixed-status families. We will meet families—like those of Aurora, Catalina, Pita, and Hazel—from Mexico and Central America known as "long-duration unauthorized immigrants."[5] This phrase refers to the settlement patterns of undocumented immigrants who came to the United States during the late 1990s and early 2000s and who, in a departure from previous migratory trends, did not move between the United States and their country of origin in a cyclical fashion because the militarization of the U.S.–Mexico border made the journey too treacherous to attempt more than once.[6] As undocumented adults have immigrated and stayed in the United States for longer stretches of time, they have also given birth to increasing numbers of U.S.-born citizen children. As a result, mixed-status families from those countries of origin now tend to include undocumented parents and older undocumented children who had crossed the border (like Aurora, Catalina, and Pita) along with a growing number of younger U.S.-born children (like Hazel).[7] We will also meet families that illustrate a revolving door–style immigration characterized by frequent travel between their country of origin and the United States. Family reunification is the primary means by which Dominican immigrants like Tere and Jenni obtain visas to immigrate.[8] Such visas enable a freedom of movement unavailable to the undocumented children in this study.

I have chosen to focus on children from mixed-status families because they are a little-known but important part of our public school population. Members of mixed-status families have extensive experience navigating differences of citizenship within their family of origin, making the immediate family unit a microcosm of national variations in immigration statuses and their attendant realities. Moreover, their growing presence in U.S. schools helps to challenge reductive or essentialized notions of Spanish-speaking immigrant families. I have often heard educators gloss over the linguistic diversity of immigrant families when they refer, for example, to a family's "home language," as if there were only one. Mixed-status families make clear that this is a misnomer in many immigrant homes, where parents and children were born and raised in different linguistic and cultural contexts.

Similarly, we tend to talk about a family's "country of origin" as if all members of a household share the same nationality. Mixed-status families highlight that millions of children in the United States do not share the same country of origin, or immigration status, as their parents or siblings. Homogenizing views of immigrant families are a problem because they limit educators' understanding of their students' experiences. This can adversely affect schooling when educators are less equipped to develop curriculum, pedagogical supports, and opportunities for parental participation that support student learning.[9] For decades, educational researchers have argued that building on children's and families' funds of knowledge to develop culturally responsive and sustaining pedagogy is an essential part of fostering children's linguistic and academic learning. Yet we know little about the sociopolitical and cultural backgrounds of this growing number of students living in mixed-status families and attending public schools.

This Study

This project took place in Brooklyn, New York, in a neighborhood that I call Vista. State and citywide demographic data make clear why Vista—and why Catalina, Aurora, Jenni, Tere, Pita, and Hazel's experiences—is representative of larger demographic trends. Around the time of this study, the undocumented population of Latin American immigrants in New York State was primarily composed of people from Mexico (19 percent), followed by the Dominican Republic (9 percent), Ecuador (8 percent), and El Salvador (7 percent).[10] In New York City specifically, most undocumented individuals came from the Dominican Republic, China, and Mexico; the Mexican population was the fastest-growing undocumented group among the three.[11] Of the nearly 1 million immigrants who lived in Brooklyn at the time, nearly 7 percent of them lived in Vista.[12] Immigrants living in this part of Brooklyn hailed primarily from China and Latin America. More specifically, Vista's foreign-born residents came from the following countries: China, Mexico, the Dominican Republic, Ecuador, and El Salvador.[13] Many Chinese families, like their Latin American counterparts, experience the harsh realities of living undocumented in the United States. This project, however, focused specifically on Vista's Spanish-speaking families with whom I was able to establish relationships of mutual trust in Spanish that are fundamental to this kind of ethnographic project.

The school-based component of this study took place at P.S. 432, a dual-language Spanish–English elementary school where classroom instruction was divided between the two languages. Despite the nearly equal numbers of Latin American and Asian residents living in Vista, this neighborhood school primarily served the children of Spanish-speaking immigrants. At P.S. 432, the average number of students labeled Hispanic and classified as English learners was well above city averages. In 2013, 40 percent of the student population in New York City and 41.2 percent of the students enrolled in the various public schools located in the Vista neighborhood were Hispanic. However, at P.S. 432, the average number of Hispanic children enrolled totaled 91 percent—again, well above these city and neighborhood averages. The citywide population of children labeled English learners was 14 percent, while the averages in Vista and at P.S. 432 were much higher, at 48.2 percent and 41.5 percent, respectively. P.S. 432's student body also reported poverty rates of 96 percent, well above the city average of 20.9 percent.[14]

This book follows Catalina, Aurora, Pita, Hazel, Tere, and Jenni from 2013 to 2015. This period spanned two academic years, including their last year of elementary school and their first year of middle school. I took a multi-sited ethnographic approach to conducting fieldwork in their school, homes, and neighborhood.[15] The first year of the project took place during the 2013–14 school year, when I visited their fifth-grade dual-language classroom on a weekly basis. My visits typically began at 8:00 AM with the start of the school day and continued until dismissal at 2:30 PM. As an ethnographer, I relied on long-standing principles of participant observation that involved joining in the everyday activities of the school while also developing ways of watching and recording these activities. As one example, I purchased a marble-cover composition notebook identical to the ones that students used, and we carried them throughout the day while working at desks, sitting cross-legged on the floor, and walking through the hallways. The children used their notebooks to complete their assignments; I used mine to take field notes. As part of my school-based data collection, I also gathered teaching materials, student work, and other curricular artifacts, as well as over two hundred hours of recorded talk among the six focal students, teachers, and peers.

In addition to the recordings, which I will discuss in greater detail in chapter 1, I also engaged in two other data-collection activities. First, I visited Catalina's, Aurora's, Pita's, Hazel's, and Tere's homes, all located in Vista within a few blocks of one another and P.S. 432. Over time, I focused my routine home visits on Pita, Aurora, and Catalina's families because each girl had been or was undocumented and because they all lived with younger U.S.-born children. While all six girls have made major contributions to the study, these three girls will increasingly become the focus of this book. I visited their homes monthly and audio or video recorded interactions between these three girls, their parents, and their siblings. In addition, I accompanied their families to immigration clinics run by community organizations, after-school and middle school programs, and local cafés and shops. Second, I adapted my fieldwork in response to the children's own desires for increased involvement. Early in the project, the girls began to ask me what I was hearing in my recordings, and they wondered if I could share the files with them. I made arrangements with Ms. Daniela and other school staff to hold a weekly after-school meeting, which I called our *grupo de análisis* (data analysis group). During these meetings, I played excerpts of the recordings so that all six focal students could hear them. We co-constructed a set of protocols for listening and responding to what we heard, always returning to the overarching question of what their experiences could teach their teachers about the lives of children from mixed-status families.

The second year of the project, which took place during the 2014–15 school year, involved weekly sessions of our grupo de análisis held at P.S. 432. By that point, all six students were attending middle school, but—after consulting with them and their parents, and with the support of Ms. Daniela and her principal—we decided to continue meeting at P.S. 432. This not only allowed this project to continue on a weekly basis but also created a familiar space for the girls to return to as they navigated the significant changes associated with early adolescence and middle school. I held a dozen group meetings in fall 2014, and I continued to meet with Catalina's, Pita's, and Aurora's families outside of school. This formal period of data collection culminated in January 2015, when I held a Three Kings Day celebration in Ms. Daniela's classroom to thank the families and teachers for their involvement. From that moment to the present, I have remained in close contact with the group in a less formal, but no less meaningful, mentoring role. The afterword to this book, coauthored with Catalina, Pita, Aurora, and Hazel, was written ten years after the project's initial phase had ended.

The two years that are the focus of this book were formative for Catalina, Pita, Aurora, Hazel, Tere, and Jenni for at least two reasons. First, the focal families' attempts to change their immigration status and household composition involved a confrontation with immigration policy that shaped the children's consciousness and our conversations. Pita's immigration status changed during these years as she and her mother became residents (officially called "lawful permanent residents"). Family members in other households worked to bring relatives to the United States, with differing degrees of success. Jenni's mother was able to obtain a visa and relocate to Brooklyn from the Dominican Republic; Catalina's grandmother obtained her first tourist visa, while Aurora's grandmother was unable to do so successfully. Hazel's older brother immigrated from El Salvador to the United States and began his life as an undocumented high schooler, while Tere traveled to the Dominican Republic to mourn the death of her grandmother. These experiences, in turn, shaped the conversations that the six children, their parents, and I had throughout the course of this study. I use the words that the girls and their parents used to describe these immigration-related processes and papers rather than translating them into the official language of U.S. immigration policy.

Second, as these six focal students graduated from fifth grade, they began to assume new levels of responsibility and independence. This involved traveling without their parents to and from home and school, thereby expanding the places where I conducted fieldwork. I gained new insights into what it is like to move through the city and borough as a student from a mixed-status family when we began to meet more frequently in the public spaces of their neighborhood. I was able to observe the real-time decisions that they made about when to participate in or withdraw from conversations about immigration as they arose in these nonschool settings.

The two years spanning 2013 to 2015 were also a formative time in the development of social movements that have shaped ongoing conversations about immigration and racial justice in the United States. The events chronicled in this book took place during the middle two years of Barack Obama's second term as U.S. president. After failing to deliver the comprehensive immigration reform known to many mixed-status Spanish-speaking families as *la reforma* (the reform), Obama signed the executive order—called Deferred Action for Childhood Arrivals (DACA)—in 2012. The undocumented, youth-led movement for immigrants' rights drove much of the conversation during this time. They focused on coming out as undocumented in an effort to draw attention to the many contributions that they and their families make to this country and to push for a pathway to citizenship.[16] The Black

Lives Matter movement established itself as a visible grassroots presence in the United States calling for justice in light of ongoing state-sanctioned attacks on Black life. Although the focus of this study ended during the Obama administration, I remained in close contact with the girls during their high school years; I witnessed how the racist, anti-immigrant rhetoric and policies of Donald Trump and his administration directly affected their lives. Throughout this book, I track how these large-scale events are registered and refracted in the focal students' everyday talk at school and beyond.

Children as Innocent

This book takes up a call issued by Carola Suárez-Orozco and Hirokazu Yoshikawa to focus empirical research on the "unique immigration-status socialization experiences" that take place during middle childhood.[17] "Middle childhood"—the period from six to twelve years of age—has been referred to as the "forgotten years of development because most research is focused on early childhood development or adolescent growth."[18] In order to fully appreciate how much children know, we first have to question the commonly held view of childhood innocence: that children remain unaware of their immigration status until they approach adolescence and young adulthood. The transitional period from elementary to middle school, which includes the developmental period of middle childhood, is formative for children in their socialization to citizenship. As I will show, during this time, they become discerning speakers with a rapidly developing metalinguistic awareness regarding when and how to talk about their and their loved ones' immigration status. Despite this reality, there is still a widely held view of immigrant children as unknowing.[19]

One of the sources of this view lies in the interpretation of the 1982 Supreme Court ruling *Plyler v. Doe,* which, as I briefly described in the preface, protects undocumented children from being denied a public education. At issue in the case was whether the superintendent of a school district in Plyler, Texas, could withhold public funds and instead charge tuition to undocumented students residing in its district. The Supreme Court held that the

Texas law violated the Equal Protection Clause of the Fourteenth Amendment by restricting free public education to U.S. citizens or "legally admitted aliens."[20] The Court held that the Texas schooling law was inconsistent with federal immigration law and policy. Unlike state restrictions on employment, for example, state and local policies restricting education on the basis of immigration status infringed on federal powers and constituted, in Justice Brennan's words, a "ludicrously ineffectual attempt to stem the tide of illegal immigration."[21] Justice Blackmun added in his concurring opinion that school officials were hardly in a position to determine which "aliens" were entitled to residence and which would eventually be deported. Any efforts to draw such lines in the context of education, he noted, would involve the State in the administration of federal immigration laws and were bound to be "fatally imprecise."[22] As a result of *Plyler,* undocumented children and youth residing in the United States were granted protection under the Equal Protection Clause of the Fourteenth Amendment for the first time.

While the Supreme Court in *Plyler* granted all students a right not to be denied a public education on the basis of immigration status—what Michael Olivas has referred to as "blanket enrollment permission"—it did not provide school districts and employees with specific guidance about how to safeguard this right.[23] In the decades since *Plyler,* federal and state governments have stepped in to provide guidance to educators on how to protect undocumented students' rights to attend public school.[24] In 2014, for example, the New York State Education Department sent a memo to school leaders warning them to avoid any actions that could "chill" or "discourage undocumented students from receiving a public education."[25] This echoed the federal "Dear Colleague" letter of the same year, which advised districts to rethink the documents they ask guardians and parents to provide during enrollment because they may deter them from completing the process. In some states, for example, schools require a driver's license as proof of district residency, but adults cannot obtain one without immigration papers. Such requests may scare undocumented families away from enrolling their children in school because not having a driver's license could be interpreted as an admission of not having citizenship.[26]

The *Plyler* ruling has been celebrated for its far-reaching impact because it set a precedent for protecting immigrant children's access to public schooling despite challenges from state and local governments seeking to deny immigrants full access to educational opportunities in this country.[27] Michael Olivas considers the *Plyler* decision significant for two reasons. First, it resolved the dispute over "whether the state of Texas could enact laws denying undocumented children free access to its own public schools." Second, the decision issued a strong protective imperative regarding a "larger, transcendent principle: how this society will treat its immigrant children."[28] The Court argued that undocumented children were "innocent" and should not be penalized for the actions of their parents.[29] Roberto Gonzales argues that "by establishing the legal inclusion of 'innocent' undocumented immigrant children in the American public school system, the ruling laid the groundwork for them to benefit from the same opportunities for inclusion that had existed for generations of schoolchildren before them."[30] Commentators have lauded the decision for allowing hundreds of thousands of children to obtain an elementary and secondary education, and for preventing anti-immigrant policymakers from restricting schooling access in order to deter immigrants from seeking opportunities and making new lives in this country.[31] Indeed, legal scholar Justin Driver has called *Plyler* one of "the most egalitarian, momentous, and efficacious constitutional opinions that the Supreme Court has issued throughout its entire history."[32]

For all the material and legal gains won in *Plyler*, however, the decision itself also reinforced exclusionary logics that glorified childish innocence in contrast to adult wrongfulness. Central to Justice Brennan's majority opinion was a view that children should not bear the guilt of their parents. "Those who elect to enter our territory by stealth and in violation of our law should be prepared to bear the consequences," he wrote for the majority. "But the children of those illegal entrants are not comparably situated." The Texas law, Justice Brennan wrote in the closing lines, was "directed against children, and imposes its discriminatory burden on the basis of a legal characteristic over which children can have little control."[33] That the child should not bear this burden was premised on an understanding that their parents should. Children's innocence in the immigration context gained meaning through a juxtaposition with "guilty" adult migrants.[34]

Innocence, of course, connotes more than the absence of guilt. It can also imply unknowingness or ignorance, as if children were unaware of their immigration status. One important reflection on this kind of innocence can be found in Jose Antonio Vargas's 2011 autobiographical essay in the *New York Times* Sunday magazine entitled "My Life as an Undocumented Immigrant," in which he recounts learning about his immigration status.[35] He chronicles key turning points in his life as an undocumented Filipino immigrant, beginning with immigrating to the United States in 1993 at the age of twelve. Vargas describes being sixteen years old and trying to obtain a driver's license using fake documents that his custodial grandfather had given him without explanation. When the clerk at the department of motor vehicles whispered to Vargas that his papers were fake and warned him never to return to the office, Vargas confronted his grandfather and learned that he was undocumented. Aviva Chomsky cites Vargas's experiences in her book *Undocumented: How Immigration Became Illegal* as evidence that "children, of course, don't usually know much about status and immigration law unless their parents choose to explain the status issue to them."[36] She attributes this to the fact that "their main interaction with state authority is through school" where children are treated equally because of *Plyler* and therefore "may never confront the issue of documentation in their daily lives."[37] As we will see throughout this book, childhood innocence is far from universal. I have observed that children growing up in mixed-status families today do in fact understand citizenship's significance, and they demonstrate just how much they know at home and at school.

Scholars like Suárez-Orozco and Yoshikawa have described how children sometimes experience "a dawning awareness of their own legal status" in middle childhood.[38] When students make social comparisons between their household and other households, a "concern over the family's legal vulnerabilities" might "seep into consciousness."[39] However, Suárez-Orozco et al. tend to view undocumented children who are "ensconced in the family and provided with public education from kindergarten through twelfth grade" as protected from "fac[ing] full on the consequences of their condition."[40] It is not, many believe, until undocumented youth realize that they are unable to participate in "social rituals" that "define personhood in early adulthood" that these young people find themselves "awakening to a nightmare" of legal exclusion.[41] This important research has identified barriers that undocumented adolescents face when they find themselves excluded from opportunities like applying for a driver's license and federal financial aid for postsecondary study. Such studies argue that the *Plyler* ruling creates inclusive conditions throughout the early years of K–12 schooling, so as a result children do not have to confront institutional barriers resulting from immigration status until they reach adolescence or young adulthood.[42]

The children in this study, along with those I worked alongside in mixed-status families in California and Pennsylvania, have a lot in common with the young people whose lives are depicted in the research and reporting cited above. But they also differ in a fundamental way: they were born nearly two decades later. The children I know well were all born around 2002, in the years immediately after the September 11, 2001, attacks in New York City and Washington, D.C. What this means is that children like Catalina, Pita, Aurora, Hazel, Tere, and Jenni have grown up in a time when an unprecedented amount of governmental attention and money has been spent on surveilling, detaining, and removing immigrants from the United States. Racism and xenophobia, coupled with restrictionist immigration policies and the militarization of the U.S. border, existed well before September 11, 2001, but that year marked a turning point. After that time, immigration policy shifted from a focus on policing exterior boundaries and ports of entry to a concerted effort to surveil, detain, and deport people already living in the country's interior.[43] It is startling to think that Immigration and Customs Enforcement—also known as ICE— was only created in 2001 with the signing of the Patriot Act. This means that for many children growing up in mixed-status families, immigration status became central to their families' kitchen-table conversations, the ambient noise of TV and radio news cycles playing in their homes and local businesses, and their dreams and nightmares.[44] Their awareness of juridical status—and their strategies for negotiating its implications—began well before adolescence, as they will recount in the coming pages.

"No Es Verdad": Children Share What They Know

What did Catalina, Pita, Aurora, Hazel, Tere, and Jenni have to say about the claim that students tend to become aware of their immigration status later in life? In fifth grade—when they were ten and eleven years old—I asked them to think with me about the discrepancy I observed between scholarly assumptions of innocence and the different kinds of knowledge they had displayed in our time together. I started with a deliberately provocative overstatement: "Almost everyone who studies immigrant children thinks that they don't realize their migratory status, let's say, if they have papers, no papers, have visas, what have you. [The research says children] don't know until they're sixteen or seventeen years old." Their first response was to shout out cries of disbelief.

Catalina:	Whoa! NO?.
Ariana:	**Porque dicen. Que:: no es hasta que ustedes soliciten un trabajo:: o una licencia:: o una beca >para la universidad< que se den cuenta. De que sí tienen o no tienen papeles. Pero-** Because they say tha::t it's not until you apply for a jo::b or a li::cense or >a university scholarship< that you realize. Whether you have or don't have papers. But-
Aurora:	**Eso es una mentira.** That's a lie.
Jenni:	°**Sí es verdad.** °Yes that's right.

I elaborated on the statement a bit further, and Aurora and Pita conjectured why some children—the exceptions, in their mind—might grow up unaware of the realities associated with their immigration status. Their first thought was that the decisions parents make to talk to their children about immigration status are personal and idiosyncratic. Aurora suggested that parents might choose to have this conversation based on their own bravery, underscoring the sense of strength needed to overcome the kinds of exclusion that mixed-status families face. She also acknowledged that parents manage information according to their beliefs about how their children will react, because the realities associated with members' immigration status shape the material conditions and the social-emotional well-being of the entire family.

Aurora: Um. Eso es una mentira. Bueno, no mentira, mentira porque algunos sí no lo saben. Otros. Sí. Lo saben. Entonces que a veces sí no se enteran, pero a veces sí como. Sus papás son valie::ntes y saben cómo controlar la situación >de decirle<- Oh oh, mi amor, no, no, °°tú no puedes, cuando crezcas, tú vas a tener que estudiar, >hacer todas las cosas posibles por conseguir papeles porque nosotros no podemos.< Hacerlo por ti. Y es muy ↑difícil. So, tú por eso, >cuando crezcas tú vas a tener que estudiar<. Y yo ↑siempre me-Yo sé que yo tengo que estudiar y cosas así porque, si no estudio ni nada, ↓entonces-
That's a lie. Well, not a lie, lie, because some truly don't know. Others. Do. Know. It's just that sometimes they don't find out, but sometimes they do if like. Their parents are bra::ve and know how to manage the situation >by saying<: "Oh oh, my love, no, no, °°you can't, when you get older, you are going to have to study, >do everything you can to get papers because we can't<. Do it for you. And it's very ↑difficult. So, that's why you, >when you grow up you're going to have to study<." And I ↑always have-I know that I have to study and do things like that because if I don't study or anything, ↓so-

Ariana: Okay. So, tú ya sabes porque tus padres te lo dicen, por ejemplo.

	Okay. So you already know because your parents tell you, for example.
Pita:	**Yo estoy de ↑acuerdo con lo que dijo Aurora. Algunos niños no saben eso, tal vez porque ↑ellos vinieron acá bien pequeños?**
	I am in ↑agreement with what Aurora said. Some children don't know this, maybe because ↑they came here very young?
Ariana:	**Um hm, es lo que dicen muchos, sí, sí, sí.**
	Uh huh, that's what a lot of them say yes, yes, yes.

They also suggested that degrees of economic privilege in the United States might inform how much children would have to confront the disenfranchising realities of living in the United States without authorization. Both Aurora and Pita offered up the idea that a child might have degrees of awareness that are based on their families' class position.

Pita:	**Y ellos crecen como que si fueran niños así de rico?, y no ↑ricos, pero <u>sí</u> que tienen mucho. Sino que, bueno, ellos no ponen mente en eso, sino que crecen >con sus ami:::gos< y todo así. They get distracted? y algunos–**
	And they grow up as if they were kids like that rich? and, not ↑rich but they do have a lot. Except that, well, they don't think about that because >they grow up with their frie:::nds< like that. They get distracted? and some–
Aurora:	**A ↑veces a mí no me gustan °esos niños, a veces, porque >luego se sienten<– ↑AY Tengo >los mejores zapatos.<–**
	↑Sometimes I don't like °those kids, sometimes, because >then they feel like< ↑ "Oh >I have the nicest shoes<."

Pita and Aurora went on to hypothesize—drawing on their first-hand experiences—that children's memories of crossing the border could shape how much they know about their circumstances. Pita explained that a traumatic border crossing experience could be indelible in a child's mind, prompting a desire to understand the circumstances leading up to such an event.

Pita: **Y algunos otros niños saben que lo que ellos pasaron porque tal vez ellos tuvieron mucho, mucho. Como cuando iban pasando tuvieron mucho di.fi.cul.ta.des, y esas dificultades siempre ellos los tienen en me:::nte. Tal vez cuando comienzan la escuela escriben de e:::so o están leyendo más de e:::so para ver qué es lo que pasa.**
And some other children know what they experienced to get here because maybe they had a lot. Like when they were crossing they had a very hard time and these di.ffi.cul.ties, and those difficulties are always on their mi:::nd. Maybe when they start school they write about tha:::t or they are reading more about tha:::t to understand what is happening.

Ariana: **Okay. So, oigo que quizás no saben porque tienen más dinero, no saben porque sus papás no se lo dije::ron.**
Okay. So I hear that maybe they don't know because they have more money, they don't know because their parents didn't te::ll them.

Aurora: **Maybe los papás tienen mucho miedo de >cómo reaccionarían<.**
Maybe their parents were very scared about >how they would respond<.

This intersectional view of mixed-status immigrant childhoods— from the perspective of immigrant children themselves—demonstrates a complex metalinguistic awareness that involves a burgeoning understanding of class, border-crossing experiences, and parental decision-making from a young age.[45] The insights offered up by Catalina, Jenni, Aurora, and Pita underscore the importance of listening to children account for their own lived experiences. As Barrie Thorne poignantly argued two decades ago in *Gender Play,* "It distorts the vitality of children's present lives to continually refer to them in a presumed distant future. Children's interactions are not preparation for life; they are life itself."[46]

Marjorie Faulstich Orellana, whose own research on immigrant childhoods has shown that immigrant children negotiate encounters with the state by translating for their parents, has asked us to reconsider our beliefs about children in light of the central role that they play as language brokers between their families and our nation's public institutions. In a study of immigrant students' displays of "transcultural and translingual competencies" in an after-school program serving elementary school students in Los Angeles, Faulstich Orellana concludes: "Their behaviors and actions revealed a *normalization* of processes and practices that may seem unusual from a dominant-culture and adult-centric standpoint. Thus, children helped make the familiar strange for all of us, so we could see and understand in new ways."[47] We can call the six girls in this study our brokers because through their words and actions, they make visible a childhood marked by an immigration status that may otherwise go ignored by adults in schools.

Children as Knowing

When I first started working as an ethnographer alongside mixed-status families in 2008, both academic and mainstream writing on immigration offered few examples of children explicitly broaching the subject of immigration status. However, there was one news-clip that I often shared with my audiences when I presented my research. The video from May 2010 contains an exchange between Michelle Obama and a second-grade student during a national tour undertaken by the first lady in support of President Barack Obama's proposed immigration reform package.[48] Seated in a circle in an elementary school gymnasium in Maryland, Michelle Obama leaned in as one young girl nervously recounted: "My mom says that Barack Obama is taking everybody away that doesn't has [*sic*] papers." Obama replied, "Yeah, well that's something that we have to work on, right? To make sure that people can be here with the right kind of papers, right?" As Obama went on speaking, the young student interjected: "But my mom doesn't have any papers." As other children excitedly waved their hands to be called on, Obama ended the exchange with, "Well, we have to work on that. We have to fix that, and everybody's got to work together in Congress to make sure that happens." At the time, this newsreel constituted the only mainstream representation I could find of immigrant children explicitly sharing their knowledge about immigration status.

There is now a growing body of ethnographic research that demonstrates how children are aware of immigration status at a young age. In her study of teasing routines in two Mexican families living in Southern California, Fazila Bhimji found that very young children were enlisted in interactions explicitly referencing the threat of deportation that families face daily. When two-year-old Esmeralda followed her mother's playful prompts to tease her aunt by threatening to call *la migra* (a colloquial phrase for immigration enforcement agents), this child communicated her understanding that la migra was a commanding authoritative presence to be obeyed.[49] In Arizona, children substituted la migra for cops in the game cops and robbers.[50] While planning the content for a zine during a collaborative storytelling project led by Jocelyn Solis in New York City, one undocumented fourteen-year-old boy drew a maze entitled "Can you get to New York without running into la migra?"[51] And in her ethnographic study of transnational motherhood, Gabrielle Oliveira explored the ways in which Facebook simultaneously fostered connections among siblings of different ages separated by national borders while also producing tension between them by making visible the material and social inequalities that they faced.[52] My own research alongside mixed-status Mexican families in southwestern Pennsylvania has shown that parents evoked threats of deportation when talking with their four- and six-year-old children about the importance of performing well academically in school.[53]

Researchers attending closely to children's language and literacy practices have also shown that children express their knowledge about citizenship—and what is at stake in having or not having papers—in a variety of ways. Solis found that the process of collaborative storytelling—which often involved creative approaches allowing children to first draw, then narrate their experiences—created opportunities for them to share their strengths and preoccupations. In one conversation between children and adolescents in the same community-based literacy program mentioned above, Solis recorded a five-year-old's narration of a drawing that represented migration from Mexico to the United States. The child described the perils of walking, not flying, to the United States, which sparked a telling exchange between two other participants about their and their families' arrival and the risks and surveillance involved in crossing a militarized border.[54] Sarah Gallo's study of undocumented fathers and their children showed how together they constructed narratives of police encounters and family deportations that they shared with their teachers and with one another.[55] Inmaculada García-Sánchez, Marjorie Faulstich Orellana, and I have all witnessed the ways in which children—through their drawings and descriptions of what they have drawn—express connections between the large-scale national context of immigration and their own childhoods.

Children's participation in everyday conversations across settings is shaped by their perceptions of the risks associated with immigration status. In some cases, young children abroad worry about becoming estranged from family members who have left their home countries to live in the United States as undocumented migrants because they know they cannot see them on a regular basis.[56] In other contexts, U.S.-born children who have returned with their undocumented parents to their country of origin fear being bullied for being outsiders.[57] I have witnessed children as young as six years old describe the ways that citizenship can limit their freedom to travel between countries, the ability to visit with loved ones, and their family members' access to health care.[58] Children do not always respond to direct questions about the risks and realities associated with juridical status; instead, they demonstrate their knowledge through drawing, play, and other means. As a result, I have learned to listen carefully to children's stories about immigration status and to attend to how those stories might encode knowledge they do not share directly.

Speech and Silence

As we have already seen, children share their understanding of citizenship's significance in many ways that do not only—or even primarily—involve explicit references to nationality or immigration status. They do, however, move between school and family contexts where the concept of citizenship saturates everyday life and where talk about citizenship can be fraught. Schools are fascinating places to study speech and silence because of the many rules that dictate teacher and student expression. Put another way, schools are highly metalinguistic spaces where talk about communication is a defining feature of classroom life. Just consider how much time teachers spend telling students when to speak or not to speak ("turn and talk with your partner" but "be quiet in the hallways"), how to initiate talking ("raise your hand and wait to be called on"), what volume to speak in ("use your indoor voice"), and even how much to say ("make a five-minute presentation" or "write a four-paragraph essay"). Homes are equally important sites for the study of speech and silence because parents and guardians explicitly and implicitly socialize children into ways of talking during everyday routines.[59] These socializing moments can occur when school forms and homework assignments are sent home, producing a confrontation between the different meanings that educators and family members assign the concept of citizenship.

We will see that children learn to make considered decisions about when and how to share the facts—as they understand them—about their and their loved ones' immigration status. Here I present a framework for studying just what children from mixed-status families know. My premise is that in order to perceive just how cognizant children are, we have to listen to their words and also attend to their significant silences. While I use speech and silence as a shorthand for the different moments when children disclose or disguise what they know about citizenship, we will explore several dimensions of verbal and nonverbal communication.

The instances of silence that we will examine in speech and in writing, across home and school settings, share two characteristics. First, they count as communication; in other words, silence is to be understood as an action rather than a failure to act.[60] Catalina, Aurora, Pita, Hazel, Jenni, and Tere grew up in families that were actively concerned about the risk of revealing their nationality or immigration status, and all six learned rules about when and where it would be appropriate to do so. Even though their elementary school teachers knew better than to ask them to discuss or disclose their immigration status, topics like birthplace and immigration came up in the curriculum. In these moments students synthesized what they knew about the setting ("should I talk about this here?"), the people ("do I trust this person?"), and the risks ("can my family get in trouble?").[61] All six had learned a set of discursive strategies that they routinely used when making decisions about whether to remain silent or speak up.

Second, a decision to remain silent may be informed by the student's sense of responsibility to others; withholding expression is not a matter of individual whim. In the case of children growing up in mixed-status families, their silences (as well as their statements) often indicate the complex social norms they have learned about when and how it is appropriate to broach the subject of citizenship.[62] Given the vast amount of social and cultural knowledge they leverage when making these decisions, students' responses tell us a lot about what they believe is at stake in possessing and displaying their knowledge.[63] As a result, children's decisions are evidence of the responsibility that they have learned to shoulder as they care for and protect members of the mixed-status communities to which they belong.[64] This book contributes to the broader project of studying children's language by paying attention to the protective role that silence can play within the sociopolitical context of their childhood.

Studies of classroom interaction have shown that student silence can render visible those unspoken assumptions that undergird classroom interaction.[65] On the one hand, teachers may treat classroom silence as a deficiency or a form of misbehavior—a sign that their students lack an interest in academic learning.[66] Educators' assumptions about the significance of silence for nonwhite student populations can lead to moralizing judgments of those students, marking them as good or bad.[67] On the other hand, Katherine Schultz and Timothy San Pedro have found that student silence in high school classrooms can function as an agentive act of resistance to mainstream curricular and disciplinary practices that place them on the fringes of classroom learning.[68] From this perspective, talk that is absent or out of place can be productive. Breaks in normative classroom conversation can prompt teachers and students to reflect on identity categories—such as race and class—that are often taken for granted in everyday talk.[69] In order for silence to stop the flow of normative classroom interaction—and in so doing create opportunities for reflection or resistance—it has to be perceptible to members of a classroom community.[70] In other words, the student silences described in these studies had to be experienced collectively in order to be understood as an opposition to the expected conventions for classroom talk.[71]

In the coming chapters, we will listen to a variety of significant silences. Some of these signifying silences will be audible—that is, perceptible, meaningful—to peers but not to teachers, and some will be missed by everyone.[72] In those cases where silence went unacknowledged in real time, the recording devices permitted me to listen and listen again to meaningful communication that we otherwise fail to perceive. It is common for a quiet student to go unnoticed within the noisy din of real-time, multiparty classroom interaction. With public school class sizes numbering upward of two dozen students to a room, student silences may be welcomed by teachers. I also consider it a type of silence when a student tactically encodes or displaces information about citizenship status, as when a student withholds one thought but shares another one instead. Students from mixed-status families may omit or reframe references to citizenship even as they express other ideas during classroom conversations or in their writing.[73] These moments constitute a kind of silence—a withholding—that may go unnoticed by teachers who do not realize that the original topic was sensitive.[74] Here, as in the studies reviewed above, silence is agentive. However, instead of being an act of student resistance felt by others within a classroom routine or discussion, reframing is a strategy for responding to teacher requests or curricular demands while also protecting themselves from disclosure.

The silence of mixed-status families—for example, a parent's failing to fill out a school form—is likewise easy to miss or misconstrue. Deepening our understanding of the kind of conversations (and anxieties) produced by the way school documents are received in mixed-status homes is essential if we are to understand how juridical citizenship shapes education. Some examples of documents that activate concerns about citizenship include report cards that include a citizenship grade, or narrative reports of student progress that refer to their behavior as evidence of being a good citizen. They may also include school lunch forms that ask for social security numbers, or homework assignments requiring students to interview family members about their immigration experience.[75] These school texts include references to state-defined citizenship (as in identification numbers indicating nationality) and to citizenship in a metaphorical sense (as in behavior and belonging). When these materials are sent home, often in a child's backpack, they enter a familial discursive and political setting where citizenship is equated with immigration status. For parents and children in mixed-status families, these materials can create the chilling effects that *Plyler* is meant to prevent. In doing so, they can produce an alignment between public school education and an immigration enforcement regime that makes parents hesitant to participate and children even more anxious to speak in school.[76] Even when school staff adhere to upholding silences about student immigration status in school, the materials that they send home can prompt anxious conversations about immigration and education between parents and children.

At various points in this study, Catalina, Pita, Aurora, Hazel, Tere, and Jenni expressed anxiety and fear when confronted with the possibility of broaching the subject of immigration in conversation with people whom they did not trust. I use the Spanish term *inquietud* (restlessness) to name these expressions—often nonverbal—of vulnerability around citizenship status. My use of the term inquietud is informed by my reading of Gloria Anzaldúa and her discussion of the emotional states associated with growing up in the borderlands. Anzaldúa describes the fear that can come from the uncertainty of living between multiple frames of reference—nation-states, languages, and more—without a clear sense of belonging which leads to silence. She writes: "Petrified, she can't respond, her face caught between *los intersticios,* the spaces between the different worlds she inhabits."[77] Anzaldúa acknowledges that such conditions can result in a state of "psychic restlessness."[78] This restlessness manifests in ephemeral expressions and fleeting silences that will become perceptible to us in the coming chapters.[79]

In moments of inquietud, the girls used communicative resources other than talk (for example, remaining silent or using physical objects to make sounds, like tapping a table with a pencil) to express how unsettling it can be to confront the unresolvable ordeal of growing up in the United States under the threat of disapproval, discrimination, and even deportation.[80] One of the interventions that I hope to make here is to introduce transcription notations that can represent the sounds and actions that attend expressions of inquietud as they co-occur with speech. Throughout the transcripts included in this book I use transcription symbols borrowed from conversation analysis because they robustly permit representation of paralinguistic communicative resources—for example, the ways that shifts in tone, volume, and speed change the meaning of the words we say. In this notation system, descriptions of a speakers' affect or actions are typically noted by the researcher in double parentheses. I have tried, whenever possible, to represent the sounds of inquietud within the speaker's turn of talk—I do so by using superscripts to integrate them within the text instead of separating them out as nonverbal information—because I have found that these sounds accompany words as communicative devices and are not simply actions that occur alongside of or external to the speech itself.[81]

All of this is to say that we have to develop new modalities of listening so that we can help attune educators to the lived experiences of their students and so that we can reexamine how and when schools are complicit in silencing students or scaring them and their families.[82] If we can develop fluency in talking about the students we serve in mixed-status communities, then we can ultimately break our own professional silences. Just as students' silences are expressive, so are our professional silences.[83] Our professional inability to acknowledge and support students from mixed-status families not only passively reinforces the idea of children's ignorance but also allows schools to continue creating materials, curricula, and policies that actively undermine our ability to serve these students well.[84]

In the coming chapters, we will follow Catalina, Pita, Aurora, Hazel, Tere, and Jenni during their routine interactions in school, as well as at home and in public spaces. Chapter 1 shows how I put theory into practice by detailing the methodology that I used to collect longitudinal ethnographic data on everyday speech and silence. I specifically focus on the ways in which I recorded talk and interaction, how the students and I co-constructed this research project, and how we negotiated ethical issues together when they arose. Although some scholars might summarize a methods overview in an introductory chapter like this one, I prefer to model a view of research in which the methodology is as the heart of the findings. I will argue that *how* we listen shapes *what* we hear in the field.

Chapter 2 takes us into Catalina's home to show how beliefs about citizenship show up in conversations that she had with her parents and younger siblings. I also examine the ways in which the circulation of documents—school forms, homework, and immigration papers—produce chilling effects as they travel between home and school settings and get interpreted in the context of a mixed-status household. The chapter also examines moments during the school day in which Pita recounted to me the process of petitioning to become a lawful permanent resident—an experience that took place outside of school and that informed our conversations during the school day. This forms an important backdrop to the rest of the book because it shows the ways that concerns about immigration travel across settings to create what I will call—building on the work of Jerome Bruner—"a spiraling curriculum" that troubles the long-standing notion of the home–school divide in educational research.

Chapter 3 explores the ways in which Aurora, Catalina, and Pita disclosed or disguised their immigration status in response to classroom assignments. I closely examine student writing samples and transcripts of classroom interactions in order to identify those moments when children make decisions about engaging in or foreclosing conversations related to birthplace and nationality. I argue that these decisions are purposeful. They are informed by students' firsthand understanding of the risks involved in speaking or writing about citizenship in a public setting where their audience included peers and teachers. Drawing on theorizations of silence as expressive, I show how the focal students and their peers communicate the importance of citizenship both when they explicitly raise the subject and when they choose to remain silent about it. The connections between what they learn at home about their immigration experiences and status shape their participation in school.

Chapter 4 examines the children's participation in a monthlong curricular unit in which they studied the Dreamer movement, visited their local high school to conduct an interview with the student-led Dream Team, and reflected on their learning. I track the ways in which Aurora's decisions to speak out about—or resist disclosing—her immigration status constituted fraught, high-stakes moments at school informed by what she learned at home. This chapter deepens our understanding of children's spiraling curriculum of citizenship by drawing connections between the ways in which families' conversations about immigration status at home shape children's talk about immigration at school.

Interludes precede and follow chapter 4, which chronicles the elementary schoolers' experiences of interviewing students at Vista High School about immigrant activism. These interludes showcase conversations that the students from P.S. 432 had with one another as they walked through the streets of their neighborhood and examine in detail their encounters with police officers both inside and outside the school buildings. The interludes highlight transcripts of student talk and still images taken from my video recordings to explore how children experience surveillance and policing, as well as how they laugh and play in their local surroundings. These interludes contribute to an ongoing conversation about "liminality"—both in the immediate sense of focusing on transitional routines and places (such as walking through a hallway between classes) and in the sense of acknowledging the ambiguous social status of undocumented immigrant youth (such as living between countries or immigration statuses). Liminality in this sense is not only negative, however; it also invites us to consider the emancipatory potential of living "betwixt and between" those social roles considered normative and acceptable.[85]

The conclusion, like this introduction, is centered on the book's themes of speech and silence. It draws on Catalina's, Pita's, Aurora's, Hazel's, Tere's, and Jenni's own words to bring the book into the present. I focus on two moments—navigating remote learning at the start of the coronavirus pandemic and applying for college—during which I helped them navigate the exclusion and anxiety that can attend being a young adult living in a mixed-status family today. The afterword was collaboratively written with four members of this study and shows that the themes of citizenship and belonging, family responsibility, speech, and silence remained constant throughout this formative decade, as the elementary students I met in 2013 grew into my coauthors in 2023.[86]

One
"Recording Everything I Say"

Over the past decade, scholars of immigration have theorized the importance of citizenship throughout the lifespan and across generations. Ethnographers of citizenship have argued for a view of belonging as processual. From this perspective, claims to citizenship are shaped by multiple phenomena at once: nation-state criteria that define who belongs to the polity, public beliefs about inclusion and exclusion informed by contemporary racial and geopolitics, and fluid and ongoing transnational relationships between communities.[1] Sociologists studying the impact of immigration status on individuals' livelihoods have shifted our view of citizenship status itself. Instead of thinking of it as a static category, we now know that state-sanctioned authorization to reside in the United States can be obtained or lost throughout a person's life, along with a sense of belonging or exclusion.[2] Rich interdisciplinary portraits of immigrant students and youth in the United States have demonstrated the persistence of what is now known as the immigrant paradox: that immigrant children's and adolescents' health, behavioral, and academic "developmental outcomes become less optimal" the longer they live in the United States.[3] The experiences of young adult immigrants are now more deeply understood within a transnational and intergenerational framework; scholars speak of an "immigrant bargain" in which U.S.-born children of immigrants are socialized to make good on the sacrifices that their parents made by achieving social and economic mobility.[4]

In the important and growing literature on youth and children in mixed-status families, there are many accounts of why researchers select one particular nationality or place or generation to study. However, it is rare to find researchers explaining why they have chosen to work with children and youth of a certain age and not another. This kind of decision matters because whom we include in our studies tells us something about whom we think we can best learn from. An example of a usefully clear methodological statement about the selection of a particular age group for their study can be found in *Learning in a New Land,* where the authors write: "To understand the experience of immigration over time, we chose to work with youngsters old enough to have developed, prior to migration, a firm sense of belonging to their country of origin. They were also old enough to articulate and reflect on their changing experiences of immigration."[5] This helpful methodological explanation makes explicit the researchers' beliefs about the relationship between age and understanding of immigration status.

Studies of immigration are invariably informed by tacit ideologies regarding childhood and development, and in the absence of a critical discussion about methodology, we risk repeating mistaken assumptions about childhood as a time of ignorance. I chose to work with children aged ten and eleven because they were on the threshold of an educational transition from elementary to middle school during which I imagined that questions of immigration status and educational opportunity would be especially salient. The ethnographic approach that I used is particularly suited to studying children. As a language socialization researcher, I began with the assumption that they are active participants in everyday interactions in which they are learning about citizenship while also displaying their knowledge indirectly.[6] (Children—and sometimes even adolescents—can find it difficult to answer direct questions like "what is a passport?" or "what does it mean to be a citizen?" Yet they often recount the significance of papers, borders, and immigration status when describing the lives of people they love. "I can go to Mexico but my sister can't," a six-year-old once told me, "because she doesn't have papers."[7])

In order to learn from children growing up in mixed-status families, we need to tackle the enduring question of whom we consider capable of reporting on lived experiences and therefore whose realities are represented in the social science literature. This chapter models a way of writing about methodology that gives equal attention to the study's procedures and outcomes. My argument is that methods and findings go hand in hand. In order to appreciate how much children know about citizenship, we first need to understand how they shaped this very research project. Because Catalina, Pita, Aurora, Hazel, Tere, and Jenni participated in this project, they also influenced the study's methodology in ways that made clear that they understood the significance of what I hoped to learn. In this sense, their co-construction of methods was also a finding about their sophisticated and metalinguistic understanding of citizenship's significance. In addition, as they navigated conversations with peers about the study's methods and tools, the students raised questions that highlighted important ethical dilemmas as they unfolded. By shaping the ways in which I studied citizenship and childhood, they revealed just how much they knew about what citizenship was and why it mattered.

Studying the language socialization experiences of children from mixed-status families requires both a real-time alertness to speech as it unfolds and a method for recording children's talk that allows the ethnographer to listen to their words after the exchange has ended. Although it was fairly straightforward for me to set up a camcorder in the families' homes, it was much more challenging to record the subtleties of speech and silence during the fluxes and flows of the school day.[8] Figuring out a way to record school-based interactions is difficult because they can be at once deeply meaningful and painfully ephemeral for researchers; exchanges happen so quickly, and the locus of attention can shift so rapidly, that one rarely finds the opportunity to reflect on and analyze what children say in real time. In what follows, I will describe in detail my methodology for studying children's speech and silences.

My goal in recording children's talk throughout the school day was to gain insight into how they understood citizenship in their own words and in a variety of contexts: responding to teachers during curricular activities and also talking among their peers. I wanted Catalina, Pita, Aurora, Hazel, Tere, and Jenni to feel a sense of ownership and agency in the data-collection process itself, so I chose recording devices that met two criteria: portability and familiarity. The devices needed to be portable so that they could travel with the girls throughout the school day. This immediately discounted audio recorders that need to be set on a tabletop for recording (such as Olympus recorders), which are still widely used in sociolinguistic and anthropological research. The devices also needed to be familiar so that I could enlist the focal students in the recording process and minimize their discomfort while wearing them. I decided on Apple iPods with the Voice Memo application because they resemble smartphones and were therefore familiar to the children—especially to children living in families in which transnational communication is often facilitated by the use of mobile technologies like telephones and tablets.[9]

In addition to the iPod touch, I equipped the girls with microphones to improve the quality of the recordings and with carrying cases to facilitate wearing the devices throughout the day. The iPod touch includes a built-in microphone that can capture ambient sound in classrooms but is less adept at isolating individual voices within multiparty exchanges surrounded by background noise. I purchased lapel microphones that would be better at recording the voice of the focal student wearing it while also being sensitive enough to record exchanges with others near the microphone. This helped me to ensure that talk could be recorded as children engaged in everyday schooling routines. In addition to having high-quality recording devices, I also needed the students to be able to take the devices with them as they traveled through their school day while minimizing their distracting presence. I purchased an off-white cotton carrying case with a strap that could be worn across the torso. I chose cases that resembled purses I had seen some students wear to school. As we will see, the excitement and novelty that they experienced wearing the carrying cases also involved managing new levels of scrutiny and questioning from their peers.

I have detailed these recording strategies because they enabled two integrally important facets of data collection and data analysis. The first was to record long stretches of talk that included students' participation during structured classroom activities as well as long stretches of child-led talk with peers and adults during transitions and noninstructional time. This allowed me to listen later to the ways in which the children negotiated peer questions about the study and the ways in which topics broached during class time echoed throughout the rest of the school day. Second, I was able to repeatedly listen to the recordings and understand the significance of children's silences as well as their discomfort. As a result, my analysis attends to those significant silences that I theorized in the introduction.[10] This includes student silences that went unnoticed during dense, multiparty schooling interactions but that became perceptible to me after listening again to the audio recordings. This also includes moments of verbal silence that were accompanied by the production of other sounds communicating the children's inquietud, such as tapping or fidgeting that might indicate anxiety. I only began to hear the silences and attend to inquietud after multiple passes at coding recorded data over time.

The Belmont Report is a core reference text used by government agencies, colleges, and universities to evaluate whether a researcher's application to launch a particular study should be approved. This text serves as a resource for institutions charged with determining what counts as human subjects research, who qualifies as a researcher, and what risks and benefits a research project poses to its participants. The Belmont Report was compiled by the National Commission for the Protection of Human Subjects of Biomedical and Behavioral Research and published by the *Federal Register* of the U.S. government in 1974. The commission was charged with reviewing the bioethical principles violated during the Tuskegee syphilis experiments conducted over a span of forty years by scientists employed by the U.S. Public Health Service. As a result of the investigation, the authors of the Belmont Report concluded that a set of ethical guidelines was needed to ensure that biomedical and behavioral scientists could prevent such abuses from being repeated. The authors describe the report as "a statement of basic ethical principles and guidelines that should assist in resolving the ethical problems that surround the conduct of research with human subjects." Since 1974, university and research-based entities have created structures and systems for reviewing researchers' plans to guarantee that they adhere to a set of rules pertaining to "informed consent, risk/benefit assessment, and the selection of subjects of research." University-based institutional review boards (IRBs) lean heavily on the Belmont Report to develop trainings, templates, and rubrics meant to guide research design and implementation today.

The report, along with the accompanying policies that have been encoded in university research practices, function at two levels: first, to protect the university from the liability associated with researcher misconduct in the field; and second, in theory, to help researchers resolve ethical dilemmas that can be anticipated before beginning their studies. However, the goals of protecting institutions from litigation and fostering authentic relationships between researchers and communities are often in conflict. For example, the IRB expects that ethical dilemmas in research can be accounted for, prepared for, and thus prevented before data collection begins. I have found time and again that this emphasis on resolving ethical issues before entering the field is insufficient. How can researchers know what ethical dilemmas may arise in the field, let alone resolve them, before beginning data collection?[11] So many of these dilemmas are relational; in other words, they arise only once researcher/participant relationships begin to take shape in real time during fieldwork. I share Eve Tuck and Monique Guishard's concern that the procedures established by IRB "represent a system of *a priori* checks without attempting to balance or disrupt asymmetrical power relationships in scientific inquiry."[12] For researchers working to redefine hierarchical relationships in order to center the voices of those not traditionally considered experts (in this case, children from mixed-status families), the framework of the Belmont Report can be problematic. It presumes that researchers can anticipate and solve ethical dilemmas without ever interacting with the communities they intend to learn from. By listening closely, we can hear the ways in which children themselves raise questions of research ethics that should shape our fieldwork.

I organize the remainder of this chapter into three sections, building on the ethical principles proposed in the Belmont Report: Criteria for Inclusion, Risks, and Beneficence. I present the data in this way not because the children used these technical terms but because the concerns and desires that Catalina, Pita, Aurora, Hazel, Tere, and Jenni expressed align so closely with these categories—dimensions of the research process that institutionally affiliated researchers are asked to anticipate and address before they obtain approval to begin their studies. By organizing the data in this way, I am better able to show how these children taught me important lessons about conducting principled ethnographic research in mixed-status school settings.

Criteria for Inclusion

One month into making my weekly visits to Ms. Daniela's fifth-grade class, I began asking Catalina, Pita, Aurora, Hazel, Tere, and Jenni to wear the iPods during the school day. Four girls wore the recorders at any given time. All of the children in the classroom had assented to being recorded, and their parents had also signed consent forms to participate in the study. However, now that the project was underway, some of the students wondered why these six girls got to wear iPods while they did not. The Belmont Report calls this an issue of "justice":

> Who ought to receive the benefits of research and bear its burdens? This is a question of justice, in the sense of "fairness in distribution" or "what is deserved." An injustice occurs when some benefit to which a person is entitled is denied without good reason or when some burden is imposed unduly. Another way of conceiving the principle of justice is that equals ought to be treated equally. However, this statement requires explication. Who is equal and who is unequal? What considerations justify departure from equal distribution?

The children raised the issue of "fairness of distribution" when they asked me to account for who would wear the iPods and who would not.[13] Ms. Daniela set aside some time for me to talk with the entire class about the project. Without using the formal language of our university IRBs, I wanted to address students' concerns about the criteria for inclusion in the study. I thought it was important to reiterate these criteria now that everyone was becoming more accustomed to the presence of these devices in the classroom.

The challenge was this: Could I talk about participation in the study without disclosing any of the children's or family's immigration status? This conversation—and the ones that followed among the children themselves—exemplified many of the very questions that my study sought to answer regarding who broaches the topic of citizenship at school, how is it broached, and when. I opened our conversation with the following explanation:

> **Yo sé que hay preguntas y les voy a explicar exactamente qué está pasando. Soy profesora en una universidad en New Jersey que se llama Rutgers University. Y allí yo preparo maestras que quieren ser maestras de ESL. Right? De inglés como segundo idioma. Y parte de mi trabajo es dar clases y hacer estudios, proyecto. Y el proyecto que estoy haciendo en P.S. 432, en la clase de Ms. Daniela, con ustedes, es un proyecto que se trata de la experiencia en la escuela de las niñas inmigrantes o hijas de padres inmigrantes. Y el enfoque de este estudio son mayormente niñas con familias o de México o de Centroamérica. Kay? So, eso explica un poco por qué cuáles niñas tienen la grabadora, cuáles no, y por qué.**

I know that there are questions and I'm going to explain exactly what is happening. I am a professor in a university in New Jersey that's called Rutgers University. And there I prepare teachers that want to be ESL teachers. Right? Of English as a Second Language. And part of my work is to teach classes and do studies, projects. And this project that I'm doing at P.S. 432, in Ms. Daniela's class, with you all, is a project about the school experiences of immigrant girls or daughters of immigrant parents. And the focus of the study is primarily on girls with families from Mexico or Central America. Kay? So, that explains a little about why which girls have the recorders, which don't, and why.

In order to maintain Catalina, Pita, Aurora, Hazel, Tere, and Jenni's confidentiality, I emphasized my role as a teacher educator over my role as a scholar of citizenship. Although the majority of the children in Ms. Daniela's classroom were the children of immigrant parents from Latin America, not all of them had been classified as English learners. Mentioning ESL teachers and English learners helped to explain why some of the students wore the iPods while others did not.

In smaller group settings, children tended to ask Catalina, Pita, Aurora, Hazel, Tere, and Jenni directly why they were wearing iPods. In these moments, the focal student had to decide whether and how she was going to talk about immigration and citizenship as it related to this project. Even when I used proxy terms for referencing the criteria for inclusion for a large group—I talked about language and country of origin—the girls who were themselves undocumented understood their participation in the project as linked to birthplace. However, they were cautious about sharing this information widely. On the first day that she agreed to wear an iPod, Aurora's device recorded the following conversation. The transcript below begins as Aurora and her peers were waiting in line to leave their classroom for lunch. In these forty seconds, Aurora drew her peers' attention to the microphone and talked with Catalina about whether she might have a chance to wear one too. The interaction exemplifies the children's meta-awareness of the project (its purpose and methods and implications for them as children). Here, they show each other (and us) what they understand about what it means to be a participant in this project.

1 Aurora:	>**Está grabando toda mi voz.**< **Like every conversation?**
	>It is recording all of my voice.< Like every conversation?
2 Catalina:	**Por qué te está grabando toda la conversación?**
	Why is it recording all of your conversation?
3 Aurora:	**Porque ella quiere investigar de qué, qué hacemos.**
	Because she wants to investigate that, what we do.
4 Catalina:	**Ohh::::↑**
5 Aurora:	**TÚ.** >**fuiste nacida aquí**<**? o** °°**fuiste nacida en tu país?**
	YOU. >were born here<? or °°you were born in your country?
6 Catalina:	**Mi país.**
	My country.

7 Aurora:	ᵒᵒSo . . . todas las que no fueron nacidas aquí van a tener esto. Para ver cómo somos nuestras vidas así. Mkay↑?
	ᵒᵒSo all those that weren't born here are going to have this. To see what our lives are like. Mkay↑?
8 Student:	>Qué es< eso:::?
	>What's< this:::?
9 Aurora:	Na::. Tú qué? Que no te importa.
	Na::. You what? It doesn't matter to you.

The first thing that Aurora told her peers about the iPod was that it was recording everything she said. In turn 1, she identified what was being recorded—"toda mi voz" and "every conversation"—in both Spanish and English. While she spoke hurriedly, she did so in two languages, as if to ensure that all of her bilingual peers could understand this important point. Catalina was particularly interested in Aurora's explanation, so she asked Aurora why I was recording every conversation, responding with a knowing "oh," as in "I get it!" (turn 4), when Aurora explained that *I* wanted to find out what *they* do. In that moment, Aurora felt compelled to explain who *they* was. In other words, she wanted to explain to Catalina precisely *whose* experiences I wanted to learn more about. As we saw above, I had already described the criteria for inclusion in terms of studying the lives of girls whose parents had migrated from particular countries. Aurora, like all the girls in the study, knew that I was specifically interested in the experience of students from mixed-status families.

At a normal volume, then dropping to a whisper in turn 5, Aurora asked Catalina if she was born here or in her country. In this classroom, asking if someone was born in her own country was tantamount to asking her to reveal their immigration status. As we will see throughout this book, the children knew that revealing immigration status was a highly personal and potentially risky proposition. Aurora's approach made her a sensitive co-researcher as she conducted a quiet and careful interview with Catalina to determine her eligibility for the study. It also revealed how intimately she understood the driving questions of this study: whether children grasp the significance of nationality and immigration status. The hushed, hurried nature of this brief exchange gives us insight into the verbal and nonverbal cues that the girls used to communicate the sensitive nature of this topic. Catalina responded with equal discretion, and Aurora found an opportunity to align with her on the basis of a shared experience of being born in Mexico. In turn 7, Aurora counted herself and Catalina among those students who "weren't born here" and who would also be asked to wear the iPod during the school day. When, in turn 8, another student approached Aurora to ask about the microphone, she gave a quite different response. She shut down any exchange by moving away quickly and punctuating her speech by emphasizing the hard vowel sounds na, tu, que, and ta, almost as if she could dispel his question with a clap of her hands or the sound of her voice.

Risks Posed by the Study

In order to obtain IRB approval to conduct research with human subjects, researchers are asked to anticipate possible risks to children and adults associated with their participation. The Belmont Report defines risk as "a possibility that harm may occur." Over time, I have come to articulate two possible risks to participation in my ethnographic studies: first, the potential loss of confidentiality or privacy if raw data revealing children's real names or identities are lost or breached; and second, the discomfort people may experience when being shadowed during their everyday lives. Although naming these risks has satisfied the IRB committee members reviewing my applications to conduct research, I don't believe that any researcher can anticipate all possible risks before beginning to spend time in the field. This is especially true for this study, where one of my goals was to learn about how children understand their own sense of risk and responsibility. Time and again, my research participants have made clear the risks and benefits posed by my research in ways I could not have known before starting fieldwork. By listening closely to the girls in this study, I learned about what they needed in order to mitigate the risks they associated with talking about their citizenship status.

Consider the following conversation about honesty and confidentiality that took place during one of our first grupo de análisis meetings. During our discussion, Aurora took the lead on establishing a set of norms and agreements:

> **Lo que a mí me agrada es que aquí todas somos honestas. Y decimos- Oh, eso no lo contará, oh no. Oh, no mi mamá consiguió papeles- y todo eso. Porque mí me choca a veces que los niños dicen- ¡Ah, sí, yo tengo papeles!- y todas esas cosas porque. ¡Ay! Están presumiendo de todo lo que tienen.**

> What I appreciate is that we are all honest here. And we say "Oh, they won't share that, oh no. Oh no my mom got papers" and all of that. Because it bothers me that sometimes kids say: "Oh yeah, I have papers!" and things like that because. Ugh! They're showing off all the things they have.

Aurora identified a number of steps for mitigating the risk of feeling ashamed or judged. The steps included calling for honesty, requesting that we agree not to share anything disclosed in this group, and asking that no one brag about having papers. She knew firsthand what it felt like to be judged for being undocumented.[14] This wasn't the only time Aurora would recount being teased. On another occasion, she reported, "A veces los niños, [dicen] eso que:—¡Ay! yo tengo papeles y tú no. Lero-lero!—Cosas así dicen" (Sometimes the children, [they say] that "Hey! I have papers and you don't. Na-na!" Things that they say). "Lero-lero" is similar to the English "na-na-na boo-boo," often heard sung in teasing sequences followed by the phrase "you can't catch me!"

Aurora's comments created an opening for the girls in the group to talk about what they needed from one another (and from me) in order to share their experiences. Catalina vouched that I could be counted on to be a nonjudgmental presence. She explained: "Yo estaba hablando de eso con Ariana y ella me dijo que no le importa" (I was talking about that with Ariana and she told me it doesn't matter to her). This turn of phrase—"no le importa"—is significant here because of its double meaning. On the one hand, she knew that having (or not having) papers mattered greatly to me because it was the subject of the study; on the other hand, Catalina was also asserting (and in so doing, asking for me to confirm) that their immigration status did not matter in how I perceived or judged them.

Once we established the norms for our group conversations—
that no one would brag or be judgmental, and that we would maintain confidentiality—Pita, Aurora, and Catalina went on to discuss
their immigration status openly. After sharing that she was born
in the United States but that her mother and brother were born in
El Salvador, Hazel circled back to a discussion of risk. For Hazel,
the risk was not solely personal; instead, talking about immigration, border crossing, and status also threatened her family members' safety because they could be detained or deported. Hazel returned to the significant ethical implications of these questions of
speech and silence, sparking the following exchange.

1 Hazel:	**Hay muchas personas porque um. Que >se meten en problemas porque<. Uno le puede decir a a::lguien que usted. Usted cree::: que they like. They not gonna tell nobody. Pero después dices no::-** There's a lot of people that um. That >they get into trouble because<. Someone could tell so::mebody that you. You thi:::nk they like. They not gonna tell nobody. But after you say no::-
2 Ariana:	**Mm::::**
3 Hazel:	**-pero algunas veces lo dicen. And I HOPE >none of you not gonna tell< NO::<u>bo</u>dy.** -but sometimes they tell. And I HOPE >none of you not gonna tell< NO::<u>bo</u>dy.
4 Aurora:	**I don't tell ºanyone. A <u>ve</u>ces se me ol<u>vida.</u>** I don't tell ºanyone. <u>Some</u>times I for<u>get</u>.
5 Jenni:	**º>A mí también<**
6 Pita:	**Mm::hhm**
7 Ariana:	**Pero es cierto. Todo lo que hablamos aquí es en confi::anza:::?-** But it's true, everything that we talk about here is in confi:::dence:::?-
8 Jenni:	**Y de la ºcámara.** And for the ºcamera.

Imagining a scenario in which a person got in trouble because
someone else shared their immigration status (turn 1), Hazel issued
a strong directive: "I hope none of you are not gonna tell nobody."

Lowering her pitch, Hazel's three negative constructions—none, not, and nobody—emphasized the prohibition against breaching the confidentiality of the group.

As if to reassure her that these forms of punishment would not befall her or her family, Aurora quickly confirmed that she would never tell anyone. As an added assurance, she explained that she sometimes went so far as to forget what we talked about in our group. Two others rushed to agree in turns 5 and 6. In a way, Aurora offered up the most honest appraisal of the situation: total amnesia would be the only way to guarantee complete confidentiality. I jumped in to reiterate the ground rule that I heard the girls articulating: that everything we shared in the group would stay in the group. In retrospect, my contributions in that moment were both affirming and tentative. I reiterated the idea of confidence, but I posed it as a question, as if I wasn't quite sure that we were all in agreement just yet (turn 7).

Interjecting another dose of realism, Jenni added that while we could agree to the norms in situ, the camera data were still being recorded and would ultimately exist beyond the confines of this conversation. Jenni's slow and deliberate emphasis on each syllable, coupled with her mention of the camera in a near whisper, added gravitas to her closing point and underscored the importance of our collective *confianza* (trust). I took this as a serious reminder of my responsibility as a researcher to uphold my commitment to keeping their data confidential and to facilitating a dialogue in which we were all accountable to one another. The weight of this conversation was understood by all of us. From a young age, Pita, Hazel, Jenni, Tere, Aurora, and Catalina were clear about the risks and vulnerabilities involved in our work together, and they took the lead in establishing the terms for our collective accountability to one another.

Beneficence: Social Capital or Researcher Surveillance?

The Belmont Report defines beneficence as a researcher's "obligation," which is encoded in "two general rules": "(1) do not harm and (2) maximize possible benefits and minimize possible harms."

During early visits to P.S. 432 and to the families' homes, I explained the indirect benefits of the study: the more I learned from Catalina, Aurora, Pita, Hazel, Tere, and Jenni, the better prepared I would be to teach teachers about immigrant students' experiences and knowledge. In the language of university IRBs, there were no direct benefits to the participants. However, during these conversations that formed part of the process of obtaining informed consent, adults shared their own beliefs about how my presence could benefit them. Ms. Daniela was happy to have another experienced educator present to think through pedagogical dilemmas and work alongside her students. The parents believed I could connect them with resources—primarily legal and academic—that could help their families, and they were eager for me to help broker their relationships with school and state authorities. Throughout these early visits, the girls and I chatted and built rapport, but they did not explicitly articulate their position about why they wanted to join the project.

When I began audio recording during the school day, the girls expressed pride in being recorded while also articulating some of the risks they associated with it. In a sense, pride and anxiety were inextricable. The focal students were honored to be among a chosen group of children whose voices mattered enough to be shared with an imagined community of teachers and adults. However, they also worried that they might have said things that adults would not approve of. Within the first few weeks of recording, I responded to these concerns by establishing a dynamic and ongoing process of assent. Instead of deciding that they had agreed in advance to constant recording, we developed a policy together in which they could decide when and where not to wear the iPods. I was prompted to do so by Catalina, Pita, Aurora, Hazel, Tere, and Jenni who sometimes would—timidly at first—tell me that they preferred to remove the microphones during particular activities (at the start of recess, for example). In order to normalize and encourage their own decision-making about when to wear or remove the recorders, I began to ask them if they preferred to continue or cease recording at key turning points in the day.

As the following example shows—taken from peer interactions during the transition to lunch and recess—the focal girls and their peers had a heightened metalinguistic awareness of the role of the recorder and its purpose. The exchange begins when Ms. Daniela announced the transition to lunch and recess. She first charged Aurora with bringing everyone's science notebooks from their homeroom to the science classroom after lunch. After a brief negotiation about when Aurora would pick up the books—she preferred to do so after lunch so that she didn't have to remember to bring them back from recess—the students continued to line up and talk as they exited the classroom and entered the hallway. Overhearing that Aurora would be returning to the classroom at some point during lunch and before science class, Tere asked Aurora to please bring her a pencil, which students were forbidden to have during the lunch and recess period.

1 Tere:	ᵒᵒ>**When you come back get a pencil for me**<. **ok?**
2 Aurora:	**Hm?**
3 Catalina:	**When um cuan >cuando vengas para atrás<? Me traes↑ un lápiz.**
	When um whe >when you come back<? Bring me↑ a pencil.

Tere had a sketch pad and loved to draw in her free time, so she wanted Aurora to bring her a pencil so that she could pass the time engaged in her hobby. Whispering and talking quickly as if that would help her voice go undetected by the iPod, Tere asked for the pencil. The children often overheard one another, so when Aurora made clear she hadn't heard Tere's request, Catalina repeated it for her in a parodic tone and in a taunting voice invited Aurora to "have a conversation" (turn 5). Aurora warned Catalina against talking about breaking the rules because *this* (the recorder) was recording everything she said (turns 4, 6, and 8).

4 Aurora:	**Con cuidado . . .**
	Be careful . . .
5 Catalina:	>**Ok. Hh: let's h: have a. a conversation**<. **No, I'm just kidding. Uhh**
6 Aurora:	-ᵒ**porque esto me está grabando todo** ᵒᵒ**lo que digo.**
	-ᵒbecause this is recording everything ᵒᵒI say

7 Catalina:	Se::cr:::et. DhHhh:::::
8 Aurora:	No digas nada.
	Don't say anything.

Catalina picked up on Aurora's warning, suggesting that they had better watch what they say because they were being recorded. She introduced the idea of a secret in a mock Spanish register that could evoke either a young person up to no good or an older authority figure who might uncover that child's covert actions (turn 7).[15] The concept of the secret recurred at many other points throughout the study, with the girls asking me at times not to listen to or share specific moments in recordings because they had said something they wished hadn't been recorded (for example, "Ms. Ariana, please don't listen because I said a secret"). Their concerns about my hearing secrets can be seen in multiple ways. One interpretation suggests that they were concerned about what I might do with this information, perhaps fearing that I would relay it to other adults or punish them for it. Another interpretation is that this confession was an invitation to me to account for what I would do with the recordings; it was a conversation starter about the role the girls themselves could play in data collection and analysis. The children wanted to be sure that they weren't going to be unjustly punished by virtue of participating in this study and assenting to be recorded.

As the class moved into the hallway, Aurora began to interact with other peers from within her class and from other fifth-grade classes in the school. She once again drew attention to the iPod, at first relishing in its novelty and then in the fact that she was in a special position as the first among her peers to wear it. When Kevin bumped into her, Aurora scolded him for nearly dropping it and reiterated that it was still recording everything they said (turn 11).

9 Aurora:	Casi la TIras. Sigue grabando . . . TODO.
	You almost DROPped it. It keeps recording . . .
	EVERYthing.
10 Kevin:	Oh Auro-
11 Aurora:	Graba to.do. lo que to.do lo que se hab-
	It records ev.er.ything we ev.er.ything that is s-
12 Juan:	Oh↑ GEE:::

13 Aurora: -la

               -aid

Students from other classrooms began asking Aurora what she was wearing, and Aurora continued to repeat in both Spanish and English that the device recorded *todo* (everything). A moment later, Juan and a number of other students yelled within range of the microphone, interrupting Aurora's thought and escalating the intensity (turn 12).

Juan asked Aurora about the iPod in turn 14; exasperated by all of the attention, she responded with a groan expressing her exhaustion with the ongoing topic (turn 15).

14 Juan: **What is tha::::t?**

15 Aurora: **Agghh. It it records everything we::'re sa::::ying.**

16 Kevin: **But . . . for what?**

17 Aurora: **Para ella escuchar <u>todo</u>. ºTO::DO::**

               For her to listen to <u>everything</u>. ºEVE::RY::THING

As Kevin—the assigned door monitor for the class—opened the door and the students began filing down the stairs, he finally asked the question that must have been on everyone's mind: why was I recording? In one breath he asked and answered his own question, turning to me and saying, "Para ver si uno dice malas palabras (To see if anyone says bad words). Right, Ms. Ariana?" Kevin, who was the only child who addressed me directly in that exchange, laughed as if he didn't believe me when I replied, "No, qué va" (No way). These last statements, while delivered lightly, were an opportunity for Kevin to test out possibilities. He was waiting for me to confirm or deny his assertions in a public peer space regarding the purpose of the recorders and recordings. These moments reminded me that I straddled various orbits of authority as an adult ethnographer spending my days with children, and that they actively wondered whether my recordings would somehow get them into trouble.[16]

The concerns expressed by Aurora's peers clarified that the onus was on me, the researcher, to justify my presence and the presence of the recording devices in their lives. I took their concerns seriously. In keeping with the work of ethnographers Shirin

Vossoughi, Danny Martinez, and Arshad Ali, I believe researchers need to listen closely to participants' metalinguistic awareness of the ways in which our data-collection methods affect their social positioning. Like these researchers, I work alongside students that experience the daily effects of state surveillance. This has led me to believe that researchers using recording technologies should be aware of how their practices interact with histories of surveillance and social control. In the absence of such awareness, our research methods can reproduce social inequity even as we intend to ameliorate it.[17] I experience this not as a burden but as a possibility. Shifting power relations in our everyday work may open up new ideas and forms of solidarity that were not possible before.[18]

This chapter—this entire study—questions the dichotomies between ignorance and awareness, as well as speech and silence, that endure in educational research on children from mixed-status families. I have chosen to devote the first chapter to methodology to emphasize how the research process and the study's findings are inextricable. The participation of the girls in shaping data collection revealed how much they already knew about citizenship. Moreover, I have argued that questions of beneficence and risk are not knowable in advance but, like citizenship itself, must be understood as processual. The guiding principle of language socialization—that we learn to use language through language use—has methodological parallels once we consider that *what* we know is inextricable from *how* we learn it. Against this backdrop, we can see that our beliefs about whom we consider to be knowledgeable experts shape the ways that we listen and observe, which in turn determine the conclusions that we draw from our research.

We have already come a long away from the idea that children growing up in mixed-status families are ignorant of the meaning of immigration status. From playground taunts to complex worries about confidentiality and surveillance, we have heard directly from children who demonstrate that immigration status is an integral part of understanding themselves and their childhood contexts. In the chapters and interludes that follow, we will continue to see just how pervasive these concerns are and how sophisticated children become as they encounter these ideas across home and school settings.

Two

A Spiraling Curriculum
of Citizenship

From a young age, children in mixed-status families learn a basic truth: that the people they love were born in different places and have different kinds of papers. They acquire this knowledge within their families, and they carry it with them as they travel between home and school settings. This way of schematizing what they know and understand about social life might be expressed by children in a variety of mundane moments: when they explain why some family members can travel to Mexico while others can't, when they describe visiting different doctors and medical clinics, and when their parents talk with them about who in their family can access certain resources like nutritional benefits.[1] In each instance, children come to understand more fully that the difference between having or not having papers means the difference between being granted or denied opportunities that matter to them. This chapter explores what I will call—adapting a phrase from the work of Jerome Bruner—children's "spiraling curriculum of citizenship." (Following many other scholars and educators, I have adjusted Bruner's original phrase from "spiral curriculum" to "spiraling curriculum" to emphasize learning's dynamic and recursive nature.) This phrase denotes how children's understanding of the significance of immigration status deepens each time they encounter evidence of the way it organizes their everyday life and creates inequalities between their U.S. citizen and undocumented family members.

I integrate two perspectives on papers—a shorthand for juridical citizenship—throughout this chapter, drawing from the work of Kate Vieira and Aurora Chang. In her study of the literacy practices of Portuguese-speaking immigrants from the Azores and Brazil living in Massachusetts, Vieira identifies two kinds of papers significant to those families. The "weightiest" papers for undocumented families "were the immigration documents that legitimized their presence in the United States and promised them rights."[2] However, as family members entered schools, workplaces, churches and more, they learned about other kinds of documents they associated with their immigration status. This second category of papers consists of "textual objects, artifacts, and technologies that link migrants to larger institutions, such as the state, the school, and the workplace, and that allow them to move up, to move around, and to get by." Examples of papers in this broader sense include "diplomas, certificates, and time sheets," which undocumented immigrants encounter in school and work settings.[3]

Papers have symbolic as well as material value. Aurora Chang's study of immigration status and educational outcomes identifies the many moments in an undocumented students' trajectory when acquiring educational documents like diplomas serves as a form of legitimation that substitutes for obtaining immigration papers that would grant them U.S. citizenship. Chang calls undocumented students' efforts to obtain such papers a form of "hyperdocumentation": working to accumulate "documents, texts, and papers in an effort to compensate for a feeling of unworthiness."[4] Hyperdocumentation becomes part of a lifelong process by which undocumented immigrants work to refute "standard stereotypical representations imposed on them" by accumulating prestige in the form of other papers.[5]

Many kinds of papers circulate in the lives of mixed-status families that become important to parents and children of all ages. First and foremost are the state-issued immigration papers—passports and identification cards—that represent the differences in family members' national citizenship. There are also school-generated documents, like homework assignments, school forms, and report cards, that parents and children receive on a regular basis. When school-issued papers enter the home, they are interpreted from within a context saturated with concerns about immigration. Over two decades of spending time with mixed-status families, I have witnessed how families work to make sense of these documents together and I have seen the active role that young children play in these conversations.

Consider, for example, the anxious conversations that transpired in mixed-status families that I worked alongside in Pennsylvania. In two households, the oldest undocumented child was enrolled in the local public school and brought home a report card with a citizenship grade. From the school's perspective, the citizenship grade denoted two things: student behavior, and the family's record of completing homework and submitting school forms. From the perspective of undocumented mothers, the citizenship grade gave rise to anxious conversations about their children's future outcomes in this country if they were unable to become U.S. citizens.[6] In another home in the same school district, educators sent parents an invitation to volunteer in their child's classroom along with a form that required them to list the individuals residing in their household and consent to obtaining a fingerprint clearance. Undocumented parents in this district wanted to spend time in their children's schools but decided against it because the requirements risked exposing their or their family member's undocumented immigration status.[7]

In both of these examples, school forms produced chilling effects at home that aligned the school with immigration authorities and deterred undocumented parents from participating in school activities sanctioned by educators. In principle, educators send forms and materials home in the hopes of fostering connections between themselves and parents. But as these two examples show, school documents can inadvertently widen the gap between home and school by instilling fear in undocumented parents.[8] Forms that evoke juridical citizenship can lead to parents' protective silences, which educators in turn can misinterpret as families' lack of interest in their children's schooling.[9] This can heighten families' drive toward hyperdocumentation. In the absence of federal immigration reform providing U.S. citizenship, undocumented members of mixed-status families work tirelessly to amass other documents (tax forms, deeds for home ownership, certificates of completion for ESL classes, and more) that might substitute for authorization.

Young children and adolescents in mixed-status households are often called on to translate for their parents as papers circulate across settings. In these moments, children often overhear—or are directly enlisted in—conversations about their own immigration status. As we will see later in this chapter, a mother completing a school form said of her undocumented daughter, "She can't get food stamps because she wasn't born here, but her siblings can." Other school documents address students directly and prompt them to talk in particular ways at home. As an example, we will explore the dilemmas children face when homework assignments ask that they interview a member of their mixed-status family about their immigration experience. In these kinds of moments, children are socialized to beliefs about citizenship, and they consider different ways of participating in these exchanges.

I draw on Jerome Bruner's notion of a spiral curriculum to theorize the deepening ways in which children learn about citizenship's significance over time and across contexts.[10] Bruner elaborates a theory of learning in which children can intuitively grasp principles before they are able to express them explicitly. For example, they might grasp the concept of combining two numbers before they are able to explain a standard algorithm for addition. Bruner explains that children's early understandings expand—and spiral back—as they confront more and more complex situations. Children in mixed-status families know who has (or lacks) papers well before they can explain that having papers means being a U.S. citizen. In order to illuminate this spiraling curriculum of citizenship, this chapter examines moments when Catalina—with her siblings, parents, and the other children in this study—interpreted immigration papers and school documents that circulated in her life on a daily basis.

Passport Show-and-Tell

Catalina's family, the Mendozas, lived in a third-floor walk-up apartment on one of Vista's main avenues. Six family members shared this two-bedroom apartment: Juan and Jimena (parents),

Jimena's brother (*tío,* uncle), and four siblings, including Catalina (ten years old), her two brothers, Carlos (seven years old) and Toño (five years old), and her youngest sibling, Karla (three years old). Catalina lived in a typical mixed-status family: she, her parents, and uncle were undocumented immigrants from Mexico. Her three youngest siblings were all U.S.-born citizens.[11] When Jimena immigrated to the northeastern United States from Central Mexico, Catalina initially remained behind with her maternal grandmother. At the age of two, Catalina boarded a plane from Mexico City to New York City with a woman her family paid to escort her. Since then, Catalina has lived in Brooklyn with her mixed-status family.

One of the most striking instances of children demonstrating to me just how much they knew about citizenship and its importance took place during one early visit that I made to Catalina's home in April 2014. I arrived on a weekday afternoon to meet Jimena and her four children as they settled in after arriving home from school. Catalina sat at the computer table alternating between completing her math homework and practicing writing her name in bubble letters. Meanwhile, her younger siblings took the opportunity to show me all their favorite toys and books. This was only my third family visit, and the children were still getting to know me; it was important to them that I also learn more about their home and each of them.

Jimena invited me to sit beside her on the couch as she recounted details of her family life and living conditions, occasionally glancing up at three-year-old Karla, who kept repeating "mira yo, mira yo" (look me, look me) while hopping up and down to get our attention. A few moments later, seven-year-old Carlos brought over a small plastic envelope containing something he wanted to show me. He leaned against the sofa's armrest and waited until Jimena finished telling me about the repairs she wished the building manager would make to their rented apartment. When Carlos found an opening in the conversation, he stood up tall and declared, "Nuestros pasaportes" (Our passports). Jimena continued talking, Karla kept clamoring, and Carlos stood firmly, waiting for me to turn to him. A few moments later, I did. He proceeded to show me each family member's passport, one by one. These documents differed by nationality. Some were Mexican passports; others had been issued by the United States. The fact that he shared them with me on this visit underscored his understanding of their significance and my role: these papers, and which one belonged to which family member, told an important story about his family, and Carlos thought I would be especially interested in knowing.

The following two-minute conversation took place that afternoon, and the transcript presents the interaction between Jimena, Catalina, her siblings, and me. This exchange is representative of a routine I have experienced time and again during my visits to mixed-status family homes: very young children displaying their knowledge about citizenship by detailing who had or lacked papers. In this example, young Carlos integrated the knowledge of immigration status that he acquired at home with the discourse pattern known as "show-and-tell," an activity he learned in school. His command of the show-and-tell genre checked all the boxes of standard early childhood literacy development: he spoke with confidence and fluency, demonstrated prior knowledge, and demonstrated the objects while explaining why they were important to him.[12] Carlos's ability to integrate talk about citizenship with a familiar school-based literacy routine indicates the close association that he had made between immigration papers and school papers—evidence of the spiraling curriculum that we explore in this chapter and throughout this book.

1 Ariana:	°Aquí: está:::n, sí:::. So, cuéntame, de quién es de quién? Qué me estás mostra:::ndo? °Here they ar:::e, ye:::s. So, tell me, whose is whose? What are you show:::ing me?
2 Karla:	**Mira. Mira. Mira.** Look. Look. Look.
3 Carlos:	**Pero de mi tío- de mi tío no tiene.** But my uncle's- my uncle's doesn't have it.
4 Karla:	**Puedo ser como un conejo.** I can be like a rabbit.
5 Ariana:	**Uh huh**
6 Carlos:	**Mi tío aquí estáhhh. °>Pero ya se fue él a trabajar.<** My uncle hhhhere he is. °>But he already left for work.<

7 Ariana:	Él >se fue a trabajar.< Esto es Karla. Karla es su primer no::mbre?
	He >left for work.< This is Karla. Karla is her first na::me?
8 Jimena:	Sí sí::
	Yes yes::s
9 Karla:	Ahhh

The papers that Carlos showed me represented his family members' different countries of origin and national citizenship. His parents, uncle, and Catalina all shared Mexican citizenship, while he, Toño, and Karla all had U.S. citizenship. When I asked him what he was showing me (turn 1), he immediately evoked the construct of having or not having papers—"pero mi tío no tiene" (but my uncle doesn't have them) in turn 3—beginning to establish an intrafamilial difference that he would more fully explain in a moment. Carlos noted that his uncle was out working. It was typical for the undocumented adults in the family to work long hours in service industry jobs and then to study English by taking classes offered by community organizations and local libraries. These efforts helped to sustain the household and prepare its members to avail themselves of immigration reforms that President Obama promised to implement at the time. Throughout Carlos's presentation, his younger sister, Karla, continued playing, and I continued talking with Jimena. On seeing Karla's birth certificate, I turned to Jimena to confirm Karla's full name (turn 7). I was still getting to know the family and had, till then, only heard her referred to by her middle name. Jimena confirmed Karla's full name, and on hearing it, Karla cooed (turn 9).

Feeling the weight of the conversation that we were having, I introduced a bit of levity by joking about the awkwardness of taking passport photos. Looking at the next document that Carlos handed me, I joked and made a funny face as I exclaimed, "Yo siempre salgo horrible en las fotos!" (I always come out terribly in photos!). Carlos chimed in with "yo también" (me too), and Jimena laughed as she concurred with "a mí no me gustan" (I don't like them). Twelve turns later—after bantering about silly faces on passport photos—we continued our conversation about the process of getting the children's passports. Jimena referred to a previous conversation we'd had about preparing Carlos and Toño for a trip they were making to Mexico that summer. Jimena was planning to have a trusted adult—one of the boys' *madrinas* (godmothers) who had papers—accompany them to Mexico and back. The sisters would be staying home that summer: Catalina could not travel internationally because she was undocumented, and Karla would not go on the trip because she was too young. Jimena and Carlos recounted when and where the family went to have the U.S.-born brothers' passports issued.

10 Jimena:	**Lo sacó cuándo fuimos-**
	We got them when we went-
11 Ariana:	**Sí:::::**
	Ye:::::s
12 Carlos:	**Fuimos a QUEENS.**
	We went to QUEENS.
13 Ariana:	**Lo sacaron a todi- a ustedes?**
	You al- you (plural) got them?
14 Jimena:	**A los tres, que fuimos-**
	((sale del cuarto para la cocina))
	The three of them, when we went to-
	((left living room for kitchen))
15 Carlos:	**A QUEENS.**
	TO QUEENS.
16 Catalina:	**Era en Manhattan.**
	It was in Manhattan.
17 Ariana:	**En Manhattan. Ah ha.**
	In Manhattan. Uh huh.
18 Karla:	**Ahhhhh.**
	((playing and talking loudly, hard to hear))
19 Toño:	**Mi hermana.**
	((señalando a Catalina))
	My sister.
	((pointing to Catalina))

20 Ariana: **Tu hermana. Oh:::. °Seria.**

((riendo))

Your sister. Oh:::. °Serious.

((laughing))

21 Catalina: **Ahhh. I don't like that photo↓**
22 Ariana: I don't like mine either. Ever.

((laughing))

In turn 13, I started to ask a clarifying question about who had gone for their passports that day—was it all of them or some of them?—and I paused when I couldn't quite figure out how to ask the question without excluding Catalina. Without hesitation Jimena clarified by saying "los tres [hermanos]" (the three [siblings]) in turn 14, marking the fact that the three youngest siblings shared U.S. birthright citizenship while Catalina did not. Carlos stayed focused on the fact that they'd gone to the neighboring borough of Queens for this important event (turns 12 and 15), while Catalina noted a different location. Her mention of Manhattan (turn 16) is notable because it is where the Mexican consulate is located—the offices Catalina would visit if she was ever able to change her own immigration status. In that moment, little five-year-old Toño interrupted the display of their U.S. passports to point out Catalina's Mexican passport (turn 19). Catalina picked up on my earlier comment about passport photos and noted that she didn't like hers either.

In the closing stretch of conversation, Carlos began to put away the family's important documents. Karla—the youngest of the bunch—listened in closely and clamored to see her passport too.

23 Karla: **Y la mía? Mira yo. Y la mía? Mira yo, mira yo.**

((saltando))

And mine? Look me. And mine? Look me, look me.

((jumping))

24 Carlos: **Cuando estaba bebé estaba-**
When she was a baby she was-

25 Ariana:	**WO:::::W, qué mucho ejercicio haces. Y la de Karla?**
	WO::::::W, you do a lot of exercise. And Karla's?
26 Toño:	**OH. Mi hermana también–**
	OH. My sister also–
27 Carlos:	**Pero nomás el de Karla. Y lo vamos a recoger.**

((Sacando papeles de la mano de Ariana para guardarlos en el sobre))

But only Karla's. And we are going to pick it up.

((Taking papers out of Ariana's hand and placing them back in the envelope))

28 Ariana:	**Sí::: y los guardas siempre, ah? Dónde lo pones?**
	Ye:::s and you always safeguard them, huh?
	Where do you put them?
29 Karla:	**EE::::: Mira yo, mira yo.**
	EE::::: Look me, look me.
30 Carlos:	**Allí, esa bolsa donde dice– "Come on, Baby."**

((señalando una bolsa colgada en un gancho sobre la pared))

There that bag that says– "Come on, Baby."

((signaling toward a bag hanging on a hook high on the wall))

Karla insisted on knowing where her passport was (turn 23) but wasn't getting an immediate answer, so I repeated her question (turn 25) while Carlos started to say something about one of his siblings as a baby. Toño chimed in, but Carlos spoke over him to explain that the only passport yet to be issued was Karla's, and he began to remove the documents from my hands, effectively ending the exchange. I noted that he was putting them away and I asked where they were stored (turn 28). Carlos tucked the documents back into their plastic envelope and returned the envelope to the glossy gift bag that hung on a hook high above the sofa. It was striking to me—given the relation of birth and citizenship—that he was storing these important documents in a gift bag meant for a baby shower decorated in pastel colors with the words "Come on, Baby" written along the side (turn 30).

As he hung the "Come on, Baby" bag on the wall, Carlos stated matter-of-factly: "No me acuerdo, pero teníamos los papeles cuando crecimos. Entonces Catalina no" (I don't remember, but we had papers when we grew up. So Catalina did not). This was Carlos's most explicit declaration of the meaning of the passports he'd just shown me: that he and his younger siblings shared the same birthplace and were therefore in possession of the same documents while his older sister Catalina was different because she was born in Mexico and so lacked papers. Carlos's reference to being too young to remember suggests that he is talking about being born or being a baby, underscoring his grasp of the relationship between birthplace and citizenship, an association made vivid by the "Come on, Baby" bag. The fact that Carlos knew where the documents were stored and that he solemnly displayed and then stowed them demonstrated just how central these papers were to the family. Yet this sophisticated display was only possible at home because Carlos would never bring these documents to school.

Although Catalina—the oldest child and the only undocumented sibling in the Mendoza family—was largely quiet during this exchange, she welcomed the opportunity to talk more about it with me a few months later, after Carlos and Toño had made their trip to Mexico. One afternoon as I walked her home from school, I brought up Carlos's passport show-and-tell; she remembered that visit clearly. I described how surprised I'd been when he shared the family's passports with me so early on in our relationship; it had seemed to seamlessly follow his display of favorite toys. I explained my theory—that somehow Carlos knew this was an important set of objects in the house—and I asked Catalina for her sense of why Carlos had chosen to share the papers. Did she think he understood their importance? She offered:

> I think he does know because they [our parents] showed him
> that when he was six or seven. He left to Mexico, yeah, and
> um, he said that um this book, they showed them to a man
> and there was other papers that they showed. That's what he
> said so that he could go to Mexico.

Catalina went on to explain that Carlos and Toño had been sent to Mexico with a trusted adult so that they could visit their grandmother. She wished she had been able to make that trip to visit the rural part of Central Mexico where her *abuela* (grandmother) still lived, and where she herself had remained when her parents left Mexico for the United States. It was only after they had crossed the border and found some stability in New York City that they sent for Catalina; without papers, it was too risky for Catalina to attempt a visit to Mexico.

I probed further, wanting to know why Catalina thought Carlos would share the family's papers with me on that day. It was one thing for him to have an awareness that family members had different papers, but it was another for him to find this information meaningful enough to share with me. She explained that even though Carlos knew those papers were important, he didn't care much about them. Seeing that I didn't really understand her distinction between knowing and caring, she offered up an analogy:

> It's like my dad's car. I know that it's important but if it gets stolen I don't really [care]. I do care but it's not that important for me because it's not mine. . . . It's not a big deal for me, it's only a big deal for my dad because it's his.

The conversation continued:

Ariana:	So the an<u>alogy</u>:: with the <u>pa::</u>pers is it's your brother knows >but it's not that important to him<?
Catalina:	Yeah if it- if- if it gets wet? he's like (sarcastic) oh wo::::w, and he doesn't-
Ariana:	Right, right, right, right. Well and how about for you?
Catalina:	For me its gonna be a <u>big deal</u> hhh
Ariana:	Right, righ, righ, righ, right. Why would it be a big deal?
Catalina:	If it was mine I would be. I would be like °that's not cool.
Ariana:	Mmhmm why cuz what would happen if something happened to yours?
Catalina:	If you can't get another one that would be. That would be so like uhhh

((like the sound of getting the wind knocked out of you))

Across these exchanges, Carlos and Catalina shared fundamental ideas about documentation and what it meant for them. First they made it clear that they know their family members have different types of immigration status because they were born in different places. Building on that basic fact, the siblings understood that having different kinds of papers leads to different opportunities: family members with U.S. citizenship can participate in activities that other family members are barred from (for example, traveling to see loved ones in Mexico). Additionally, they understood that loved ones born in Mexico live with uncertainty about being able to remain in the United States and obtain U.S. citizenship. Finally, and above all, both children expressed just how much they knew about the significance of immigration status, and—at the young ages of seven and ten—they showed us how it shaped their view of the world, their place, and each other.[13]

The spiraling curriculum of citizenship—how children as young as Carlos begin to understand the significance of papers, an understanding that deepens as they grow—becomes more visible to us as undocumented parents and children interpret the school documents that are sent home. Even though the important protective mandates issuing from the *Plyler* ruling prohibit educators from inquiring about students' immigration status, the topic of citizenship arises regularly throughout a student's educational trajectory. As children move between school and home, they facilitate the circulation of papers that are not as "weighty" as passports but are nonetheless significant in practical and symbolic ways. School documents that travel home can produce the chilling effects that *Plyler* is meant to prevent, prompting conversations in mixed-status families about how to participate safely in educational programs and activities.

We turn now to two kinds of school documents that circulate in mixed-status families' homes. We will first examine forms that address parents as the primary audience, as in the case of school lunch forms that public school parents are asked to complete in order to enroll their children in the federally funded free and reduced price lunch program. We will then turn to homework assignments that address children in their role as students, prompting them to broach the subject of immigration with their families.

School Lunch

At each stage of her educational trajectory, Catalina's understanding of what it means not to have U.S. citizenship has deepened as she has had to make sense of documents circulating between home and school. As she has grown older, she has continued to experience firsthand the ways in which different immigration statuses mean different levels of access and opportunity for her and her siblings. Educators often use the language of citizenship metaphorically—to mean a child's good behavior or participation, or to attempt to enlist parental involvement—but in mixed-status homes, the term citizenship conjures up much more. As children move between school and home, they facilitate the circulation of papers that travel with them in their backpacks and school folders. As these papers circulate, they often spark a confrontation between the various meanings of citizenship (as juridical status, as belonging, as a standard of behavior).[14] Listening in as Catalina and Jimena interpret school documents helps illuminate the disconnect between the educators' intended meanings and what the documents signify within a mixed-status household.

Jimena asked me if I would help her with interpreting school forms because, in her words, "a Catalina le había dado flojera" (Catalina had a bout of laziness). I have found that in homes where I'm present as an ethnographer, parents will often ask me to play this brokering role instead of their child. On this day, Catalina was present as her mother and I discussed the packet of documents sent home at the start of the school year, which included the school lunch form. Before looking at this particular form, Jimena noted—gesturing toward Catalina, who was sitting beside us—that we would probably need to take into account the fact that "como ella no nació aquí no le dan cupones" (since she wasn't born here they don't give her food stamps). Using the colloquial term (*cupones* in Spanish and food stamps in English) for the federal Supplemental Nutrition Assistance Program (SNAP), Jimena indicated one of the impacts of the differing immigration statuses among her children: as the Mexican-born undocumented child, Catalina was denied access to the same social services that her siblings were entitled to as U.S. citizens.

Shown below is an excerpt from the application that Jimena

needed to complete in order to enroll Catalina and her three younger siblings in the free or reduced price lunch program at P.S. 432. The materials included instructions, starting with the following words, which appeared capitalized and underlined at the top of the page:

TODO NIÑO, SIN IMPORTAR SU ESTADO MIGRATORIO, TIENE DERECHO A PARTICIPAR EN EL PROGRAMA DE COMIDAS ESCOLARES Y EL PROGRAMA DE LECHE GRATIS

ALL CHILDREN REGARDLESS OF IMMIGRATION STATUS, ARE ELIGIBLE FOR THE SCHOOL MEALS PROGRAM AND THE MILK PROGRAM

Despite the form's bold, bilingual assurance about eligibility, the document nevertheless provoked confusion and anxiety. Translation of these sentences alone proved insufficient because the form went on to ask for information that encoded immigration status, thereby undercutting the family's confidence in the inclusiveness of the program.

After completing the form with her children's information, Jimena was instructed to enter her name and the last four digits of her social security number. There was also an option that read: "If you do not have a Social Security Number check this box." At this point in the form, Jimena hesitated and asked me to advise her. She was worried about completing the form because in her mind, entering her name and checking that box was akin to disclosing her undocumented status to the school administration. She was torn. She knew her four children would benefit from participating in the school's nutritional program (the entire family would, in fact, be better off if they could save money by enrolling), but she also feared sharing her undocumented status because she did not know where this form would end up once submitted. Despite the bold type informing parents and guardians in mixed-status families that their children had the right to receive the food and milk distributed by the school, there was nothing to reassure undocumented adults that they could safely complete the form and secure their child's place in the free lunch program without risking disclosure, detention, or deportation.

Our conversation that afternoon was inconclusive. I explained to Jimena that I understood her concern and that I did not know if anyone outside of P.S. 432's school staff would ever see the form. I also suggested that Jimena check in with the school's parent coordinator—a staff person whom I knew she trusted—for additional reassurance. Jimena did not complete the form in my presence. Instead, she set it aside and noted that she would ask me for additional advice in the future, saying, "Voy a poner los papeles en mi folder para que tú me los lea" (I'm going to put these papers in my folder so that you can read them for me). I heard an intergenerational echo here of Carlos's language when he finished showing me his family's passports—"los voy a guardar" (I'm going to put them away)—indicating their shared preoccupation with safeguarding any documents that might relate to immigration status. Jimena did ultimately submit the free lunch form.

Jimena and I had this conversation several years before Donald Trump would try to explicitly marry immigration policy to nutritional benefits provided through schools. In 2020, his administration attempted to amend the public charge rule, which is a criterion by which the U.S. government evaluates applications for legal permanent resident status or U.S. citizenship on the basis of whether the government considers an individual an economic burden to the country.[15] The proposed change to the rule would have made a child's enrollment in a nutritional benefit program like SNAP or the free lunch program a strike against their parent or guardian's application to become a legal permanent resident or U.S. citizen. This change was never approved by Congress, but the proposal alone received wide media attention and scared immigrant parents away from enrolling in this long-standing social service provided daily in public schools.[16] This is only one example of the way in which mixed-status families may come to fear participating in public schools when schools appear aligned with immigration authorities that are punitive and potentially destructive to family life.[17]

This exchange recalls Vieira's discussion of moments when "the border thickens" in the lives of mixed-status families—the many moments when policies that seek to deter or detain immigrants move from the border to affect the everyday lives of families living within the country's interior.[18] The Mendoza family's discussion about a form that ostensibly had to do with nutritional services opened on to other topics relevant to access and belonging. Having noted the difference between Catalina and her three younger U.S.-born siblings, her parents talked more about other schooling-related topics that linked with her immigration status. As Jimena put the school lunch form away, her husband, Juan, talked about how Catalina "necesita echarle ganas en la escuela para graduarse y entrar en college" (needs to put in effort in school in order to graduate and be admitted to college). Although he hoped that all of his children would do well in school, this advice was relevant "especialmente a ella" (especially to her), referring indirectly to Catalina, who was still sitting with us. Juan went on to explain, nodding toward Catalina once again, "Yo fui a una clase de inglés en Jay Street a ver si podría hace preguntas sobre ella" (I went to an English class on Jay Street to see if I could ask questions about her). Juan was pursuing his own study of English to maximize his own eligibility for policies that might grant amnesty to undocumented immigrants, but he was also keen on figuring out whether Catalina herself was eligible for the new DACA program. She did meet the eligibility requirement of having immigrated to the United States before 2012, but she was too young (ten instead of fifteen years of age) to enroll in the program. As a result, her postsecondary options were still unclear, and her need to put in effort in order to overcome the structural inequities she faced was paramount to her and her parents.[19]

Homework

A big part of being successful in school is completing assignments and homework, and Catalina, along with Aurora, Pita, Hazel, Tere, and Jenni, were all attuned to the importance of getting good grades and high praise for their schoolwork. We will see signs, as the study progresses, of Chang's hyperdocumentation, as the children and their families expressed their deep investment in educational documents (report cards, diplomas), conceiving of them either as steps toward obtaining juridical citizenship or as symbolic substitutes for the legal documents that remain out of reach. Still, academic progress in school was fraught—not only because of the complex associations they made between educational progress and self-worth, but also because of the ways in which the school materials they were responsible for completing evoked anxieties about citizenship.

Let's now turn to a homework assignment that several of the girls encountered in sixth grade, after having graduated from P.S. 432, as part of a district-wide social studies curriculum used in their respective middle schools. I first saw the assignment on a visit to Catalina's home. It required her to interview a family member about their experience of immigrating to the United States. The homework sheet included four questions, followed by space for the student to write answers to the following prompts:

1. (a) What countries does your family come from? (b) What continents does your family come from?
2. Who in your family moved to the United States (grandma, uncle, great-grandfather, and so on)?
3. How did your family come to the United States?
4. Why did your family come to the United States?

School mandates prohibiting educators from inquiring about students' immigration status do not, of course, prohibit teaching about immigration. However, an assignment like this one, designed to foster home–school connections with immigrant families, can inadvertently produce a chilling effect.

In addition to these scripted interview questions, the homework sheet included an assignment overview, a rubric, and sample text that the students could use as a model for writing their own family immigration stories. The overview connected the students' study of geography to their family's experiences of immigration, beginning with the statement: "Geography includes us! While we live in New York, not all of our families' [sic] have origins in New York." This claim to a shared immigrant experience was followed by a metaphorical view of citizenship—"we are citizens of the world!"—meant to communicate a sense of equal belonging.[20] The rubric detailed the steps that children needed to complete to fulfill the assignment and included language that could be especially stressful for undocumented students living with the realities of surveillance and deportation: "I tracked my families' migration," "I collected and recorded my families' interview answers," and "I brought in a photo." Although the final project was meant to celebrate classroom diversity, for students aware of birthright citizenship, juridical differences, and their attendant risks, the assignment evoked surveillance as much as community building.[21]

After learning about this assignment at Catalina's apartment, I took a picture of it to share with Aurora, Pita, Hazel, Tere, and Jenni at our next grupo de análisis meeting. Aurora had an interpretation of the assignment that I found significant. She associated this homework assignment with other clerical systems that she was familiar with. The "blue card" that she references below is a document that all families enrolled in New York City public schools must complete and update annually with their address, demographic information, and emergency contacts. Aurora explained:

> **Que la escuela quería saber un poco de su pasado de los estudiantes y la manera en que vinistes. Como aquí dice: How did your family come to the United States? So, quieren averiguar un poquito cómo fue tu experiencia viniendo a este país. A mí también me preguntaron esas preguntas, y es como . . . quieren saber un poquito más de lo que tus padres filled out en el blue card. Like un poquito de tu pasado, fue de la inmigración, que es lo mismo. Solo están preguntando: Ohhh, cómo . . . por qué tu familia vino a los Estados Unidos? Que por una mejor vida o por dinero? Cosas así.**

> That the school wanted to know a little bit more about the students' past and the way in which you came. Like here it says: How did your family come to the United States? So, they wanted to find out a little bit about what your experience was like coming to this country. They asked me these questions too, and it's like . . . they want to know a little more than what your parents filled out on the blue card. Like a little bit about your past, it was about immigration, which is almost the same thing. They're just asking: Ohhh, how . . . why did your family come to the United States? For a better life or for more money? Things like that.

Although the assignment seemed to assume that the children themselves are U.S. born (it did not ask them to recount their own immigration experiences), Aurora went on to imagine that she was being interviewed. She explained that when asked where she is from, "I would say from Mexico but when they ask me if I have papers I say yes." Aurora, in other words, immediately associated this assignment with questions of birthright citizenship, which made her uncomfortable, and she was frank about how she would misrepresent her immigration status if asked. In her interpretation of this homework document, Jenni also assumed that it was about papeles and *residencia* (residency).[22]

This wasn't the first time Aurora had spoken about resisting the pressure to divulge her immigration status.[23] Consider this excerpt from an exchange we'd had after a previous grupo de análisis meeting.

Aurora:	ᵒCuz I'm not like my cousins I'm ↑different. From ↑all my cousins, almost all my cousins were born HERE and I wasn't. I'm <u>tot</u>ally Mexican.
Ariana:	Yes. Yes.
Aurora:	Not American. Mexican.
Ariana:	Yep, yep.
Aurora:	But I don't have papers. I'm just gonna put that I'm American cuz it makes me more opportunities but just because of that because the rest I'm totally Mexican.
Ariana:	Totally. Yep yep yep.
Aurora:	Yeah. At the same time I think sometimes that it won't be that hard-
Ariana:	Uh huh
Aurora:	-to grab [get papers].
Ariana:	Uh huh
Aurora:	Cuz hhh it's been like. Like if I was ↑born here hh cause almost yeah hh.
Ariana:	Cuz you've been here so long you mean?
Aurora:	Yeah hh
Ariana:	Right
Aurora:	And. I've not really FAILed ↑a:::nything.

Here Aurora displayed a complex understanding of intrafamilial differences arising from birthplace, and of the relationship between having papers and having opportunities. She also indicated how questions of juridical and cultural citizenship intersect, and how her understanding of belonging is inextricable from her sense of self-worth. Having come to the United States before the age of two, Aurora felt "it's like I was born here almost." Given her good academic record of "not really [having] failed anything," she felt that she deserved U.S. citizenship. This echoes other conversations I've had with children in mixed-status homes who equate being eligible for citizenship with the idea of being good—something that can be proven by staying out of trouble, purchasing a house or car, and being part of a household that contributes to society economically.[24]

This chapter has shown how children in mixed-status families embark, from a young age, on a spiraling curriculum of citizenship in which they come to understand the significance of immigration status, often before they're capable of expressing such knowledge explicitly. It is a curriculum that unfolds during the course of everyday life and deepens over time as children encounter different kinds of papers that matter to them. School documents sent into mixed-status families often inadvertently evoke anxiety and provoke conversations that further expose children to the realities of their and their loved ones' juridical statuses. As we will see in subsequent chapters, the relationship between immigration papers and educational documents only grows in symbolic value across the lifespan. In chapter 3, as we return to the classroom setting, we will hear more from Catalina, Aurora, Pita, Hazel, Tere, and Jenni about how and when they evoke, through both speech and silence, immigration status at school.

Three
Speech or Silence at School

How do students draw on the lessons learned from the spiraling curriculum of citizenship during the school day? How are their responses to classroom assignments and activities informed by what they know about citizenship, and what they want others to know or not know? Having considered some of the ways in which papers circulate between home and school and accrue meaning in the lives of children, let's now return to the classroom to consider how students describe—or refuse to describe—their immigration experiences at school.

This chapter builds on two key insights that we have gained thus far. The first is that children from mixed-status families are cognizant of their immigration status and have a deepening understanding of what it means to have or lack U.S. citizenship. Second, children learn that talking about their citizenship status can pose risks to their loved ones or themselves, so they are intentional about when and how they disclose it. Building on these lessons, we will engage in a close reading of how Catalina and Pita narrated their immigration experiences for a school assignment. In so doing, we will learn about how they made sense of their early childhood experiences of migration and how that shaped their hopes for the present and future. We will also consider what their narratives tell us about when they disclose or downplay their own stories of migration. Finally, we will examine teacher and peer narratives about diversity and immigration co-constructed during classroom interactions and consider a revealing moment when

Aurora redirected a classroom activity in order to avoid being forced to disclose her undocumented status.

Narratives are a core part of how we make sense of our lives and articulate our place in the world. Telling stories helps us to "imbue life events with a temporal and logical order, to demystify them and establish coherence across past, present, and as yet unrealized experience."[1] Throughout this study, I heard Pita, Hazel, Aurora, Catalina, Jenni, and Tere retell and revise core narratives related to their immigration experiences. By telling these stories, they tried to make sense of the differences they perceived between themselves, their siblings, and their peers. These narratives did not just refer to the past and present; they also communicated the girls' imagination of their futures. Teachers and students in school also reproduced and revised narratives about citizenship and belonging. One common narrative—which we noted in chapter 2 with the "citizens of the world" homework assignment—is that the United States is a nation of immigrants. By universalizing the immigrant experience, this narrative erases specific histories of colonialism and enslavement while projecting an imagined present and future society in which immigrants assimilate, with existing social inequalities and power hierarchies magically disappearing.[2]

The stories that we tell do much more than chronicle a series of events; they also reveal what we believe to be right and wrong, good and bad. As Elinor Ochs and Lisa Capps observe, narrative is an important "medium for determining moral truths, through either consolidation of what members believe or reasoning that calls into question existing moral horizons."[3] The personal memoirs and classroom narratives examined in the coming pages involved a set of risks unique to the particular sociopolitical context of mixed-status childhoods. Sharing stories about crossing the border or living undocumented always entails a risk of moral judgment, especially at a time when the criminalization of immigrants permeated mainstream political discourse, news media, and everyday conversations. The girls were attuned to the immediate risks involved in disclosing their own or their loved ones' immigration status. In a context of heightened anti-immigrant sentiment and punitive immigration policies, they feared that their family's efforts to migrate, settle, and survive in this country could be suddenly upended by detention or deportation. As a result, they experienced—and communicated—different degrees of inquietud when the subject of immigration was broached at school.

Personal Memoir

Ms. Daniela started her fifth-grade language arts curriculum with a unit on personal memoir writing that lasted for the first two months of the school year. She had two main goals: to develop students' written fluency and to foster classroom community by asking students to share stories with one another. A core pedagogical principle of this unit was that children would be better able to learn new writing skills if they were permitted to write about topics familiar to them. The assignment read, "Tell the story of an important time or event in your life." The assignment was introduced in English, but unit activities were conducted in both English and Spanish, and students were given permission to write in either language, or both. Throughout the unit, Ms. Daniela introduced her students to narrative conventions, including reported speech and dialogue, adverbs marking temporal transitions (such as "then" and "when"), and descriptive language using simile and metaphor. The format for the writing assignment was teacher led, but the content was completely student directed; in other words, students were not instructed to share a memory related to any particular theme or topic.

The personal memoir unit divided the writing process into various stages. First, students brainstormed a list of *recuerdos* (memories) that were important to them. Second, as Ms. Daniela conducted a series of lessons on narrative conventions—for example, the rules for representing dialogue in English versus Spanish texts—students were encouraged to draft several different narratives that incorporated what they had learned. Third, students were asked to choose one personal narrative that they wanted to revise and publish; they would prepare a final draft of their story to share with their classmates during a publishing party. These final texts would also be displayed publicly in the school on bulletin boards for students, teachers, and family members to read. As a result, choosing which story to write also involved making explicit decisions about what memories students felt comfortable sharing with a wide audience.

I collected data from the personal memoir unit by photographing the pages of the writing notebooks that Ms. Daniela required each student to use throughout the school year. In their black-and-white composition notebooks, the students drafted stories and responded to Ms. Daniela's prompts to brainstorm ideas, engage in freewriting, and reflect on their writing. Here my goal is not to assess Catalina's or Pita's writing but to explore the ways they narrated moments that they considered central to their lives. I have reproduced the students' original writing in bold. My translations attempt to reflect the unique features of their writing. In what follows, I will juxtapose the published and unpublished memoirs, examining what the writers withhold from wider circulation. Publishing is a form of making public, and this assignment unintentionally provoked students to consider the dilemmas associated with disclosure. Strikingly, both Catalina and Pita recount their younger sisters' birthdays—memories that are metonymic of the complexity of growing up in mixed-status families because citizenship is primarily determined by birthplace.

Catalina

Let's first take a close look at Catalina's unpublished personal memoir. This untitled story describes living in Mexico with her abuela when her mother migrated to the United States. Catalina was three years old when her mother left Mexico, and it was several years before Catalina was able to join her in New York.

Sin titulo

Mi primera vez que mi mama me dejo sola en Mexico no mas lloraba y lloraba en la noche tambien al segundo dia yo casi no lloraba visitaba a los vesinos pero las noches lloraba porque mi mamá no estuvo con migo ese dia y aveses me portaba bien. Tambien siempre perdia las chanclas de mi mar abuelita porque jugaba con ellos y despues se me olvidaban donde los dejaba. Me portaba mal porque no me dejaba bañarme mi abuelita me decia que me bañara y

yo no la obedecia tambien yo me despertaba temprano y pedia tacos para comer me sentia sola porque mi mamá no estuvo con migo tambien porque no tenía con quien jugar y. Un dia mi abuela dijo "que no haga esto y lo hice" porque yo queria poner masa en la tortillera para hacer tacos y despues por acidente meti mis manos en la totillera y me machuque. Y me dolio muy fuerte mis abuelos me llebavan por todo el pueblo para ber tiendas y beia la grande iglesia tengo una prima yo no me llevaba bien con ella porque hagarraba mis jugetes y no me gustava siempre me peleaba con ella no le emprestaba mis juguetes y un dia cuando mi tia se hiba a la escuela yo no quería que se fuera y yo la abrasaba y mi abuelita decia que la deje que se le hacia tarde para la escuela y no queria dejarla y me regañaron. Me senti muy triste cuando mi mama me dejo cuando tenia 3 años.

Untitled

The first time that my mom left me alone in Mexico I just cried and cried in the night also the second day I almost didn't cry I visited neighbors but at night I cried because my mom wasn't with me that day and sometimes I behaved. Also I always lost my ~~mar~~ grandmothers slippers because I played with them and then forgot where I left them. I behaved badly because I didn't let her bathe my grandmother said bathe and I also didn't listen because I would wake up early and asked for tacos to eat I felt alone because my mom wasn't with me also because I had no one to play with and. One day my grandmother said "don't do that and I did it" because I wanted to put the mix on the tortilla maker to make tacos and then by accident I stuck my hand in the tortilla maker and I got smashed. It hurt me very badly and my grandparents took me all around the town to see stores and a big church. I have a cousin I didn't get along well with her because she grabbed my toys and I didn't like it I always fought with her and she didn't borrow my toys and one day when my aunt was going to school I didn't want her to go and I hugged her and my grandmother said that I let her leave she's going to be late for school

and I didn't want to let her go and they scolded me. I was very
sad when my mom left me when I was three years old.

Asked to write about an important moment in her life, Catalina
recounted part of the origin story of her mixed-status family. The
story opens with Catalina being left in her grandmother's care
in Mexico when her mother migrated north to the United States.
This event marked the beginning of Catalina's own migration
story, because her mother, Jimena (whom we met in chapter 2), left
Mexico for the United States with the goal of establishing herself
and sending for Catalina.

The first line of Catalina's narrative begins with feelings of sadness ("I cried and cried") and foreshadows that the rest of the pas-
sage will focus on her own conduct ("and sometimes I behaved").
Catalina recounted a series of events that she described as mis-
behaving in the care of her abuela. She provided six examples in
all: losing her grandmother's slippers, not allowing herself to be
bathed, waking up too early and asking for tacos, cooking without
permission, fighting over toys with a cousin, and hugging an aunt
for too long, causing her to be late for school. This last detail is consistent with the rest of the story while also marking a different vision for her future: Catalina clung to her aunt who was running
late and had to leave; in so doing, she expressed a longing to be held
closely by a loved one whom she did not have to separate from. The
final sentence of the story returns to Catalina's mother, whom she
missed dearly and wanted to be reunited with.

Catalina's tender personal memoir checked all of the boxes for
detail and descriptive language that the assignment required, but
she decided not to publish it. Catalina instead chose to draft a different personal memoir to submit for wider circulation. As we will
see in the next story, her published narrative focused on celebrat-
ing her younger sister's birthday a few years later in Brooklyn.
Examining her writing over time, we find a significant elision between this first story and the second: Catalina never accounted
for how she went from Mexico to New York City, and she makes
no mention of her own immigration experience or juridical status. This is not to say that she never talked about these things. In
our grupo de análisis, Catalina shared, "Yo no tengo papeles, pero
yo vine en avión. Porque me prestaron papeles. Me prestaron un

papel. Sí por mí yo no vine caminando" (I don't have papers, but I came by plane. Because they lent me papers. They lent me a paper. Yes, for me I didn't come walking). Although she shared her story of crossing the border during our small research group meetings, she decided not to share those details in the personal memoir assignment, which she knew would be viewed by her classmates and teachers.

Catalina's published personal memoir details her family's efforts to prepare a birthday celebration when her younger sister turned three. In her writing notebook, Catalina explained why she chose to publish this recuerdo: "Yo elejí esa memoria porque es muy especial para mi cuando conoci a mi hermanita era mi primer hermanita que tenia esta muy alegre" (I chose this memory because it is very special to me when I met my sister. She was my first sister and I was very happy). Catalina's shift of attention to her U.S.-born sister's birthday didn't erase immigration as a topic. Instead she encoded it. Without ever referring directly to migration or citizenship, the excerpt below pinpoints stark differences in their early childhood experiences linked to their respective immigration statuses.

El primer cumpleaños de mi hermana

MANA!!! AY grite "Feliz cumpleanos Karla" le dije a mi hermanita "hoy es enero 6" dije, mi mamá y papá estaban decorando la casa pense por mi misma ohh hoy van a hacer los cumpleanos de mi hermanita ya habian puesto las mesas para que los invitados se sienten mi mamá dijo a mi y mis hermanos que nos quedemos en la casa porque hiban a hir a comprar unas cosas para poner en la mesas y hiban a comprar una piñata. Mi papá me dijo "limpia las mesas porque hestan susios" "ok" dije. agarre baunty y windex para limpiar cuando termine me fui a mi cuarto a ber (Goosebums) ese era mi mejor show cuando mi papá y mama bino vi que compraron una fonda de mesa y unas flores que briyan y tambien compraron una piñata tenia un dibujo de una persona de caricatura que se llama (pitufina). Despues pasaron minutos y despues tocaron la puerta Nok Nok abri la puerta y era mi madrina bino para ayudar a mi mama a cosinar comida cuando mi papá vino

habia traido chiken nugets mi mamá nos dio comida que
era espageti y chiken nugets despues cuando habia ter-
minado de comer tocaron la puerta otraves me pregunte
quien sera?. Lo abri la puerta era mi hamiga que conosia
nosotras estuvimos. Juntas desde Kinder hasta terser
grado yo le dije vamos a jugar mi 3PS nos fuimos al cuarto
y empezamos a jugar despues le hablo a su mamá vamos a
comer ella se fue a comer. . . . Jugamos con mi hermanita
porque no tenia con quien jugar. Mi mama me dijo que le
ponga su vestido porque vamos a tomarles fotos le puse su
camiseta y sus zapatos despues su vestido azul con blanco.
Mi papa siempre le compra vestido azul porque como mi
papa le gusta el color azul cuando termine de cambiarla
mi mamá la peino y le puso su corona que tenia el numero
3 despues mi papá saco el pastel era de Hello Kitty con un
muñequita que prende en la noche.

My sister's first birthday

SIS!!! OH I screamed "happy birthday Karla" I told my little
sister "today is January 6" I said, my mom and dad were deco-
rating the house and I thought to myself ohhhh today is my
sister's birthday and they had already set out the tables for
the guests my mom said to me and my brothers that we would
stay at home because they were going to buy somethings to
set on the tables and they were going to buy a piñata. My dad
said "clean the tables because they are dirty" "ok" I said. I
grabbed baunty and windex to clean when I finished I went to
my room to watch (Goosebums) that was the best show when
my dad and mom came I saw that they bought a table cloth
and flowers that shine and they also brought a pinata that had
a cartoon on it named (Smurfette). Then a few minutes passed
and they knocked on the door Nok Nok I opened the door and
it was my godmother who came to help my mom cook when
my dad came he bought chicken nuggets my mom gave us food
which was spaghetti and chicken nuggets after we finished
eating someone else knocked on the door and I asked myself
who could it be?. I opened the door and it was my friend who
I've known we've been. Together from kindergarten until

third grade and I said let's play my 3PS we went to the room
and started to play then her mom told her to come eat and she
went to eat.... We played with my sister because she didn't
have anyone to play with. My mom told me put on her dress
because we are going to take pictures I put on her t-shirt and
her shoes then her blue and white dress. My dad always buys a
blue dress because he likes the color blue and when I finished
changing her my mom combed her hair and put on her crown
which had the number 3 after that my dad took out the cake
made of Hello Kitty with a little doll that lit up at night.

I am struck by the important detail—mentioned quickly toward
the end when Catalina described her sister's birthday outfit—that
Karla was turning three years old. The fact that she was the same
age here as Catalina was in the previous story intensifies an implicit contrast between the sisters' childhood experiences. Against
this backdrop, the birthday party served as a site for Catalina to
think through the meaning of birthright citizenship. In her family,
U.S. citizenship was celebrated as the fulfillment of the promise of
migration, affording Karla a range of opportunities unavailable to
Catalina and her parents as undocumented immigrants. Catalina
managed to express all of this for anyone capable of reading between the lines while also hiding it from those she feared might
use knowledge of her juridical status against her.

The symmetry of the protagonists' ages underscores other key
points of comparison between Catalina's and Karla's childhoods.
The two stories convey opposing sentiments. The first begins
with Catalina crying into the night because her mother had left,
while the second begins with screams of joy because it is her sister's birthday. In addition, the relationships depicted suggest that
Catalina felt less of a sense of belonging in her pueblo than in New
York City. She described fraught relations with her grandmother,
cousin, and aunt, whereas in Brooklyn she was surrounded by her
parents and siblings along with her godmother and a close school
friend. Finally, Catalina described her own behavior quite differently before and after her own migration. Whereas in Mexico she
was a mischievous young child who lost her abuela's slippers, in
the United States she was an obedient older sister who cleaned the
house and tended younger siblings. In both narratives, Catalina

communicated her desire for a future characterized by family closeness uninterrupted by separation across borders.

The differences in these personal memoirs produce contrast-
ing portraits of citizenship and childhood. It would be misleading,
however, to conclude that Mexico is only characterized by sadness
and scarcity whereas the United States is only filled with love and
abundance. In fact, Catalina relished many aspects of her grandparents' care, and she often longed for them, the land, and the ani-
mals that surrounded her in their town. She, Jenni, Tere, and Pita
could remember being young children in Mexico, the Dominican
Republic, and El Salvador, and they often lamented that Brooklyn
life meant being cooped up in apartments without the freedom to
play on their own like they once could.

In choosing which story to publish, Catalina encoded her complex knowledge about citizenship without explicitly disclosing her
own immigration status. The spiraling curriculum of citizenship
not only influences what a young person knows about birthright
citizenship but also what she does with that knowledge—if and
when and how she shares it with others. A reader who assumed
Catalina was too young to understand citizenship's significance
would miss how much insight her narrative communicated about
growing up undocumented in a mixed-status family. We'll turn
now to another birthday story told by Pita, the eldest sister in her
mixed-status family.

Pita

Pita, like Catalina, also came to the United States as an undocumented child, and she also wrote a personal memoir recounting
her younger U.S.-born sister's birth. This is Pita's unpublished and
untitled personal memoir:

> **Sin titulo**
>
> **Era un día soliado escuche el telefono.—¡Halo! ¿Hola
> mamá como esta?—Yo le pregunte. Ella me dijo—Bien
> bien! ¡Y sabes que, que voy a tene un bebéééé!—No lo pude
> creer. Entonces le pregunte—¿n verdad?—Yo brinque y
> brinque!! ¡Grite de emocionamiento! Yo le pregunte—¿Va
> hacer niña o niño?—Ella me contesto—¡Niña!—Yo me emo-**

cione más en lo que estaba. El dia siguiente me desperte
fui al baño me lave los dientes y me di un baño caliente. Y
cuando sali le pregunte a mi papa con encanto—¿Podemos
ir hoy a visitar a mi mamá al hospital por favooor?—Y el
dijo—ok—todavia dormitado. . . . Cuando llegamos yo le
entrege el telefono a mi papá. Yo le pregunte a una muchacha (enfermera)—¿Adonde queda el cuarto de Amaya?—
Ella me contesto—¡Recto al final a la derecha!—Yo le
dije—¡gracias!—. . . Cuando entre no lo podia creer mi
mamá estaba en la cama con mi hermana en los brazos. Yo
le pregunte—¿Mami puedo aguantar mi hermanita?—Ella
me dijo—¡¡Claro que si!!—Y esa fue mi primera vez que yo
la aguante y la sigo aguantando hoy día, presente!
   FIN!

Untitled

It was a sunny day I heard the phone. "Hello? Hi mom how are
you?" I asked her. She told me "Fine, fine! You know I'm going to
have a babyyyy!" I couldn't believe it. Then I asked her "really?"
I jumped and jumped!! I screamed with emotion! I asked her
"Is it going to be a boy or girl?" She answered "Girl!" I got even
more excited than I already was. The next day I woke up I
went to the bathroom brushed my teeth and took a hot bath.
And when I came out I asked my dad with joy "can we visit my
mom in the hospital pleeease?" and he said "ok" sleepily. . . .
When we arrived I gave my dad his phone. I asked a woman
(nurse) "where is Amaya's room?" She told me "straight to the
end on the right!" And I said "thank you!" . . . When I entered
I couldn't believe it my mom was on the bed with my sister in
her arms. I asked her "Mom can I hold my little sister?" She
said "Of course!" And that was the first time I held my sister
and I continue holding her until this day, presently!
   END!

Even though this story doesn't narrate migration across national
borders, it is nevertheless saturated with questions of citizenship.
The narrative begins with Pita receiving a call from her mother,
Amaya, who delivers the news of Pita's sibling's birth. Pita then
navigates the short but significant journey from her home to her

mother's bedside in the hospital. As the linguistic and cultural broker between her father and the institution, Pita was responsible for speaking with the nurses and asking for her mother's hospital room. It was her presence that enabled them to arrive quickly and joyously at her mother's side. It is notable that Pita ended her memoir with a subtle but significant detail that extends this memory into the future: by holding on to her U.S.-born sibling, Pita also symbolically held on to the promise of obtaining U.S. citizenship. Like Catalina, Pita's desire for belonging within her family was inseparable from the caregiving role that she had for her younger sister.

In contrast, Pita's published personal memoir, entitled "Frontera," is a marked departure from the subtler references to migration that we have read thus far. Here, she explicitly narrated a story that she recounted at many points throughout the study to me, in our small group data analysis meetings, and to her class. This is an excerpt from Pita's story of crossing the U.S.–Mexico border on her way from El Salvador to the United States to reunite with her mother.

Frontera

Cuando yo cruze la frontera primero me llevaron a una casa para que descansara. Despues agarramos una troca y empezamos a recorrer. El sol estaba más caliente que agua hervida. 2 dias despues en la frontera, alguien vino corriendo y a la misma vez gritando—¡¡la patruya viene!!— Todos empesamos a correr. Yo y la muchacha no corrimos caminamos rapido. El policia nos agarro. Nos dio agua, un sandwich de queso y jamon. Y despues nos scepararon y fuimos a un lugar quenos cuidan mientras alguien viene para recogernos.

Border

When I crossed the border first they took me to a house in order to rest. Then we grabbed a truck and started the trip. The sun was hotter than boiled water. 2 days later on the border, someone came running and at the same time screaming "the police are coming!!" We all started to run. Me and the girl didn't run we walked fast. The police grabbed us. They gave us water, a ham and cheese sandwich. And then they separated us and we went to a place where they take care of us while someone comes to pick us up.

Pita's border crossing story recalls the birth story reproduced above through its step-by-step chronicling of a significant moment. We can almost imagine that her sister's birth story—tinged with urgency and uncertainty even amid happiness—was an allegory of her own migration experience and reuniting with her mother in the United States. In both cases, she moved from one place to another, traversing boundaries: crossing a border from one country to another, and crossing a threshold from the domestic space of her home into the institutional hospital setting. Here too it is striking that her narrative ends with being picked up—a phrase with multiple meanings that echo across her stories, from lifting her sister in an embrace to waiting for someone to come for her at the border. These narrative moments express a desire for a future in which family members could be permanently united.

Unlike Catalina, who quietly omitted any mention of her own migration experience from her personal memoirs, Pita expressed a strong sense of responsibility to share this story with others. Pita was motivated by a desire to improve the public's perception of immigrants and was enabled by the comparatively higher degree of safety she now had as a permanent resident.

As she explained to me many times:

Yo decido compartir esta historia para que gente sepa que yo fui una de esas, que yo pasé por eso, que no soy una niña que crece acá. Tengo una aventura que no todos tienen. Cuando gente ya sabe dice—oooh—y cuando van a la casa y se quedan pensando, y suena el teléfono y dicen—yo escuché este cuento de una niña—y la gente escucha y pasa, para que otra gente lo conozca bien.

I decide to tell this story so that people know that I was one of those, that I went through that, that I'm not a girl who grew up here. I had an adventure that not everyone has. When people know they say "oooh," and when they go home they keep thinking, and the phone rings and they say "I heard a story about a girl," and people hear this and it spreads, so that other people know this well.

The new privileges that Pita had acquired as a lawful permanent resident were accompanied by a sense of accountability to
her mixed-status family and community. Having participated
in the process of changing her own immigration status at such a
young age, she was keenly aware that she no longer faced the risk
of deportation—even though loved ones close to her did—and she
thought that she could help other immigrants by changing public
perception of them.

The moral undertones of Pita's immigration narrative are inextricable from the experience of getting her papers. The year I
met Pita—the same year she wrote these recuerdos—she had just
obtained her green card (officially called "lawful permanent resident" status).[4] Although Pita was no longer undocumented, her
mother was still actively involved in the process of applying for
a green card for herself. These firsthand experiences were at the
forefront of Pita's mind and shaped her understanding of the importance of birthdays and birthplace. During our many conversations over the length of this study, Pita explained to me that in
order to obtain her residencia, she and her parents had to meet
with lawyers and go before a judge to *pedir el perdón* (ask for forgiveness). This entailed appearing in court in person, answering
questions about her life and family (for example, the name of the
school she attended and her sister's birthday), and waiting for the
judge's decision regarding their case. This notion of asking for forgiveness for wrongdoing is built into the language of the immigration process and made a lasting impression on Pita. It left her with
this idea that obtaining papers consisted of more than following
steps in a legal process; it was also an act of moral repentance in
which the migrant asks for forgiveness and the state absolves them
of wrongdoing.

When school reopened after spring break that fifth-grade
year, Pita shared with me that she had obtained new papers with
a stamp signifying her change in immigration status. She told
me that once she had the official documents, "mi mamá me dio
un abrazo y me dijo—oh, ahora que tienes tus papeles te sientes
mejor" (my mom gave me a hug and said to me "oh, now that you
have your papers you feel much better"). Pita was to feel better not
only because she was safer with papers but also because she could

set aside the shame and guilt that she and her mom had expressed to me in other moments. For Pita, the experience was complicated: "En verdad me sentí muy oh my God. It's like, there's no feeling for that. Es como un montón de cosas, confused, excited, porque en verdad uno no sabe lo que van a decir, si le van a preguntar una cosa que uno no ensayó o algo así. So it was really lucky" (The truth is I felt very oh my God. It's like, there's no feeling for that. It's like a bunch of things: confused, excited, because really you don't know what they're going to say, if they're going to ask you something that you're not prepared to answer or something like that. So it was really lucky). Pita expressed her excitement, but also her sense of being "lucky" that she was granted a green card instead of being stumped by unexpected questions from an immigration judge. Bypassing the moral vocabulary of good and bad, we have seen how Pita carried concern for those who haven't been so lucky.

Catalina and Pita made decisions surrounding speech and silence—choosing to disguise or disclose their immigration experiences—according to their juridical status. Their understanding of the significance of citizenship and the risks involved in revealing their immigration status shaped their decisions about what stories to publish for the personal memoir unit. Catalina, aware of her vulnerabilities as an undocumented student, encoded her status in the story of the birthday. Pita, with the confidence and sense of obligation surrounding being one of the lucky ones with papers, used publication as an opportunity to support and advocate for her community. Both girls reacted to the pressure of publication and publicity with a sophisticated understanding of risk. We have come very far indeed from a notion of young people as ignorant of the implications of immigration status.

Classroom Conversations about Diversity

We turn now from student writing to group conversations that took place in Ms. Daniela's class. We will listen in to a set of conversations focused on themes of diversity, difference, and acceptance—concepts at the core of P.S. 432's social emotional learning curriculum. We will take a close look at two interactions representative of the kinds of classroom activities led by the social emotional learning teachers at the school. The first took place in the spring, when fifth-grade students were asked to define diversity by working in small groups to create a word web representing their ideas. The second took place near the end of the school year, when first graders participated in a diversity panel hosted by Ms. Daniela's class and shared their experiences of being bullied at school. We will consider the kinds of pressure and inquietud that Aurora and her peers felt during these interactions, where references to birthplace entailed implications about immigration status that made the girls feel exposed to moral condemnation or state surveillance. We will also take a multisensorial look at how Aurora's considered refusals to communicate—to write, speak, or stand—were themselves communicative.

Defining Diversity

In the activity that follows, the teacher asked students to work in small groups to define the term diversity. Aurora, Nellie, and Sara—with some guidance from the teacher—worked together to create a word web on a large sheet of chart paper that would be displayed for the class to see. They wrote the word "diversity" in the center of the chart paper and drew a big circle around it. As they brainstormed ideas associated with that keyword, they added lines radiating out from the circle. Aurora held the marker and wrote down her group's ideas.

For students in this mixed-status, mixed-race classroom, skin color, national origin, and language were some of the first themes to emerge. The opening lines involve multiple negotiations: choosing to write the words "countries," "immigrant," or "cultures" and debating the phrases "skin tone" or "color."

1 Nellie:	Countries, COUNTRIES, Don't write immīIGRANT? Write COUNTRIES
2 Aurora:	CULTURES instead
3 Teacher:	Cultures, cultures, cultures
4 Aurora:	Cu::ltu:::res
5 Nellie:	Uniqueness
6 Aurora:	Someone have this ((holding out a marker))

7 Nellie:	I'll rewrite it, rewrite it
8 Aurora:	Countries. Um. I have another one. Um. Likes?
9 Nellie:	↑Colors. ↑Colors.
10 Aurora:	I already put ↑SKIN TONE.
11 Teacher:	Colors? U::m
12 Aurora:	Colors over there–
13 Nellie:	Colors TOO
14 Aurora:	I already put ↑COLORS.
15 Sara:	You can discriminate by saying I don't like blue either
16 Aurora:	That's WHY we put COLORS

At this point, we have some sense of how many of the words and concepts mentioned during this brainstorm evoked questions of birthright citizenship and juridical status for Aurora. We find her in the highly charged situation of negotiating—and transcribing—in real time her feeling of what topics are permissible or too risky. If we listen carefully, we'll hear her tactically change the topic or simply refuse to write down anything at all. Nellie started off with the word "countries," and Aurora reframed with "cultures" instead. Although she ultimately wrote down "countries" in turn 8, this was her attempt to shift the conversation away from connotations of nationality and birthright citizenship and instead toward a reference to culture, which can separate belonging from birthplace.

Aurora became more explicit in her decisions about what to write when Nellie introduced the word "border" and explained her reason for bringing it up.

17 Nellie:	Border. Cause some people cross the border. And some people DIDN'T.
18 Sara:	Independence.
19 Nellie:	Yeah, independence.
20 Teacher:	Sh::::
21 Aurora:	Chill I won't put that. ᵒI'm not putting that. ᵒI'm not writing nothing. I don't wanna write anything.
22 Nellie:	Independence
23 Teacher:	Use another color
24 Aurora:	GAMES!

25 Teacher:	Use another color, use different colors. Use another color.
26 Sara:	Language. ↑ Immigration.
27 Aurora:	Awww I like green.
28 Nellie:	Oh yeah uh write language. Somebody write language.
29 Teacher:	Language
30 Aurora:	I'll write language

As we can see, Aurora responded strongly when asked to write about border crossing, choosing not to write down the word "border" in order to avoid any risk of inviting further discussion about different ways of entering the country and, by extension, the range of immigration statuses that might be represented in her classroom. When Nellie said the word "border" in turn 17, she explained that some people "cross the border" while others "didn't." In turn 21, Aurora rejected this idea, putting an end to the conversation by decisively saying she would not write it down. Nellie dropped the subject, and Aurora resumed writing a moment later when Sara said "independence" (turn 22). Aurora reentered the conversation switching to a more neutral topic—"games"—that steered the interaction in a different direction (turn 24). The activity came to a close just as Sara offered "language" and "immigration" in turn 26, and Nellie emphasized "language" in the following turn. Aurora ignored the word "immigration" but did repeat and write down "language" (turn 30).

As her peers called out terms for Aurora to write on the chart paper, she had to make real-time decisions about how to represent these ideas for her group. This exchange demonstrates just how hard Aurora worked to steer the conversation away from states and borders to other ways of belonging (culture and language) that do not depend on national boundaries. Any discussion of this type of diversity could run the risk of drawing attention to her undocumented status, so Aurora redirected the topic or outright refused to write in several important moments.

When I recently reviewed the transcript and recording with Aurora, asking her to reflect on her refusal to write down the words "border" and "immigration," she emphasized the risks involved in disclosing her undocumented status in school. She explained,

"Still to this day this [kind of conversation] makes me feel like you want me to stand out, be identified, be spotlighted," especially if we are sharing and I have to say, "I relate to this." For Aurora, being spotlighted can open on to two kinds of threats: first, people's "stereotypical judgments" about what she can or can't do, and second, and even worse, to the fact that "anyone knowing could ruin the life that I have here." For Aurora, "having to choose between answering or not answering is really hard," so her strategy was to avoid the subject altogether.

This fleeting but formative moment is representative of many that Aurora encountered in elementary school. Classroom prompts about diversity meant to foster students' personal connections by drawing on their prior knowledge often served to make Aurora retreat. She was at once central to the activity—serving as her group's scribe—and marginalized by the conversation itself. Depending on the students' and their families' citizenship status, the stakes involved in broaching these topics was quite different. When Nellie, who is Puerto Rican, raised the subject of the border, Aurora chose nonparticipation. And when Sara (a first-generation U.S.-born child of Dominican descent) offered up "immigration" and "language," Aurora ignored the former and wrote only the latter. This moment of silence only becomes audible when we recognize how much Aurora knows about the broader sociopolitical context of her own immigrant childhood.

Seeing Diversity

During diversity panels at P.S. 432, teachers arranged for students to visit different classrooms throughout the school to talk with their peers about the harmful effects of bullying. On this day in June, a teacher brought a panel of first graders to visit Ms. Daniela's class to talk about their experiences. After the panel discussion, the teacher asked all of the boys in the class to stand up in order to "see how diverse we really are." As the male-identified students stood before their peers, the teacher summarized the lessons she hoped children would take away from this activity:

Difference is part of life. We need to really have freedom for who we are and respect one another. Even if you don't agree, even if you don't like it. It's important to just accept who we are. It's a world that's not gonna change. It's important to embrace everyone and to learn about each other. To learn. Ask questions that are meaningful and important and say I'm sorry that was not- that was ignorant of me. And you know, please forgive me but I want to learn, and I make mistakes. But at least be real and not make fun and take responsibility.

The teacher's goal in producing a visual display of classroom differences was to foster students' acceptance of them. In her view, social categories like gender were fixed and unchangeable; as a result, she advocated for resignation and tolerance. Turning to the children who remained seated, the teacher asked, "So what do you notice girls, women?" Instead of listing out gender-specific descriptors, students reframed the prompt and began to share ideas about diversity that echoed the word web activity conducted just a few months earlier. Maysi began with, "Um most of the things that are differences between us, um well there technically all of us not just among the boys is skin color, uh, the country, size." Aurora added, "Feelings, uh, uh, feelings, point of views, heights, cultures." Just like she had done during the diversity word web activity, Aurora replaced the word "country" with the word "culture" in order to avoid talking about birthplace.

Picking up on the word "country" from Maysi's list, the visiting teacher proposed a final activity where she would name countries of origin that she believed to be represented among the students in the class. Hazel added that they should all stand up when they heard their country called, but no one clarified what it meant to "come from" any of them. Let's observe how Aurora, Catalina, Jenni, and their peers responded to an activity explicitly focused on identity, country of origin, and belonging.

1 Teacher:	I'm gonna do this very quickly. Um, people? I'm gonna name some of the countries that we come from. Okay?
2 Hazel:	And stand UP
3 Teacher:	Stand UP if you are from Mexico.

((chairs dragging across the floor))

4 Brandon: Oh that's me
5 Teacher: Okay
6 Brandon: **Párate**

((dirigido hacia Aurora, quien no se paró))

Stand up

((directed to Aurora, who did not stand))

((many students talking))

7 Teacher: Quietly:: <u>Sit</u>. >Sit. Sit. Sit.<
8 Aurora: What? Literally
9 Teacher: Uh anybody. Uh. From the Dominican [Republic.
               Quietly

((Jenni stands up))

10 Students: WOO:::hhh BR::::

((cheering and clapping))

11 Jenni: **República Domĺinicana**
12 Teacher: Just stay quiet. Quietly
13 Student: Maysi that's- that's my personal space
14 Teacher: Quietly, I'm speaking
15 Aurora: Woo-de-de-de-de-ne-nee-ne-ne

((making a rhythmic electronic sound like a rock guitar solo))

16 Teacher: All right, sit down. Puerto Rico. Anyone from
               Puerto Rico? Okay
17 Hazel: Mi::::ss Ariana:::::!

For these knowledgeable students, the question of what country one is from immediately evoked birthright citizenship. Within a public school setting where teachers might assume that children were unaware of or unconcerned with questions of immigration status, this visiting teacher's activity was premised on the misguided idea that evoking national origin would simply produce a sense of cultural pride. It might be an easy assumption to make in an immigrant community like Vista, where flags of several different Latin American countries hung in storefront windows, were painted on food trucks, and were used as curtains in apartment windows. But these expressions of affiliation are quite different than being asked to share your birthplace in a school setting.

This kind of pedagogy—attempting to foster student participation in school by asking them to draw on knowledge they bring from home—is not uncommon when teachers try to be culturally relevant in their teaching. In this instance, however, the educator was underestimating the students' knowledge. We see a clear collision between students' spiraling curriculum of citizenship and the educator's assumption of their innocence. The students were cognizant of the risks involved in revealing immigration status, but the teacher was apparently unaware of these vulnerabilities. We saw evidence of this in chapter 2 with the oral history homework assignment, which Aurora also experienced as threatening. In this mixed-status classroom context, the activity proposed by the visiting teacher instilled a range of feelings in students ranging from pride to anxiety to fear.

As the teacher called out country names, students had to decide whether to stand or remain seated. This was similar to other moments in which being asked to stand was synonymous with expressing national pride: "All rise for the singing of the 'Star Spangled Banner,'" for instance, or, "Please stand for the Pledge of Allegiance." The children in Ms. Daniela's class knew each other so well at this point in the school year that they began to call on each other and the adults present when they thought they should stand. The command *párate* (stand up) became an important part of this activity, as we can see in turn 6, when Mexico was called and Brandon turned to Aurora and told her to stand up. Aurora replied in disbelief, preferring not to draw attention to herself by remaining seated. After quickly rising and sitting again, Aurora began humming loudly to herself, as if to drown out the discussion. In contrast, when the Dominican Republic was called next, Jenni jumped up excitedly to the sounds of cheering and clapping from her peers (turn 10). These various ways of participating in the activity are indicative of the focal students' different views on what is at stake in displaying their nationality: to be from Mexico implied an experience of border crossing, whereas to be from the Dominican Republic did not conjure up questions of immigration status. The next country was Puerto Rico. This time Hazel called my name as though she were awarding me a prize in a pageant ("and the winner is . . . !") and I stood up (turn 17).

In the last minutes of this "countries we come from" roll call, a number of children in the class vocally challenged the teacher's narrow focus on birthplace and nationality as tied to immigration. Having noticed that the two African American students in the class had not had a chance to stand up, one student called out "African American," and another followed with "United States!" Let's take a close look at two more stretches of talk and the impact of this activity on Aurora and Catalina in particular.

19 Student 1:   The >United States<

20 Student 2:   Okay

21 Teacher: But that's what we have in common, right?-

                 ((laughter))

22 Aurora: °Stupid

                 ((pencil scratch sound))

23 Student: We were all born here.

24 Teacher: So you can all see-

25 Aurora: °Not really

26 Maysi: Not all

                 ((for all to hear))

27 Aurora: Not all

                 ((into the mic))

The visiting teacher's question—"but that's what we have in common, right?"—either indicates her own assumption that all of the students in this classroom were U.S. citizens or, and I believe this is more likely, indicates her belief that children of this age would be unaware of the connections between birthplace and immigration status. In turn 23, a student made explicit what the teacher proposed to be a shared characteristic of everyone in the class— "we were all born here"—at which point the teacher was ready to move on (turn 24). But Aurora and Maysi refused to move on, refuting that false universalism. First, Aurora quietly challenged this claim, her words inaudible to everyone except Maysi, who repeated Aurora's words ("not all!") loud enough for everyone to hear (turns 25 through 27). The children themselves resisted a facile notion of diversity that would have dissolved their actual differences into an imaginary American melting pot.

Quickly improvising one last set of instructions that would give students not born in the United States a chance to stand, the teacher called out, "Stand up if you were not born in this country." The teacher assumed that this would be a noncontroversial directive, but she was wrong.

28 Teacher:	No not really. Well? No. We're not all we're born here? Stand up
29 Maysi:	↑This is why they are called immigrants
30 Aurora:	°Duh::
31 Maysi:	Stand up if you're an <u>im</u>migrant
32 Aurora:	°Puh- I'm not standing up
33 Teacher:	Hello::? Can we have one voice. So stand up if you were <u>not</u> born in this country. <u>Not</u> born in this country.

((sound of chairs dragging across the floor))

34 Maysi:	That's an ↑<u>im</u>migrant.
35 Aurora:	**Si <u>no</u> naciste en este país, <párate>, si nacis-** If you <u>were not</u> born in this country, <stand up>, if you were born-
36 Student:	**Jenni- párate** Jenni- stand up

((students laughing))

| 37 Teacher: | Okay, have a seat, have a seat |

Aurora's participation in this activity is revealing of the anxiety that accompanied it. Despite having called attention to the fact that not everyone in the room was born in the United States, Aurora refused to stand (turn 32). This—like the previous—moment of refusal is all the more significant when we contrast it with Aurora's ongoing participation in the activity. In keeping with the classroom role of language broker for newcomer students that

Ms. Daniela had assigned her at the beginning of the year, Aurora turned to her classmates to translate the teacher's directive. She rightly assumed that the nuances of this conversation were hard for Jenni to understand, so she repeated the teacher's prompt in Spanish (turn 35). And just like above, a student commanded, "Párate." Jenni stood up in a comic way that garnered laughter from her classmates (turn 36). Jenni, a newcomer student from the Dominican Republic for whom revealing birthplace did not correlate as strongly with juridical status, rose without hesitation.

Jenni and others stood up and sat back down; the air was full of the sound of chairs dragging across the floor as Aurora maintained her position and did not rise. Seated across the room, Catalina, who was Aurora's counterpart in their shared Mexican origin and undocumented status, also chose to remain seated. Whispering strongly and hissing loudly so that Catalina would hear while also keeping her volume low enough in the hopes of staying under the radar, Aurora addressed Catalina in a way that could have potentially revealed her nationality.

38 Aurora: Catalina, you were, ↑you were born HERE?
              Catalina psssst
39 Teacher: Oh, right, ok, so we're gonna wrap up, but the
              life is . . . I would say some advice-
40 Catalina: Aurora

                ((Catalina glanced firmly at Aurora))

41 Aurora: What?
42 Teacher: -but not to give you another task or anything,
              but write a couple of sentences or a drawing or
              something or maybe even your story-
43 Aurora: °Ay ay ay ay ay
44 Maysi: °°your stuff

            ((sound of chairs dragging across the floor))

45 Teacher: -at another time
46 Maysi: from her chair
47 Teacher: But for now I would like a couple of people to tell
              me how was this experience. What did you think
              of what you just shared? Sharing?

Aurora began to call out Catalina's name, asking her if she was born here (turn 38). Her quiet but assertive bids for Catalina's attention made it clear that Aurora wanted to communicate directly with her without anyone else's noticing. Catalina, however, ignored Aurora and kept silent until she grew tired of Aurora's attempts to get her attention. Finally, Catalina turned back to Aurora, saying her name and giving her a stern look that silenced her (turn 40).

As the teacher regained control of class and issued a closing prompt, Aurora lamented "ay, ay, ay, ay, ay" (turn 43)—perhaps because she realized that she'd upset Catalina, or perhaps because the teacher's invitation to "tell your [immigration] story" was the last thing she wanted to do. Finally, the teacher invited the children to reflect: "What did you think about this experience? What did you think about sharing?" (turn 47). Aurora shared her thoughts with the whole class: "I think it's a good experience because you might be like maybe you knew something about this, but you never said it and right now you feel like you feel terrible and—" Interrupting Aurora, the teacher thanked her for sharing and offered her own commentary: "Now you feel that you're sorry cuz you offended anyone." Aurora was remorseful, whispering "yeah" into the microphone. In this—the only moment that Aurora spoke up in class—she was, in fact, speaking to Catalina and apologizing for drawing attention to her in an upsetting way that she understood all too well. Aurora knew that she had potentially revealed an aspect of Catalina's identity that she was supposed to guard in confidence.

Throughout this exchange, we have witnessed a profound disconnect between the teacher's imagination of what it might mean to evoke birthplace in this classroom and the students' sophisticated awareness of the risks involved in displaying their nationality in a public setting. Although the teacher worked to make differences visible while fostering inclusion through the sit/stand activity, the undocumented children in the room experienced the activity as threatening. Educators may assume that students will feel comfortable talking about their identity during activities meant to elicit multicultural perspectives designed to honor their culture and experiences in school. However proud students may be about their nationality, these kinds of classroom conversations can actually serve to marginalize rather than foster inclusion for undocumented students.

The assignments and interactions we've examined throughout this chapter make it clear that children's awareness of the significance of citizenship saturates school life. We've seen how a student's awareness of her juridical status influences her classroom participation—what she shares, encodes, or withholds. For example, Pita's change in status prompted her to tell her border-crossing story in the hopes of positively influencing public opinion on immigration. And Catalina, while writing nothing explicit or potentially incriminating about immigration in her published story, nevertheless encoded her hopes and fears about citizenship status in sophisticated, if implicit, ways. During classroom interactions, Aurora and Catalina maintained a protective posture as undocumented students, while Jenni, who at the time possessed a visa, did not hesitate to publicly proclaim her birthplace.

For all the inquietud the students might experience, I want to emphasize their agency here. The girls protected themselves and their families by refusing certain topics of conversation (like Aurora's choosing to not write the word "borders"); they rejected simplistic assumptions that public school students are all born in the United States (as seen in Aurora and Maysi's exchange about "not all" children being born "here"). As we will see, these students' speech, along with their purposeful silences, regarding immigration status only grows more complex as they approach their elementary school graduation.

Interlude I
"Cállate"

On a sweltering June day in 2014, I accompanied Ms. Daniela's students, along with three other fifth-grade classes from P.S. 432, on a field trip to their neighborhood high school. Aurora, Catalina, Hazel, Pita, Jenni, and Tere were among this group of fifth graders on their way to interview student leaders of the Vista High School Dream Team. The Dream Team was a mixed-status group of high school students committed to building solidarity by advocating for equitable educational opportunities and immigration policy reforms that would provide a pathway to citizenship for their undocumented peers. The fifth graders had been building toward this moment for months. Since the start of the yearlong curriculum, entitled *Resistencia* (Resistance), they had studied different historical moments in which groups of people had resisted injustice and advocated for their rights. Now, they were working on a final unit entitled *Causas de Quinto* (Fifth-grade causes).

After researching contemporary social causes that they would be (in Ms. Daniela's words) "willing to fight for," these ten- and eleven-year-olds were going to visit Vista High to talk with local teenagers about a cause they had chosen to learn more about: immigration reform. (Recall that while teachers cannot ask about students' immigration status, immigration is considered a standard part of social studies curricula.) In order to support Ms. Daniela in her planning, I had introduced her to Ms. Janet, a teacher at Vista High School and faculty advisor to the Dream Team, in the hopes that they could bring their students together to talk more about youth-led participation in the immigrant rights movement. The interview that Ms. Daniela's students conducted with Ms. Janet's students—the focus of chapter 4—was the culminating project in the Causas de Quinto unit. For now, let's walk alongside the children and listen to what they notice on the four-block walk from P.S. 432 to Vista High School.

Before we set out from P.S. 432, Ms. Daniela and the students gathered in the hallway outside of the cafeteria. I pressed record on the Voice Memo app on the iPods that Aurora, Catalina, Pita, and Hazel were wearing just as the teachers tried and failed to arrange dozens of students into two straight lines. The students clamored to leave the stuffy hallway and scolded one another before embarking on their short walk: "Don't lose that pencil," "I was next to her," "No you stand over here," and "Who is using the f-word?" When a handful of students lined up near Hazel whispering about a note being passed around—"Pick it up, pick it up! did they give it to her?"—Hazel sternly admonished one of her classmates: "My God, forget it. No Christi gave it to Jenni, Jenni gave it to Martin to throw it out. But you don't know what happens. They could be writing about you, me, anybody. So that's why before I throw anything out that's a paper, I read it."

Childhood routines like passing notes in school accrued a sense of urgency in a community where the state might demand to see your papers at any moment. For Hazel, reading and interpreting papers was a serious responsibility. She expressed concern not about the specific content of a note being passed among her peers but about "anything that's a paper" containing information about "anybody." (As we've have seen in chapter 2, interpreting and translating school forms and safeguarding papers relating to immigration are crucial components of the spiraling curriculum of citizenship.) After Hazel's warning, we filed out of the school.

We walked down one of the main north–south avenues cutting through the neighborhood while the children offered a running commentary on the people and places we passed. English, Spanish, and Mandarin—the three main languages that make up the linguistic landscape—were visible in the local businesses and shop signs. Within just one block, we passed Lucky Noodle Kitchen in Chinese characters and in English, Vega Deli Grocery, legal offices with the signs "Attorney/Abogado" and "Real Estate," and Angel Restaurant, which specializes in "carne y pescado" (meat and fish). When Ms. Daniela gestured toward a looming building— "this is where we're going"—Aurora was incredulous.

Aurora:	Th<u>IS</u> is a hi↑gh school?
Student 1:	↑Yeah
Aurora:	>I never °knew that<

Student 1:	You thought that was [name of local middle school]?
Aurora:	No::: I thought this was like a building of a <u>fac</u>tory or something-
Student 1:	WHhhat! Oh my gosh Aurora you're so-
Aurora:	I'm so:::rry, ssss not MY fault

How is it, I wondered at the time, that Aurora didn't know it was a school, that she thought the building was a "building or a factory or something like that?" Unlike her peers, Aurora had never been to the high school, even though she passed it regularly when she entered the subway station just one block over. This was not because her parents weren't invested in her education. They had taken her to visit the neighborhood middle school she'd be attending next year; they had received and carefully read school correspondence regarding extracurricular activities held at Vista High. However, not only did Aurora's work schedule prevent her from attending such events—Aurora worked three out of five days a week with her parents selling textiles at a flea market—but her parents also felt uncomfortable, given the uncertainty associated with being undocumented, leaving Aurora in the care of others. Aurora's inability to see the building as a school struck me as a metaphor for the difficulty of imagining a future education, given her family responsibilities and the risks that attended her lack of papers.

Once it became clear to Aurora that this building was a high school, she began, with excitement, to imagine one day attending it. "We're gonna be here in like four or three years," she said as she set the school's name to a tune that she sang as we entered the building lobby. "I would love to go to this high school," she cooed, and a student named Brandon who was standing next to her agreed. Meanwhile, Ms. Daniela worked to reorganize the children into line formation as we waited for Ms. Janet, our host. Having been instructed to stand at the front of line beside each other, Brandon and Aurora took in their surroundings.

For the next four minutes, while she stood directly in front of the security desk in the center of the school lobby, Aurora's voice and actions changed dramatically. Here, a school safety agent—an employee of the New York City Police Department assigned to

Figure 1. Standing in front of a school safety officer in the Vista High School lobby.

work in a public school—sat behind a desk covered in signs addressing visitors. Some of the signs directed behavior ("You must sign in and show ID to enter"); others invited visitors to aid the police in prosecuting those accused of graffiti or vandalism ("REWARD for arrest and conviction"). Observe the changes in Aurora's demeanor as Brandon began to read a sign in Spanish and Aurora became aware of the officer's gaze.

Brandon:	**Hasta quinientos dólares de recompensa**
	Reward up to five hundred dollars
Aurora:	**Oh <u>WO</u>AH**
Brandon:	**I guess that's worth . . . Hi policeMAN**
Aurora:	**Cá.lla.TE**
	Sh.ut. Up

((Brandon continues to read the signage))

Brandon:	No students allowed in the mai:::n.

((switching topics))

I can't ↑wait to meet my <u>bro</u>ther.

Aurora: °Ohh::. I do not ca::re.

As the students' excitement increased, the school lobby grew noisier. Ms. Janet instructed us on how we'd arrive at the classroom on the fourth floor. She directed small groups of students to head toward the elevator, while Brandon and Aurora continued their exchange near the security desk.

Brandon: <u>He</u>llo cop!

((the muffled male voice of the school safety officer addresses the group of children standing in the lobby))

Ms. Janet: Next group

Student 1:   Next gr<u>oup</u>?

((children's laughter))

Student 2:   ↑Yeah!

Ariana: Yeah, should we go with that? She's our host today. You're making this happen. Thank you!

Brandon: He↑llo

((addressing officer as we continued to wait by the desk))

             Yay

Aurora: **Shhhh. °<u>Cállate</u>:::**

             Shhhh. °<u>Sh</u>ut u::::p

Brandon: Oo, business-

Aurora: **<u>Cá</u>llate:: Shhh::::: Brandon. °<u>Please</u>**.

             <u>Sh</u>ut up Shhh::::: Brandon. °<u>Please.</u>

Aurora shushed Brandon as they stood in the gaze of the school safety agent whose uniform and disposition were hard to distinguish from those of the police officers they passed outside on the street. When she failed to silence Brandon, she became silent herself. For several minutes, Aurora's mic caught only the sound of her classmates bantering.

Finally, Ms. Janet called Aurora's group. We walked past the security desk and waited for the elevator as Ms. Janet explained the rules of elevator use at Vista: high school students were generally forbidden from taking it, but the school had made an exception for P.S. 432's students. We stood and watched the floor numbers light up as the elevator descended. Once we were in the elevator and the thick metal doors had closed, Aurora seemed to gain a sense of safety as we gained distance from the police officer.

Student 3:	The high school kids go here?
Ms. Janet:	Usually not. We're:::: This is a special case cause you're our visitors. Usually the high school kids have to walk up the stairs.
Aurora:	↑What?
Ms. Janet:	Only the teachers are allowed in the elevator but I have a ↑pass. So I'm letting you in.

((bing of doors opening))

Brandon:	Yay elevator!
Aurora:	Oh!
Ms. Janet:	I can take about half of this group.
Aurora:	Yeah, take it EASY

((bossy and assertive))

Student 3:	Take it EASY
Ms. Janet:	Right. Can you press four for me?
Aurora:	Which ↑one?
Student 4:	Four.
Aurora:	Oh.

As she moved farther away from the security desk, Aurora's confidence and talkativeness returned. Compare Figure 1 with Figure 2. While in the officer's line of sight, Aurora tried to make herself small, but here—on the fourth floor of the school—she looked straight ahead at the camera, making a sweeping gesture, as she led her peers down the hallway.

Figure 2. On the fourth floor of Vista High School.

Four
An Interview with the Dream Team

Aurora, Catalina, Pita, Hazel, Tere, and Jenni understood the significance of citizenship from multiple vantage points: their own personal experiences of migration, their awareness of the differences between themselves and other members of their mixed-status families, and their senses of responsibility toward a broader immigrant community. In this chapter, we explore their developing sense of political consciousness by examining their participation in the Causas de Quinto unit that marked the end of their fifth-grade social studies curriculum. This series of culminating activities—in particular, the interview that the P.S. 432 fifth graders conducted with members of the Vista High School Dream Team—provides us with an opportunity to hear how elementary- and high school-age students made connections between the macro context of immigration policy and the micro familial and educational contexts in which they were growing up. At this point, we have seen how children learn from a spiraling curriculum of citizenship and how the lessons they have learned shape their participation in school. By now it is clear that the girls approached this unit of study with a deep understanding of how their lives and their families' lives are affected by immigration policy and status. A teacher or researcher unaware of those forms of knowledge might easily think meeting the Dream Team would be a first encounter with these issues, but we know that these students already had extensive experience negotiating the concerns that would now become the explicit object of study in their closing curricular unit.

During the Causas de Quinto unit, Ms. Daniela taught her students about federal legislation called the Development, Relief, and Education for Alien Minors, better known as the Dream Act. This law, which was first considered by Congress in 2001, proposed to provide a pathway to legal permanent resident status for eligible undocumented immigrants.[1] It garnered the support of union leaders, immigrant advocates, and undocumented youth activists and was passed through the Senate, but—after seven years of political debate and organizing—members of the House of Representatives failed to pass the law in 2010. In the absence of comprehensive immigration reform at the federal level, President Barack Obama used his executive power to create the Deferred Action for Childhood Arrivals (DACA) program in 2012. DACA did not provide a pathway to U.S. citizenship, but it did make a subset of the undocumented young adult population eligible for work authorization and financial aid for higher education. Undocumented youth activists who had become the face of this immigration justice movement became known as Dreamers: undocumented students eligible to attend college who could not afford to enroll because they were prohibited from obtaining federal or state financial aid. The term Dreamers was prevalent in the mainstream media at the time of this study, but many activists and scholars have criticized the name for reproducing the view that some immigrants—often students and children—are more innocent and deserving of protection than others.[2]

Although the federal Dream Act failed to become law, undocumented youth activists and allies throughout the country also worked to enact pro-immigrant legislation at the state level.[3] While preparing for their interview with the Vista Dream Team, the fifth graders learned about the New York Dream Act (NYDA). NYDA was first introduced to the state legislature in 2013, taking six years for it to become law in 2019.[4] This policy offers in-state tuition assistance to undocumented students pursuing higher education, but it does not provide them with a pathway to citizenship. The New York State Youth Leadership Council (NYSYLC), or YLC for short—the first undocumented youth-led organization in the state of New York—took a leading role in drafting, presenting, and advocating for NYDA at the state level. One of their early political strategies was to support teachers and students in starting school-based Dream Teams that would build community and campaign for legislation. Dream Teams often include undocumented students and their allies—peers and teachers with papers—committed to advocating for policy change that would widen educational opportunities and provide a pathway to citizenship for undocumented students.[5] Although YLC members did not use the term "Dreamers" to refer to themselves, preferring the label "undocumented," they did call these school-based groups "Dream Teams." The Vista High School Dream Team that we will meet in this chapter was one of the groups supported by and connected to the YLC's network of youth activists.

In the following pages, we will listen in as Aurora and her classmates discussed immigration—and immigrant rights—in the Causas de Quinto conversations leading up to the visit with the Dream Team. The teachers' decision to develop a unit responsive to the students' interests and focused on immigration is especially interesting in light of the rules regarding how and when the topic of immigration can be broached in public school. As we know, the guidance that school districts provide to school administrators prohibits teachers and school staff from inquiring about students' and their families' immigration status because of the chilling effect this may produce. *Plyler* does not, however, limit educators' ability to teach about the subject of immigration in school. In fact, many states include immigration as part of their mandated curriculum standards. Teachers are therefore faced with the challenge of teaching about immigration, but without encroaching on their student's very real experiences of immigration. This is a particular challenge for educators committed to developing culturally relevant curricula that honor and draw on their students' lives. During the Causas de Quinto unit, the process of preparing for, conducting, and reflecting on the interview prompted explicit conversations about the significance of U.S. citizenship.[6] With their graduation from fifth grade rapidly approaching, Ms. Daniela's students saw images of their own possible future reflected in the high school Dream Team members whom they met.

Injustices That We Want to Change

I want to begin by describing the classwork that laid the foundation for the fifth graders' interview with the Dream Team. Over the course of the school year, the fifth graders had studied U.S. history from 1860 to 1970, with an emphasis on the history of race and racism; they focused on topics such as slavery and abolition in the nineteenth century and Jim Crow and the Civil Rights Movement in the twentieth century. This integrated humanities curriculum was called "Resistencia," and the teachers wanted to end the year with a unit they named "Causas de Quinto," which they would base on students' ideas about pressing contemporary social and political issues. The teachers polled the fifth graders to find out which social issues they felt most connected to by asking students to complete a form entitled "Injusticias Que Queremos Cambiar" (Injustices that we want to change). The instructions read: "Hagan una lista de las 10 injusticias más importantes que quieren cambiar en el mundo" (Make a list of the 10 most important injustices that you want to change in the world). Students completed the sheet by writing down the social issues that they cared most about and numbering them in order of importance from 1 to 10.

On the day her students completed the form, Ms. Daniela talked with the class about the activity and how it represented the culmination of their curriculum. The conversation began as Ms. Daniela posed the guiding question:

So, la pregunta es qué injusticias existen en el mundo hoy en día. La reunión de hoy es seria, porque todo lo que nosotros hagamos desde ahora hasta fin del año va a ser basada en la actividad que hacemos hoy. Vamos a decidir qué causas queremos defender. ¿Qué es lo que realmente nos pone como bien apasionados que queremos luchar por esa causa? So, es en serio. Okay. So la primera pregunta es- y queremos solamente tres o cuatro lluvia de ideas. ¿Qué injusticias existen en el mundo hoy en día?

So the question is what injustices exist in the world today. Today's meeting is serious, because everything that we do from now until the end of the year is based on the activity that we do today. We are going to decide which causes we

want to defend. What is it that really gets us very passion-
ate so that we want to fight for that cause? So, this is serious.
Okay? So, the first question is- and we want only three or four
brainstorms- what injustices exist in the world today?

I wasn't present for this morning meeting, but by this point in the
school year, Ms. Daniela helped me with data collection by recording classroom conversations that she knew I'd be particularly interested in. We had agreed to audio record all of the lessons in the
Causas de Quinto unit, and I had left her an extra recording device
to use on days I wasn't visiting the school. That day, Ms. Daniela
sent me the following note about the conversation:

> Hi Ariana,
> Just wanted to share that immigration status came up a lot
> today with Aurora, Pita, and Hazel during a lesson where
> kids generate a list of injustices they want to change in the
> world. . . . Aurora shared again about the discrimination she
> faced as a small child at school. This story came with more
> details and her conviction that by speaking up, her mom
> was the voice for Latino kids whose moms hadn't spoken up
> in previous years. Aurora also told some interesting stories
> about her grandparents applying to get Visas as teachers but
> not being able to, and how her grandparents are professionals
> but (I think this is on her mom's side?) "none of their kids
> were successful" or something like that. Hard to remember
> the exact language since this was all in Spanish. . . . Anyway
> I thought it was interesting that all it took to get the kids
> talking about immigration, Latino identity, etc. was an open-
> ended invitation to list the injustices that still exist in the
> world today. Makes so much sense, and yet happens not so
> frequently in school.
> —Dani
> Sent from my iPhone

There are many classrooms in the United States where teachers
would fear raising the subject of immigration in school, but Ms.
Daniela's was one where children felt comfortable talking about
the injustices of family separation across national borders and
their experiences of racial and linguistic discrimination. As I read

her email, I was reminded of the personal memoir unit from earlier in the year. Ms. Daniela's mention of the students' responses
to her "open-ended question" recalled how the focal girls took up
general questions about childhood memories as opportunities to
express the realities of growing up undocumented in mixed-status
families (see chapter 3). The next day, I visited Ms. Daniela's classroom to pick up the recorder and audio files. Let's listen together
as Aurora shared two injustices:

> **Okay. Las injusticias que somos. . . . Es que si ya eres
> como un poco mayor- pero en verdad no eres tan, tan y
> si no eres tan como viejita y por eso no te dan tu visa.
> Y cuando, y cuando eres maestra, porque mi abuela es
> maestra y mi abuelo también. Ni uno de sus hijos fueron
> nada importante, so eso salió mal, y entonces sí mi abuela
> como maestra y ella quiso agarrar a su visa para venir a
> visitarnos a mí y mi mamá y mi papá. Se lo negaron siete
> veces. So, trató siete veces, y mi mama quiere que ella
> intenta de nuevo, pero ella dice—para qué si me lo van a
> negar otra vez—porque ya se la bajaron sus ánimos de que
> es un injusticia que no dejen pasar.**

> Okay the injustice that we are. . . . Is that if you are a little
> older but not that, that, that- and if you're not so old and
> because of that they don't give you your visa. And when, and
> when you are a teacher, because my grandmother is a teacher
> and my grandfather too. None of their children became
> anything important, so that came out badly, and then yes my
> grandmother as a teacher wanted to access a visa to come
> visit me, my mother, and my father. They denied it seven
> times. So, she tried seven times and my mom wants her to try
> again but she says "why if they're going to deny it to me again"
> because her spirits are down from this injustice that they
> don't let pass.

Aurora had not seen her grandmother since she left Mexico with
her mother at the age of two, and both she and her mother longed
for her grandmother to visit Brooklyn. Aurora and her parents
could not visit Mexico because the risks of crossing the border into
the United States a second time were too high; instead, her family

tried to obtain a tourist visa for her grandparents to visit them in New York City.

As Aurora shared her story, she was also thinking out loud about the relationship between different kinds of status and belonging. She associated a right to immigration status (being granted a visa) with social, professional, and educational status (it was unfair that her grandmother, a teacher, was unable to obtain a visa). Just as Ms. Daniela had noted in her email, Aurora strongly associated professionalization with authorization—hence the injustice of a teacher's not being granted a visa. This strong symbolic connection between educational achievement and the right to be in the United States is also central to Aurora's second injustice. She continued:

> Otra es- sorry- otra es que, um, aquí nosotros y los que pue- los que tienen oportunidad de venir de allá y aquí- aquí no les dan oportunidad a veces. Es que yo. Es que yo- yo en el primer año yo sufrí porque un injusticia que algunos americanos o cosas así que no les gustan los latinos y son maestros como muchas. Yo me- mi mamá se dio cuenta y yo también que una vez había esta maestra que, uhm, no, no quería que yo pasara solamente porque yo era la única latina de la clase. Y, entonces eso- después todo- cuando mi mami di- cuando mi mamá le habló con ella y con la principal para decirle—¿cómo es posible?—porque mi mamá notó que- porque la maestra dijo que- yo pienso que ella no va a pasar y so- y mi mamá se dio cuenta que yo era la única latina y por esa razón sí era. Y ella decía por- que no sabía nada. Y me hicieron un examen y mi mamá pidió que fuera con una maestra de otra escuela para que- porque tú ves que la maestra puede hablar con otras maestras y así. So, mi mamá decidió que hacer con otra y saqué noventa y nueve punto nueve. So, es- y después el siguiente dí- al siguiente año yo me fui para New Jersey y fui- um- saqué mi diploma de estudiante del mes. Y se lo fuimos a enseñar al, la, la principal para decirle cómo es posible que mi maestra no me iba a pasar de año y saqué examen cien y diploma del mes el otro año. Y ella se llevó el diploma y se lo enseñó a la maestra. Cómo es posible que no me iba a dejar pasar.

Another is- sorry- another is that, um, here we and those who ca- those who have the opportunity to come from there and here- here they don't give them opportunities sometimes. It's that I. It's that I- I was in first grade and I suffered because an injustice that some Americans or something like that they don't like Latinos and they're teachers like many. I- my mom realized and I did too that once this teacher didn't want to pass me because I was the only Latina in the class. And then after everything- when my mom said- when my mom talked to her and the principal to say "how is it possible"- because my mom- because the teacher said that, "I think, she's not going to pass" and my mom realized I was the only Latina and that was why. And she said it was because I didn't know anything. And they gave me a test and my mom requested that it be with a teacher from another school because you see this teacher could talk to other teachers. So, my mom decided to try it with someone else and I got a ninety-nine point nine. So, then- and then the next day- the next year I went to New Jersey and I got- um- a student-of-the-month diploma. And we went to show it- to the- the- principal from the previous year to say how was it possible that she wouldn't let me pass when I got one hundred and diploma-of-the month in the following year. And she took the diploma to the teacher and showed her. How was it possible that she was not going to let me pass.

Aurora recounted this story often during fifth grade because it allowed her to describe the adversity she experienced in the United States without disclosing her undocumented status.[7] There's an interesting change in pronouns that shows her real-time negotiation of belonging and disclosure. She started with a "we" that she quickly corrected to a "those" and then spoke, albeit hesitatingly, in the first person. This *testimonio*—in which Aurora linked her personal experience up to a broader struggle faced by "those who have the opportunity to come from there to here"—underscores her view of the redemptive power of papers (her "student-of-the-month diploma") as a way to prove that she ("the only Latina in the class") could successfully achieve a sense of belonging in school.

It is significant that the verb *pasar* (to pass) is central to both stories. The first injustice described attempts at passing through borders, while the second recounted passing from one grade to the next. In both cases, Aurora and her family were denied an opportunity because of their country of origin. Moreover, in the absence of immigration documentation, Aurora's stories focused on the importance of obtaining other papers, like teaching degrees and student-of-the-month diplomas. As mentioned in chapter 2, this emphasis on what Chang calls "hyperdocumentation"[8] is typical of mixed-status families' attempts to pursue educational achievement as a kind of substitute for papeles and as a pathway to acceptance and belonging. Although the fifth graders had become accustomed to hearing a number of refrains about their own education as they approached graduation—"you can do anything you put your mind to!"—Aurora knew that in addition to her own individual choices, she would confront a number of institutional barriers linked to immigration status that would affect her future. As a result, she associated education with a pathway to belonging while also knowing the differences between papeles and diplomas. Let's see how her thinking developed as the class turned to preparing interview questions for the Dream Team.

Preparing for the Interview

Once the fifth-grade students completed the worksheet to rank the social causes that mattered most to them, the teachers set about planning. The student-generated topics ranged from bullying and racism to animal abuse and climate change, but the majority of students across the four fifth-grade classes listed immigration— or a related phrase like *derechos de inmigrantes* (immigrants' rights)—as their top choice. For the students in Ms. Daniela's classroom, immigration was a defining aspect of their families' everyday lives even though the majority were born in the United States. They all lived in a distinctly immigrant neighborhood; they were tuned in to national debates over immigration reform. Just that year they had welcomed newcomer students Tere and Jenni, who had immigrated to Brooklyn in September. Ms. Daniela thought of this unit as an opportunity for her students to meet older immigrant youth who could inspire them to take civic action as they entered middle and high school, and so she hoped to find student activists working within the national movement for immigrant justice that her students could learn from directly. When she told me about this idea, I introduced her to Ms. Janet, an ESL teacher at the neighborhood public high school who was also the faculty advisor to the school's Dream Team. Together, Ms. Daniela and Ms. Janet arranged for the fifth graders to visit the high school and interview members of the Dream Team.

Ms. Daniela prepared the class for their visit at the high school in two ways: first, teaching about youth leadership in advocating for inclusive immigration policy reform; and second, co-constructing a set of questions and norms to guide the interview. To develop shared knowledge of the movement, Ms. Daniela drew on news coverage and digital footage of interviews with the group of students they called Dreamers. Drawing on the language used in these clips, Ms. Daniela and her students employed the vocabulary of the Dreamers and the Dreamers' movement to refer to the youth activists that they were studying. The day before the interview, the class watched a video depicting key moments in the political campaign to pass the federal Dream Act. Ms. Daniela gave students a two-column chart to organize their thoughts into categories—what they knew about activists in the Dreamer movement and what they wanted to know—and she instructed her students to take specific notes on the policy goals, political strategies, and outcomes that they heard mentioned.

Ms. Daniela paused occasionally to ask questions: "So, what strategy have you guys heard so far in this video?" "Can you guys see what they're doing here?" To these questions, the children replied, "Marches, planning, graduates, leaders." Ms. Daniela made explicit connections to other social movements that they had studied: "Yeah, the Civil Rights Movement. It's a sit-in. So they're going to a government office and they say: 'We're gonna sit here until you listen to us.' So make sure you have it in your list of strategies." When one child asked why the students in the *New York Times*-produced video "Pushing the Dream" were wearing graduation regalia, Ms. Daniela paused to invite student ideas, and Aurora jumped in to answer.[9]

1 Brandon: But didn't . . . ? Why they're wearing their
                 graduate costume?

2 Ms. Daniela: Hm::: I wonder who can figure out why they're
                 wearing?-

3 Aurora: Yes because exactly. In the other one they were
                 asking for **diplomas?** So that's how they show
                 that they <u>really</u> ar:::e like **grad↑uados** and they
                 <u>really</u> wanna pay for college. And. So. I think
                 what they're fighting for is pa:::pers? to:: uh let
                 them work to pay their ↑college?

4 Ms. Daniela: Hm:::

5 Aurora: And also to stop deportations.

6 Ms. Daniela: Ok<u>ay</u>. Good ↑pick up.

7 Aurora: Oh!

8 Ms. Daniela: So let's see if there's anyone who can add theories.

Aurora was excited about sharing just how much she knew with
the class; she sounded assertive and animated as she explained
that the graduation gown iconography represented a call for educational access, U.S. citizenship (papers), and an end to deportation.
Graduation ceremonies, like birthdays (as we saw in chapter 3),
evoked questions of belonging linked to citizenship, nationality,
and the threat of being forcibly removed from the United States.
In turn 3, Aurora switched to Spanish when saying *diplomas* and
graduados, using language that reminded me of conversations I'd
had with her mother, Marta, earlier that year.

Marta often raised concerns about what opportunities Aurora
would have as an undocumented student if the family remained
in the United States:

> **Aurora tiene su meta de que ella va ser abogada. Y que no**
> **le importa que si ella es inmigrante o no. Que ella tiene**
> **fe en Dios que algún día le van a dar una oportunidad en**
> **los Estados Unidos y que ella va ser <u>alguien</u> que le pasen**
> **en la televisión y digan—Aurora Sánchez es un orgullo**
> **hispano—Que es lo que ella quiere escuchar. Ajá, enton-**
> **ces es, ese es su propósito de ella. Y, bueno, gracias a Dios,**
> **mira hoy estamos con el cuarto diploma de que ella está en**
> **honores este año. Cuatro veces. Entonces, ¿tú cómo le vas**
> **a decir a tu hija que te trae esos honores de la escuela que**
> **no? ¿Algo que ella quiera?**

Aurora has the goal of being a lawyer. And it doesn't matter if she's an immigrant or not. She has faith in God that one day she'll be given the opportunity in the United States and that she is going to be <u>someone</u> that will appear on TV and they're going to say "Aurora Sánchez is the pride of all Hispanics." That is what she wants to hear. Uh huh, yes then, that is her goal. And, well, thank God, look today we're here on her fourth honors diploma this year. Four times. So how are you going to say no to your daughter who brings honors home from school? Something that she wants?

Taken together, Aurora and Marta's comments remind us of the spiraling curriculum of citizenship described in chapter 2. In Aurora's shifts between English and Spanish, she demonstrated that issues of education and juridical status were discussed both at home and at school. Marta and I had had many conversations like the one transcribed above, often when Aurora was present—conversations in which Marta expressed a hope that educational documentation (diplomas) could in fact substitute for immigration documents. The goal of being a lawyer—a person assumed to have U.S. citizenship who also has expert knowledge of the legal system and advocates for immigrant rights—and the fantasy of publicity ("will appear on TV") show the powerful association between educational achievement and citizenship. It is important to note here that Marta's belief in the importance of educational achievement and educational success—referenced above in Aurora's second injustice—runs counter to enduring deficit views of immigrant Spanish-speaking families as uninterested in their children's education.[10]

The prospect of visiting the Dream Team, a group of high school students explicitly linking education and a pathway to U.S. citizenship, activated for Aurora long-standing concerns about papeles both juridical and academic. The myth of educational achievement in which honors diplomas can solve inequality—a discourse reinforced in the family but also everywhere in schooling—is evident in both Aurora's and her mother's words. What we see in Aurora's and Marta's comments is a hope, however tenuous, that educational achievement will ultimately lead to U.S. citizenship. The idea that education will result in belonging and that public education will equalize students is present in the *Plyler* ruling.

Justice Brennan summarized the court's view that education "is a principal instrument in awakening the child to cultural values, in preparing him for later professional training, and in helping him to adjust normally to his environment. In these days, it is doubtful that any child may reasonably be expected to succeed in life if he is denied the opportunity of an education."[11] The prevailing justices argued that denying undocumented children access to a K–12 public school education amounted to "penalizing these children for their presence within the United States."[12] To an extent, what Aurora was navigating was the persistence of this rhetoric of equalization and access without a mechanism for full citizenship. She had both internalized the emphasis on education as a pathway to belonging and already encountered the reality of institutional barriers to her advancement that no diploma can remedy. These are the ambitions and anxieties about her own future that Aurora carried into her visit with the Vista High School Dream Team.

The next steps for Ms. Daniela's class were to draft their interview questions and to develop a set of guidelines for conducting the interview. Drawing on what they had learned about the Dreamer movement, the fifth graders wrote their questions on index cards, and Ms. Daniela prominently displayed them in the classroom. The questions ranged from topics focused on goals ("Did they get in a university?" and "How will there lifes [sic] be with no deportation?"), community organizing ("What was your strategies?" and "Do you use words or violence to fix your problem?"), and emotions ("How do the Dreamers feel?" and "Are you happy the way you work?"). After compiling these and other questions, Ms. Daniela initiated a discussion of which types of questions would be appropriate to ask during the interview. She introduced the idea that there were "two kinds of kids" on the Dream Team, referring to the fact that some of the students were documented and some were undocumented. For Ms. Daniela, this was important for the fifth graders to consider when deciding what to ask and how to ask it. She explained to the class:

> So I put the questions that are here because you guys did a really nice job of phrasing them in a way that kids who are in the Dreamer Club at the High School I think will feel comfortable answering. So one thing to know about this Club is that

it has two kinds of kids. It has kids who would be considered Dreamers; meaning they themselves are immigrants who came over and they're trying to get the Dream Act law passed to like personally benefit them. This Club also has kids who are what's called allies, which means they're like supporters of the Dreamer Movement. Now, to be sensitive to the allies and to the Dreamers, we're not gonna ask them questions about whether or not they are a Dreamer or an ally. If they choose to tell us their personal story. Like, for instance, if one of them chooses to tell us, you know, "I came over the border when I was five years old and I don't have documents." That's their personal choice to tell us that, but we're not gonna ask because that's something that's very personal and um private and they might not feel comfortable sharing that information with a group of strangers.

Ms. Daniela was not the only teacher to describe the composition of the Dream Team in this way. The following day, during our visit with the high schoolers, Ms. Janet—their teacher and faculty advisor—also told the fifth graders, "The Dream Team is not just Dreamers, though. So we're a group and we are Dreamers or undocumented students but we're also allies. This means like friends and supporters. So not everyone in our group is undocumented." Ms. Janet's self-correction, from "Dreamers" to "undocumented students," can be attributed to the many conversations she'd been part of in which members of the YLC and students at Vista High decided to adopt the term undocumented over Dreamers. She and her students followed the YLC's lead in choosing "undocumented," a term that was both more inclusive of students who were not as academically high achieving and of undocumented loved ones that were not students at all. Emphasizing the mixed-status nature of the Dream Team meant that the audience couldn't presume the immigration status of any particular member, thus allowing participants to make their own decisions about disclosing or withholding immigration status. It was also a broader political strategy that invited us all to get involved by modeling ways in which directly affected students and their peers might work together in solidarity.

Here, both teachers drew the fifth graders' attention to the strategic silences that student members of the Dreamer's movement used to avoid revealing their or their peers' status in public set-tings. This is not the top-down silence mandated by the guidance issuing from *Plyler* in order to protect undocumented students by not inquiring about students' immigration status in schools. It is instead a grassroots strategy in which individuals choose to dis-close or not disclose their undocumented status as part of a col-lective effort to bring about visibility and change. The decision on the part of activists to break that silence, to speak out, is central to the Dreamer movement. As Genevieve Negrón-Gonzales explains:

> As the potential consequences of discovery are so severe, silence is a fundamental part of the undocumented experi-ence in this country. Undocumented children learn, gener-ally following the lead of their parents or older siblings, the importance of guarding information about their status. Yet more and more, a generation of these young people is coming out of the shadows, demanding to be seen, proudly donning the label "undocumented, unafraid, and unapologetic."[13]

To study the Dreamers is to study a movement for immigrant rights explicitly predicated on the idea of taking risks to disclose one's un-documented status in order to push for change.[14] As we have seen in chapters 2 and 3, the fifth graders in Ms. Daniela's classroom had ample experience negotiating the risks of disclosure when it came to the question of juridical status at home and school.

Here we see the children developing their own research meth-odology for the study of citizenship and schooling, reckoning with how to both solicit speech and protect a right to silence. The focal students had always been active participants—not just passive subjects—in our study. They asked to review what their iPod de-vices had recorded, and they helped me collect and analyze data. But here the children themselves became the interviewers, think-ing through in their own terms many of the questions I had faced as they developed interview protocols and considered the ethics of elicitation for their own research on the Dreamers. Not unlike the questions of informed consent and confidentiality that concerned the students at the start of this project (chapter 1), the students were especially interested in the idea that the Dreamers' decisions to share their immigration stories and statuses were personal choices. The following conversation about disclosure and trust took place as they puzzled through what was at stake in talk about citizenship and status.

1 Maysi: It's their choice cuz it's their lives.
2 Ms. Daniela: It's their choice cuz it's their lives. Thank you, Maysi.
3 Manuel: But Ms. Daniela >we are a community<.
4 Ms. Daniela: That's true. We are their community but. They don't know us that well? A:::nd. >They don't know us that well?< And there's real reasons why they might not wanna share that information. Okay?
5 Aurora: Cuz they might think. Oh::: they are gonna °tell people
6 Ms. Daniela: Shhhh! Um can you guys think about what's a reason why they might not want to share that information? What do you think?
7 Aurora: I think maybe that. Maybe it happened before? Or::: somethi:::ng maybe::: like one kid went in there and asked who wa:::s and their names and all. They're like Oh:: °>this is your ID?< Okay. And maybe they told the police or something. ↑Oh >he's an immigrant.< °You may arrest him. °°Take her back.

This interaction began with Maysi echoing Ms. Daniela's own words—"it's their choice"—and adding "it's their lives." Maysi's use of the deictic pronoun "their" made clear that the reality she described was not her own. Manuel countered Maysi's idea that "they"—the Dream Team members—would not share their immigration status by appealing to the idea of a collective identity among the students in the class. Manuel was the U.S.-born son of immigrant parents, and his bid for an inclusive "we," with an emphasis on the word "community," appealed to a sense of camaraderie and solidarity (turn 3).

Ms. Daniela worked to acknowledge her students' sense of connection to one another ("we are a community") while also reiterating that disclosing status involves risk ("there's real reasons why they might not wanna share"). In turn 5, Aurora jumped in to elaborate on why an undocumented student would choose to guard that information closely. The level of detail she furnished in this brief story indicates just how familiar she was with the hypothetical situation that she recounted. In turn 7, Aurora slowly worked up to depicting a scene that escalated quickly from a student being asked for a name, to being asked for ID, and then being punished for being "an immigrant." The way she spoke mirrored the content of her story. Starting slowly, she elongated her vowel sounds ("or something maybe") but began to speak much more quickly as she quoted the language used when police demand papers ("your ID" and "he's an immigrant"). The final words in the story—shifting from the police officer's command "you may arrest him" to "take her back"—uttered in increasingly hushed tones is as close as Aurora came to articulating what she actually feared might happen to her.

As we know, Aurora's spiraling curriculum of citizenship commenced at a young age. On biweekly trips to flea markets in and around the city with her parents to sell women's clothing, Aurora had witnessed them being asked for their documents; at times federal agents would ask them to show their driver's licenses at traffic checkpoints set up by the U.S. Customs and Border Protection agency, while at other times local police would ask them to display their vendor licenses at the markets.[15] The anxiety produced by these encounters is evident in the stories that Aurora told throughout the Causas de Quinto unit. At the same time, Maysi and Manuel, U.S.-born peers with immigrant parents, also worked to articulate their connections to what the class was studying. The students' differing levels of vulnerability to surveillance and deportation, evident between U.S.-born and undocumented members of Ms. Daniela's class, shaped their preparation for the interview, and they carried this awareness into their visit with the Dreamers the following day.

Interviewing the Dream Team

As we know from Interlude I, the walk from P.S. 432 to Vista High School was fraught with Hazel's concerns about papers and Aurora's revealing uncertainty about which of the buildings we passed were factories or schools. Once we arrived at Vista High School, Aurora's anxiety was palpable as we stood for several long minutes in front of the security desk under the school safety officer's gaze.[16] Ms. Janet met us in the lobby to sign us in to the building and then escort us to the fourth floor. The fifth graders could not contain their excitement as they walked through the fourth-floor hallway; they whispered loudly about the high school students we passed, and they shouted out things they noticed (like the lockers they imagined using in the future).

We entered the classroom where the interview would take place, where three Dream Team members awaited us, seated at a long table at the front of the room. The fifth graders took their seats and took out their notebooks. The high school panelists started the interview with a formulaic introduction that each of them repeated: "Hi. My name is ___. I am a ___ grader, and I am part of the Dream Team." However, they quickly turned to a more substantive description of their group. Nina, one of the panelists, explained:

> Okay. So the Dream Team is a group uh- of stu- a group of students. Undocumented students and supporters who- Wait, okay. We're a group of undocumented students and supporters. We just basically try to make- Okay. Oh gosh! I'm nervous. Okay, so, yeah, we just try to make this space as like comfortable for everyone, for undocumented students especially and it's a confidential space. So everything stays within the group.

These brief opening lines communicated a lot: Nina's version of the "two kinds of kids" formulation that we heard from the teachers ("undocumented students and supporters"), her own sense of anxiety ("Gosh! I'm nervous"), and one of the key purposes of the Dream Team—to "create a comfortable space for everyone" and "for undocumented students especially." Her metapragmatic commentary about the group's norms—"it's a confidential space so everything stays within the group"—underscored the importance of mutual trust and discretion. By sharing this rule with us at the start of the interview, Nina was in effect asking us to follow it as well. I asked permission from the three Dream Team members to publish interview excerpts here; two students, Sula and Nina, agreed to have their voices included in this chapter.[17]

Throughout the course of the interview, the high schoolers talked about their activism. Their testimonios—just like their

introductions—started out in general terms and grew more specific over time. This paralleled a shift in the questions that the
fifth graders asked, beginning with broad ones like "why is this
important?" To this, the high schoolers described the importance
of taking political action. One of the panelists, Sula, explained that
she "wanted undocumented students to feel like there's like people
all over the place that supports them with like their situation,"
while Nina recounted that "a lot of undocumented students want
to have a better future. So that was a way of showing support and
like a way of showing how like they really want this too, like they
wanted this to like really like pass." The students articulated the
many ways they could support one another—by creating student
clubs founded on confidentiality, by showing up to protests together, and by calling on local and state politicians to support leg-
islative reform that would create opportunities for undocumented
students to apply for financial aid to pursue higher education and
ultimately provide a pathway to U.S. citizenship.

As she spoke more about the group's activities at Vista High
School—specifically their work in recruiting new members to join
the Dream Team—Nina talked in greater detail about her peers
and herself. Gaining visibility and welcoming new members was
important for the Vista High School Dream Team because, Nina
went on to say, "in our school there are some undocumented students as well. So for them to know that there's someone here for
them. And there's a group that they can join." She shared that her
motivation for being a part of the group was personal: "I joined
it because it benefits me and then I wanted to learn more about
it and like what can I do not just for myself but for my family as
well." With each student's turn, we learned more about why the
high school students chose to be part of the Dream Team: to take
actions in the present that could lead toward a better future,
and to advocate for educational opportunity and citizenship that
would benefit them, their loved ones, and the broader communities that they belonged to.

One of the final questions posed during the interview was
"What made you brave to do this act?" This question was simple,
but it communicated an understanding of the risks involved in disclosure. It also opened on to the following exchange between the

Dream Team members Nina and Sula and Ms. Daniela's student Maysi.

1 Nina: OH! We were brave enough because. We didn't really care what people thought. We just- we just went there. So::. To like. To- to show our sup<u>port</u>.

((Ms. Janet prompted with other examples of brave things they've done, such as speaking to policymakers and learning from the YLC community organizers))

2 Nina: Oh ↑yeah. And we went to talk to other students. So, I mean, for us. Well, for ↑me that was <u>ch</u>allenging because like I can be like very shy:: so. Yeah.

3 Sula: But what was it like >when it was all of us<. When everyone started <u>talk</u>i:::ng. You felt more <u>com</u>fortable.

4 Nina: We just wanted to let- let. We just wanna spread the wo::rd of what is the Dream Act. And the situation that's going on.

5 Maysi: So you said that um. That you don't <u>care</u>? what other people think? So::::. Did you say something to them?

6 Nina: No, it's not <u>that</u>.

((students chuckle))

It's like. What I'm trying to say like. ↑Like for us we don't like really care what like other people think based on like ↑immi<u>gration</u>. Some people think it's like a ↓<u>bad</u> thing. So you shouldn't think <u>that</u> way? You should think like a <u>positive</u> way? Get me?

7 Sula: ↑Yeah. Just because you're an immigrant doesn't mean anything. You can be proud °of what you <u>are</u>. Not <u>care</u> what people <u>say</u>.

Nina and Sula focused on the sense of collective purpose that they felt as a way of explaining how they had surmounted any individual hesitation that they experienced as activists. Nina described the importance of the interpersonal relationships involved—talking with other students (turn 2), working to positively influence public perception about immigration (turn 6), and advocating for the Dream Act (turn 4). Earlier in the interview she had also mentioned how much she had learned from the YLC community organizers who had worked closely with Ms. Janet and the Dream Team members over the last year.[18] Sula added that speaking out as a group instilled pride in her and countered the negative perceptions or responses that they faced during public demonstrations (turns 3 and 7).

The students repeatedly made connections between the personal experience of growing up in a mixed-status community and the political context in which undocumented members of that community are denied access to rights and opportunities. As they vacillated between these micro and macro perspectives, they co-constructed a set of conditions—of camaraderie, trust, and confidentiality—in which they and other students could talk about their undocumented loved ones.

8 Maysi:	I just usually ↑think that it's like unfair? And I also think that the ↑world belongs to everybody? So. Most people come here anyway. For example, like. My parents? They're both um immigrants. >One's from El Salvador and one's from Dominican Republic.< And I think that um to stay in um >United States< you have to be an American citizen and have to do this <u>test</u>. So I usually say like. Like let them be there. Let them just stay here. Like no <u>test</u> just stay here. Like no <u>test</u> just stay here fo:::r-
9 Nina:	Yeah. I ↑agree with <u>you</u> because I have an undocumented mother as well? So I feel like everyone should be equal and everyone should be able to like have the same rights. So <u>yes</u>.
10 Sula:	It's almost the same. They're just <u>people</u>.
11 Maysi:	Like if my parents stayed as like people that don't come from here? that mea::ns me and my sisters would be lonely? because both of my parents are from um different places like

from <u>not here</u>. So that means like if they aren't American citizens then we wouldn't be here either. Cuz like if ↑they weren't here? then ↑me and my sisters wouldn't be here.

12 Ms. Janet: You should join the Dream Team when you come here.

13 Maysi: Yeah. Um my sister comes here. So I like to follow my um older sister's footsteps? So yeah um she came to our school and now she comes here so I want to come here too.

Maysi shared her parents' immigration status and attempts to pass the citizenship test (turn 8), while Nina mentioned her undocumented mother (turn 9), making clear that her involvement in the Dream Team connected her to a broader immigration rights movement that also affected them in a deeply personal way. The connection between parents' and children's previous immigration experiences and their futures was strong. For Maysi and her peers, this interview and the visit to Vista High School foreshadowed their own sense of possibility about whose footsteps they would follow and which rights they would have access to.

Writing Thank-You Letters

The day after the fifth graders' interview with the Vista High School Dream Team, Ms. Daniela asked them to write thank-you letters to the high school panelists. Ms. Daniela asked her students to consider why this might matter: "I want you to think what are all the reasons why it's important to thank <u>these</u> high schoolers for <u>their</u> activism." The children talked in pairs. Aurora and Maysi had the following exchange in which Aurora referred to her undocumented status. Although Aurora had shared this before in the private small group conversations that took place in our grupo de análisis meetings, this was as close as she'd come to disclosing her status out loud in the classroom.

1 Aurora: I think that it's really important because apparently. Um. I think it's really important because apparently.[djun djun djun] I think it's[scritch] really impor[scritch]tant. I think it's really impor-

2 Brandon: ↑HI

((speaking into the microphone))

3 Aurora: I think it's really important because apparently
hhh. >I keep on saying apparently< hhh. Cuz-
parently. Um::: Uhh that ↑not becau::se it's just-

4 Maysi: Apparently?

5 Aurora: Yeah, I was ga-na-say-dat hhhh. But, come on.
So I think that. U::::parently. And also that. Also
that they're gonna also that they're gonna.

((turning to read from the message board where Ms. Daniela
had written the prompt for this class activity))

°°I can write a thank-you letter to the Vista
High School Dream Team.

6 Maysi: So I think that because of-

7 Aurora: Well. >It's important because it's gonna ↑help
us?< °Some of us are not. **in.doc.** >some of us
don't have documents< and >if they do that
maybe< then later on when ↑we're hh high
school? and we're gonna turn to college that is
↑already gonna be there? so that's gonna. really
↑help us a lot? So they're not just doing it by
their- for themselves. To know they're doing
it for the gene↑rations that are coming.

Aurora jump-started the conversation with Maysi right away while
also grappling with what she would say. Fidgeting with the iPod
in turn 1, the recorder picked up muffled sounds as she covered
the lapel microphone (djun djun) and rubbed it against her shirt
(scritch scritch). Across turns 1 and 3 Aurora repeated the phrase
"I think it's really important" five times—as if to work up the courage to state her next thought—and she kept repeating the word "apparently" while also noting that she was doing so. This chatter was
a kind of hedging; Aurora was both asserting the importance of
this letter-writing activity and what she was about to say while
also dismissing her own ideas as merely speculative ("apparently"). At the same time, Brandon spoke loudly into the microphone, further heightening Aurora's awareness that what she was
about to say would be heard by others.

After taking a momentary break from talking to reread Ms. Daniela's instructions, Aurora began to describe an "us" that recalled the Dream Team strategy of claiming membership in a mixed-status community without necessarily divulging individual status. But as she spoke, that "us" began to sound more like a "we" that specifically situated her within an undocumented group of students. Starting off hurriedly, in turn 7, Aurora began her disclosure with the phrase "some of us are not. in. doc." switching between English and Spanish with the start of the word *indocumentado* (undocumented, as she had earlier with graduados). Then, in the same turn, Aurora changed her pace noticeably—speaking loudly and at a more normal speed—to explain that the Dream Team's work was important because it would "help" students and future generations. Her change in delivery paralleled a change in topic; she had moved from talking about her own lack of papers to describing her future as a student ("later on when we're in high school and we're gonna turn into college"). We can see, however, that Aurora understood the Dreamers' activism in relation to her own uncertain future and to the future of other undocumented student "generations that are coming."

Ms. Daniela—who had been walking around the classroom listening to the conversations among the pairs—overheard Aurora's contribution and exclaimed, "That's so powerful!" Surprisingly, Aurora asked if she could share her ideas with the whole class. When Ms. Daniela regained her students' attention and asked for pairs to share their ideas with the whole group, Aurora was the first one to be called on:

↑Um? Hhhh. That? I think they're- I think the Drea^taptmers^taptap? are^tap not just^tap doing it by.^tap by their act?^tap The Dream Act? they're not just doing it for themse:::lves? to get. ↑to get a better future::: and for. but if^fffya? But I think they're also^taptap doing for the gene^taprations^tap that are^tap coming^tap cuz, apparently hhh. If if^ffff mmmiffff If we were just growing up- right? and what they're doing right now? like they^scritch win^scritch what they wanna do? they.^taptap how you^tap say it?^taptap They reach^tap their^tap goal^tap what they^tap wanted to do? so that's really gonna help us when we wanna go to hh college hh cuz then we're not gonna be fighting anymore^ffff. °That's ri:::lly cool^swissshhh yeah^swissshhh

cuz we're °°not ri:::lly gonna be:::fighting. Yeah. taptaptaptaptap
Ne-na:::h-no-you-di-nnnn-t.

((speaking with an electronic-sounding robotic voice))

Wha::t?

The shift between what Aurora said to Maysi and what she chose to share with the class is telling: Aurora chose not to repeat the more direct reference to herself as also being undocumented ("some of us don't have documents") when she addressed her peers. Aurora muttered her closing comments to herself—"that's really gonna help us" and "we're not really helping"—as she grappled with the uncertainty that she felt about her own role in the Dreamer movement. She both acknowledged her indebtedness to the Dream Team for bravely taking a stand and worried that she might not herself be capable of "fighting" and "coming out" in order to advocate for change.

Working to make principled choices about what to disclose or disguise, Aurora communicated her inquietud. She replaced the nervous chatter from her conversation with Maysi (her repetition of "this is important" and "apparently") with fidgeting (represented in the superscripts above), which was picked up by the microphone as she addressed the class. Toward the end of her turn, Aurora spoke so quietly that her speech was recorded by the iPod but was inaudible to her peers. She began to speak in a slow, staccato, and distorted way, as though imitating a robot. Perhaps Aurora's robot voice represented the voice of the device itself, scolding Aurora for the discourse it had just recorded ("Nuh! No, you didn't")? Or perhaps she was distancing herself from the emotional intensity of the moment by speaking in a nonhuman voice. This moment was not so private either, as another student looked at her strangely and she responded, "What?" For my part, I heard Aurora's adoption of this artificial voice as a way of expressing the dehumanizing force of restrictive immigration policies that reduce people to mere legal categories.

A look at the letters that Aurora and Maysi wrote that afternoon highlights which of the themes raised during the Causas de Quinto unit they most wanted to convey to the high schoolers. Both girls made personal connections between immigrant rights,

student activism, and the possibility of social change. I have transcribed their letters below:

> May, 28, 14
> Dear [__] High School Dream Team,
> Thank you that you answerd all of our questions. Also that
> you were honest saying if you had documents or not. I know
> that you feel terrible that familys get seprated for deportacion.
> What I like is that you use words to express yourself. Like
> showing a movie about a family seperating for deportation.
> Thats a way of getting people to be inspire. Your goal is
> everybody goal.
>
> > Sincerely,
> > Aurora
> > Dreamers Rocks

> Dear [__] High School Dream Team,
> I want to say thank you so much for teaching me what and who
> is The Dream Team. You showed me to stand up for imagent's
> and me, it's mostly what is right not wrong, anybody can be
> in American, and mostly that I can be a dreamer. Because of
> you guy's/The Dream Team I want to be in the Dream Team so
> thank you so, so, so much.
>
> > Sincerely + Love
> > Maysi

The children's letters are revealing of their own lived experiences. As an undocumented student, Aurora honed in on the significance of the high schooler's disclosures ("you were honest")
and expressed a firsthand understanding of the pain caused by
family separation ("I know that you feel terrible"). It is also notable that Aurora tried to imagine a solidarity in which difference
disappeared entirely: "your goal is everybody goal." Meanwhile,
Maysi—a U.S.-born student with immigrant parents—emphasized
her plans to join the Dream Team as an ally ("you showed me"
and "because of you . . . I want to be"). These two pieces of writing exemplify the "two kinds of kids" trope that we heard from
Ms. Daniela, Ms. Janet, and Nina throughout the interview process. For both types of students, the interview itself involved visions of their own future selves.

Every part of the encounter with the Vista High School Dream Team reveals the depth and sophistication of these fifth graders' understandings of how their own futures are inextricable from questions of birthright citizenship and the possibility of immigration reform. Listening in on the class preparations, their visit, and their processing of the experience also vividly demonstrated how the students are capable of constructing metapragmatic norms for discussion of immigration status. And we have also seen the fifth graders reveal both their deep association between educational advancement and belonging and their ambivalence about this association—their knowledge that, despite the rhetoric of equalization, barriers to their educational, social, and economic advancement persist.

The preparation for the interview itself was a fascinating instance in which the children in this study became researchers. As they learned about youth leadership in the immigrant rights movement, they developed ethical standards for talking about citizenship, including a set of norms for asking interview questions that preserved students' rights to silence. They were able to enter into these rich discussions about the metapragmatics of talk about citizenship precisely because they were so attuned to the importance of U.S. citizenship for themselves, their families, and their community. These students made explicit the need for confidentiality, they varied deictic language to encode a sense of proximity to or distance from the undocumented experience, and they managed their own disclosure through more and less explicit references to their and their loved ones' immigration status.

Before and after the interview, Ms. Daniela's students expressed their appreciation of and admiration for the Dream Team student activists. Across these exchanges, we observed the students' multiple expressions of solidarity with the immigrant rights movement. In these moments, the children also communicated their own sense of uncertainty. Some children proudly took up the role of ally, while others, like Aurora, grappled in sophisticated ways with how to balance self-protection and solidarity. Aurora was clear that if NYDA were signed into law, her life could meaningfully change because she would have more educational opportunities in the near future. She was also ambivalent about whether she would be brave enough—in the words of her peers—to run the risks of public disclosure and political action on behalf of her community. The visit with the Dream Team inspired her most public disclosure but also her most palpable expressions of inquietud. The girls in this study had been living with a deepening spiral of understanding their own immigration status and its implications for education and belonging for many years. This knowledge was inextricable from their senses of their past, present, and future.

Interlude II
"There's Always Police"

At Vista High, as at most middle and high schools, there is something called passing time. It's the time when students move between classes, navigating common school spaces with relative freedom, without teachers regulating their behavior as closely as they do in the classroom. However, passing time—whether transitioning between periods or walking back from Vista High to P.S. 432—is not empty time. Instead, given the opportunity to listen in, we can hear how these liminal spaces and transitions are saturated with knowledge and anxiety about citizenship. Let's take our place alongside the fifth graders as they return from encountering a possible image of their future (high schoolers, activists) back to their present elementary school. Let's pay attention to their sensory experience of surveillance. Let's also hear them singing.

Listen In

Once the interview was over, the elementary schoolers filed out of the classroom just as the high schoolers' passing time was starting. The older students moved through the hallway, largely ignoring our presence, caught up in their own conversations. Lined up against a wall on one side of the hallway and awaiting instructions from their teachers, the P.S. 432 students commented on what they saw. "Ooh they were kissing," observed Catalina, as Ms. Daniela asked that she and her peers "stand up against the wall and stand up straight." Nellie replied, "Hellooo it's high school you gonna be doing that too." "Middle school," Catalina quickly corrected, clarifying that they were on their way to middle school, not high school, the next year. Maybe she was eager to emphasize they had plenty of time before they were expected to behave like the high schoolers they were witnessing. Meanwhile, Nellie relished the social capital she accrued by claiming to be acquainted with some of the high school students who passed us: "That was so-and-so, I told you I know them."

As we exited the building, the humidity reasserted itself. The fifth graders sang their graduation song—"Brave" by Sara Bareilles— spontaneously practicing for their upcoming graduation just a few weeks away. The graduation would bring them back to Vista High School because the ceremony was scheduled to take place in that school's auditorium. Because it was much bigger than P.S. 432, the high school could accommodate all the students, teachers, family members, and friends expected to be in attendance for the event.

> Say what you wanna say and let the words fall out.
> Honestly I wanna see you be BRAVE!
> I just wanna see you ooo.

From the outside, it may have seemed like they were just belting out the latest pop song. In fact, the children were rehearsing for what they and their families considered a major educational milestone.

Look Around

As we exited the school onto the sidewalk, some of the children no-ticed that I was recording our walk. My camcorder was just one of the many devices recording people's actions along the city streets that afternoon; other cameras were in apartment building vesti-bules, in the doorways of local businesses, on lampposts, in pass-ing cars, and in smartphones. The images below illustrate the various ways that students responded to the many modes of sur-veillance that surrounded them. After these fleeting moments, the students' attention shifted back to the streets we were now walk-ing through, and they began to narrate what they saw.

The camera picked up two synchronous audio tracks: talk in Spanish about behavior and continued singing in English. Seeing someone a few years older than them and smelling smoke from the lighted cigarette in his hand, Catalina commented on his smoking while a friend told her not to climb along the ramp leading down to the street. Ignoring that warning, Catalina sang back—her words timed to a merengue beat—tempting her friend to tell on her.

Catalina:	**MIRA, mira, está fumando**
	LOOK, look, he's smoking
Hazel:	See you be brave-

Figure 3. Children respond to the camera #1.

Figure 4. Children respond to the camera #2.

Figure 5. Children respond to the camera #3.

Students:	**No se suban**
	Don't climb up there
Hazel:	See you be brave-
Catalina:	**Ya me subí y qué, ya me subí y qué**
	I just climbed so what, I just climbed so what
Hazel:	Wanna see you ooo-

The sound of a passing police siren entered into one boy's stream of consciousness. He stopped chatting, and I overheard him saying, in a singsong manner matching his light hopping movements, "If you wanna run away from the cops, why don't you play with me." His friend—another male student—looked over and put his arm around his shoulder, as if to pull him to safety.

The police presence intensified as we rounded the corner from the high school to the main commercial strip leading back to the elementary school. Just as Aurora had immediately noticed the presence of the school safety officer (Interlude I), Catalina commented on the police officers patrolling the streets on which we were now walking. Both school safety officers and police officers are employed by the New York City Police Department. The differences between them are registered in the subtle variations of their uniform's shade of blue and the far less subtle difference that only the latter carry guns. These differences were not lost on these children. Sara and Nellie—whom we met in chapter 3 as they worked alongside Aurora to complete the diversity word web activity—also joined in here.

Nellie:	Yo I almost died can someone get me out the street. Thank you.
Catalina:	There's always police around this school
Ms. Daniela:	Can you get with your partner? Please go with your partner? Thank you.
Nellie:	Oh wait they're in front of us. I'm missing my partner.

((Sara waves to police officer))

Notice everyone's hands. The girl waving—Sara—extended her hand as she said hello to the police officer while another hand—Nellie's—reached out to hold her back. Male friends in the class placed their arms around each other's shoulders and walked closely together. The police officer rested his right hand on his gun. Without stopping, and in a whisper, as if she had been dared, Catalina asked the police officer his name; he did not respond.

The girls' voices bubbled up in a release of nervous energy as they processed their fleeting interaction with the officer.

Figure 6. Passing a police officer while walking through the neighborhood.

Catalina:	I just made a new _friend_!
Sara:	Yo Nellie, Nellie wait
Nellie:	I can't believe you just said that
Sara:	Nellie Nellie. He was ugly yo.
Nellie:	Yo::: but the way you _said_ that.

((giggled))

Ms. Daniela:	Are you with your partner?
Students:	Yeah
Ms. Daniela:	Who's your third?
Nellie:	Shit, come here. Stay here.
Students:	That's right!
Nellie:	I was like WOAH you gave me too much information.

Ms. Daniela raised her voice in order to restore order to the lines. The officer stood quietly alongside the buildings, but his presence was loud. The children responded to passing him in a variety of ways: with silent yet anxious gestures, and with words unlikely to be audible to the police officer but registered by my audio recorder. Catalina asked his name. Perhaps she thought she could humanize him by transforming the abstract representative of police power into an actual individual. Or maybe she was playing with reversing the usual interrogation routine, so that if he did speak, it would be on her terms. The girls' exclamations indicated how significant the brief interaction was. They played and they teased, sarcastically claiming, "I made a new friend," then countering with, "He was ugly, yo." They expressed disbelief at Catalina's daring ("I can't believe you said that") and a sense of danger and transgression ("Shit, stay here"). As the class continued walking, the police remained on the children's mind—not just because of the individual officer but because of the siren sounds and flashing lights as cop cars passed us.

While Catalina, Sara, and Nellie played with the idea of being noticed by a police officer, Hazel demonstrated profound anxiety about that prospect. Hazel, who boisterously sang "Brave" in the streets, did not tolerate Jenni's taking risks in the public space. Although she was often bossy with her friends, Hazel rarely tattled to her teachers, preferring instead to assert her own authority. But when she worried that Jenni was scribbling graffiti on a lamppost, she began yelling, threatening her friend with the risk of being stopped by police for defacing public property, and turned to Ms. Daniela to recount what she had witnessed. For these girls, peer interactions were infused with a sense of the risks involving state authority.

Hazel: **No hay que subirte a eso porque la policía te va ver-**
            There's no reason to climb on that because the police is going to see you-

Jenni: **Ajá, no puede ser. Llámalo now.**
            Uh huh, can't be. Call them now.

Hazel: **Yo dije ↑la policía te va a llamar la atención.**
            I said the police are going to notice you and call you out.

Jenni: **La policía-**
            The police-

Hazel: **Escucha, limpia tus oídos.**
            Listen, clean out your ears.

Jenni: **Sí. <u>Okay</u>**
            Yes. <u>Okay</u>

Hazel:	**No estoy jugando. Ms. Daniela, Jenni was writing on the WALL.**
	I'm not playing. Ms. Daniela, Jenni was writing on the WALL.
Jenni:	**↑No. I don't have a pencil ↑you see.**
Hazel:	**Hmmhmm**
Jenni:	**Yo lo bote allí**
	I threw it out over there
Hazel:	**Mmhhmm en la boca lo tienes.**

(((con firmeza))

And let the words fall out

(((cantando))

Mmhhmm it's in your mouth.

(((sternly))

and let the words fall out

(((singing))

Hazel wanted to take the words—and the instrument of writing— out of Jenni's mouth, to make sure that she didn't say or write something that would put her at the risk of attracting the attention of the police. So she returned to singing "Brave." But what does it mean to be brave on these streets, in a childhood inflected with both song and surveillance, where schools are mistaken for factories, in which decisions about speech and silence take place against a backdrop of sirens?

Conclusion
A Lifetime of Knowing

We have been listening to the voices of Pita, Hazel, Catalina, Aurora, Jenni, and Tere, who are among the 16.7 million people currently living in mixed-status households.[1] We've heard them directly and indirectly discuss the significance of citizenship in their lives, revealing a deep understanding of the relevance of immigration status to their past, present, and future. We've learned to listen to their meaningful silences, to those moments when their refusal to disclose or discuss citizenship has spoken volumes. Grasping the significance of citizenship when it comes to schooling can help educators, policymakers, professors, and researchers to more fully realize the promise of *Plyler*. Notably, mixed-status families were among the plaintiffs who—having experienced first-hand the inequalities produced when their undocumented children were denied a free public education while their U.S.-born children could attend public school—risked retribution and deportation to participate in the trial.[2]

Plyler's important protections, however, have come at a cost by producing domains of silence where we should instead be vocal advocates for students from mixed-status families. By prohibiting educators from inquiring into families' immigration status when they register for school, state and local education departments have instituted a kind of "don't ask, don't tell" policy. Educators may remain ignorant of their students' immigration status, and project this ignorance onto their students, assuming that awareness of its significance only dawns on young people as they approach legal majority. Our silences have left this growing student population to study in the shadows.³ Meanwhile, students engage in a spiraling curriculum of citizenship with their peers and family members. Their always deepening, if not always explicitly expressed, understanding of how juridical status affects their lives is often missed or underestimated.

School policymakers' and educators' overfocus on implementing *Plyler* when families register for school—an attempt to secure children's rights to a public education by ensuring that they can attend without needing to disclose immigration status—may give the impression that citizenship only arises for parents and guardians as an issue at the time of enrollment. This book demonstrates that immigration and education policies are in fact inextricable throughout students' experiences of schooling. We have gained a deeper understanding of the material and symbolic connections between these domains of policy and have seen how, from a young age, they shape children's perceptions of themselves and their families while coloring memories of their past and thoughts about their future. We now know that children of all ages, starting as young as seven years old, are engaging in conversations about their birthplace and immigration status. And we have learned that whether they choose to speak out or remain silent in school, children make real-time calculations about the risks associated with disclosure out of a deep sense of responsibility to their families and friends. Recognizing both the knowledge and inquietud of these children is essential for understanding the complexity of the contemporary public school classroom in the United States.

Chapters 1 through 4 provided ethnographic accounts of the study's methods and findings. In chapter 1, I argued that the ways in which we collect data (our methods) are directly related to the conclusions that we reach (our findings). This is especially important for understanding this book's contribution to the existing literature on immigration. By conducting longitudinal participant observation with children, I have been able to observe how and when they demonstrate the significance of citizenship in ways that they would have been unable or unwilling to report during interviews. Relying on direct elicitation can lead to a view of children as ignorant of citizenship's significance and reproduce a long-standing view of childhood as a time of innocence. I have also shown how elementary-age students took up co-researcher roles in this ethnographic study and shaped my thinking about the ethics of research about citizenship. In so doing, they demonstrated precisely how much they knew about what was at stake in talking about citizenship outside of their families. Together, the focal students and I developed approaches to ongoing informed assent and consent through collaborative data analysis that infused this ethnography with participatory approaches to recording everyday life. We have seen the ways in which audiovisual research methods could both resemble and run counter to the surveillance technologies with which these children are accustomed to living.

Chapter 2 theorized a spiraling curriculum of citizenship, the learning process by which children gain ever-deepening understandings of what it means to have or lack papers over time and across settings. Two sets of examples demonstrated how and when papers circulate in the lives of children and how conversations about papers that take place at home affect children's learning about when to broach the subject at school. First, we examined the moment when Catalina's younger brother launched a show-and-tell sequence of their family's passports during one of my first visits to their home. This exchange exemplified how school literacy practices and immigration documents shape conversations at home about citizenship, access, and belonging from a young age. Second, we examined the ways in which school documents sent home evoked undocumented parents' and children's concerns about the potential for disclosure. The school lunch form and the middle school social studies homework assignment shaped Jimena's (Catalina's mother) view of the school and also prompted Catalina, Aurora, Jenni, and Pita to consider what they would do if they were asked to reveal their immigration status. As adults and children encountered these dilemmas, they co-constructed a set of norms for speaking out or remaining silent about their immigration status that then shaped their participation in school.

Chapter 3 offered us a view of the focal girls' classroom experiences during their fifth-grade school year, focusing specifically on the ways in which they expressed the significance of immigration status through writing, talk, and silence. I first chronicled the ways in which Catalina's and Pita's written accounts of their important early childhood memories—of their families of origin, of border crossings, and of sibling's birthdays—were inflected with their pre-occupations about citizenship. In their written responses to school assignments that did not directly mention immigration, they explicitly and implicitly referenced the ways in which formative moments in early childhood were also moments of reckoning with their sense of belonging in the United States. Crucially, we saw how the prospect of publication—that is, of more widely disseminating these assignments—led to different responses by Catalina and Pita that correlated with their juridical status. Catalina, who lacked papers, encoded her published narrative so that only a careful reading could yield insight into the implications of her story. Pita, who had recently obtained papers, published an explicit story of crossing the border that sought to challenge negative perceptions of immigrant families. Both the form and content of these assignments therefore revealed a sophisticated reckoning with citizenship status and disclosure. The second part of the chapter focused on the ways in which Aurora and her peers reframed classroom conversations that oversimplified complex terms like diversity and nationality while also raising their fears about disclosure. I described the dilemmas of disclosure that Aurora faced in real time, the inquietud she felt in those moments, and the resourceful ways she responded.

Chapter 4 examined a monthlong study of immigration reform which culminated in an interview with members of their local high school Dream Team. I attended closely to the ways in which Aurora inflected this school-based project with preoccupations about her future as an undocumented student. We followed Aurora's real-time adjustments to—and refusals of—an assignment that would both force disclosure and identify belonging with birthplace. We also tracked her expressions of inquietud as the assignment unfolded. At the time of the study, Aurora and her classmates were about to enter middle school, and they were attentive to the ways in which policies like DACA and the Dream Act might open up new educational opportunities in high school and beyond. We also saw them vividly display their metalinguistic awareness about the significance of citizenship and the ethics of speaking out and remaining silent.

Interlude I and Interlude II, preceding and following chapter 4, respectively, move with the children throughout and between school settings to better understand the landscapes and socio-political contexts of their daily lives. The interlude as a form was meant to draw attention to the liminal but crucial spaces that the students traverse—spaces outside of (but never unrelated to) the classroom. The interludes sought to bring students in mixed-status settings out of the shadows by illuminating the complex topics that they are grappling with even in their casual conversations with peers. Taken together, the interludes chronicled the children's walk through their neighborhood on our way to and from the interview with the Vista High School Dream Team. By attending to their speech and body language, we learned about the children's perceptions of the buildings we passed, the law enforcement officers that we encountered, and one another. As we walked alongside them, we witnessed their fear, listened to their songs, and observed their playful attempts to move through a neighborhood that is home to their families while at the same time full of risks inextricable from their immigration status.

I began this book with a consideration of how institutional criteria for ethical research—encoded in concepts like criteria for inclusion, risks posed by the study, and beneficence—took on new meanings as I listened to the students talk about this study. As I have explored elsewhere, researcher training in conducting qualitative educational research tends to focus on gaining access to study sites and establishing trusting relationships with potential gatekeepers.[4] University IRB committees, along with core textbooks in our field, are primarily concerned with resolving ethical dilemmas before a researcher's study is approved—in other words, before the researcher begins fieldwork. I have argued that this emphasis on the research design phase results in our overlooking important ethical concerns that arise when we are ready to exit the field. In addition to addressing ethical issues that arise as we establish relationships with children and families, it is also essential that we consider the ethics of reciprocity and beneficence after the completion of our formal period of data collection. This is especially true in educational research with children from mixed-status families who are threatened by the traumatic and forced exit of deportation and whose access to social services are always precarious.

Now, as I both bring this book to a close and trouble the notion of closure, I emphasize the importance of rethinking exit as it pertains to beneficence: the edict that our research should do no harm and "maximize possible benefits."[5] Just as in chapter 1, where I challenge the notion that risk and beneficence were knowable in advance, I want to raise questions about exit as a hard stop in which the relationships that developed during our research suddenly dissolve. In this project, maximizing benefits has meant sustaining relationships; by looking for opportunities to establish a sense of ongoingness, I have become a mentor to and advocate for the focal girls. I am cautious about describing this as "reciprocity" because the term suggests that the girls gave me something that I can return in kind, running the risk of flattening inherent inequalities in the researcher/researched relationship. For example, after years of publishing and presenting this research, I have experienced considerable career advancement; however, I do not pretend that any amount of my expertise or advocacy could bring the girls and their families the same material and financial stability that I have obtained as a result. Instead, I think of my ongoing relationships to the girls as a lifelong process of *acompañamiento,* which Andrea Dyrness and Enrique Sepúlveda III define as "accompanying young people in their citizenship formation" in a way that centers "migrant youth as experts and co-researchers of their own experience."[6] This conclusion represents my attempt to live out this ongoingness by not merely ending the book with a discussion of the past but rather by bringing my ethnographic account into the present.

One site of my ongoing advocacy and support has been trying to help Pita, Hazel, Catalina, Aurora, Jenni, and Tere manage the shifting terrain of DACA. This has meant helping all of them to learn about the program so that they themselves could apply or share the information with eligible friends and family. This federal immigration policy was enacted in 2012 when President Obama signed an executive order providing young undocumented immigrants with protection from deportation and authorization to work. As I explained in chapter 4, Obama created this program during his second term as president after Congress failed to pass the federal Dream Act, which would have provided a pathway to citizenship for undocumented immigrants who came to the United

States as children. Although DACA does not offer immigrants a pathway to citizenship, it does provide existing DACA recipients with a social security number that temporarily authorizes them to seek employment and protects them from deportation. (Depending on where they live, DACA recipients may also be eligible for in-state tuition and financial aid for higher education, health care benefits, and driver's licenses.) DACA applicants needed to meet the following criteria: entering the United States before the age of sixteen and being younger than thirty-one years old in 2012, residing in the United States for five consecutive years since 2007, having no criminal record, and being enrolled in high school or the military or having the equivalent of a high school diploma. DACA holders are required to renew their temporary status every two years. By combining temporary authorization with educational advancement, DACA intensified the families' hopes for obtaining U.S. citizenship through schooling.

As we know from chapter 2 and chapter 4, Aurora and Catalina were aware of the promise of DACA as early as ten and eleven years old; by that age, they had already set their sights on entering the program as soon as they turned fifteen and became eligible. Yet they were equally cognizant of the contradictions in federal approaches to immigration policy that simultaneously extended benefits like DACA to a subsection of undocumented immigrants while also restricting entry and ramping up deportation for others. In 2014, as they prepared to graduate from P.S. 432, the girls and their family members closely followed news reports of protesters nationwide calling on President Obama to stop the soaring number of detentions and deportations. The girls often talked about the contradictions between Obama's pro-immigrant campaign rhetoric, his DACA program, and the punitive policies that had earned him the nickname of "deporter in chief."[7] That same year—two years after DACA started—Obama announced a related program called Deferred Action for Parents of Americans and Lawful Permanent Residents (DAPA), which would have extended similar benefits to the undocumented parents of U.S.-born or green card–holding children. DAPA had the potential to help each of the mixed-status families in this study, but it was immediately challenged in the courts and never implemented.

Because I remained in close touch with Pita, Hazel, Catalina,

Aurora, Jenni, and Tere when they started high school and turned fifteen years of age, I bore witness to their upset when Donald Trump was elected after promising to revoke DACA. On September 5, 2017—just two days before their first day of high school—Trump announced that the program would be phased out.[8] Existing DACA holders would retain their status until further notice, but only renewal applications received by that October would be considered, and no new applications were accepted.[9] From 2017 to the present, a staggering number of legal battles have ensued over the lawfulness of the program itself and over the executive authority of the president to implement or terminate the program. Immigrant advocates argue that Trump did not follow due process in revoking the program, while immigration restrictionists question whether Obama had the power to institute the program via executive order in the first place. In December 2020, the Supreme Court ruled that the Trump administration violated procedures for ending the program and reinstated DACA (without ruling on the integrity of the program itself). Between December 2020 and July 2021, there was a brief reopening of the program and new applications were accepted; however, a U.S. district court in Texas subsequently declared the program unlawful and once again barred any new applicants while granting a stay to current DACA holders.[10] President Biden's administration has since appealed the 2021 Texas ruling and, at the time of writing, a Supreme Court ruling on the program's lawfulness is still eagerly awaited.[11]

The upshot of these dizzying shifts in policy is that young people like Aurora and Catalina are still unable to participate in DACA, despite having watched for over a decade as the program was created, debated, and ultimately closed to them. As they tried to make sense of this shifting landscape, each one took a different approach. Aurora waited until Biden became president to submit her application, but, as she explained it, "my application stayed in limbo." These many years of uncertainty have felt to her like "a very huge up and down having to think about all of these plan B, plan Cs, saying to myself should I stay here or go back," leaving her wondering about whether she can pursue a career in this country. Catalina, who decided not to submit her DACA application amid such uncertainty, resigned herself to searching for alternatives to DACA because "it's been like this for a long time and it's not the only thing that's going to help me. I've been doing this for a long time."

Trump's election didn't just have implications for DACA policy.[12] The focal students' four years of high school were shadowed by the hatred, fear, and uncertainty produced by his and his administration's anti-immigrant talk and the punitive policies that they justified by villainizing the undocumented and stoking racism. "The Trump Effect"—a phrase coined in a 2017 report issued by the Southern Poverty Law Center—refers to an increase in children's experiences of being bullied and to a rise in "uncivil political discourse" at school.[13] The phrase also denotes the fear that permeates schools around the country. Students at all grade levels began vocalizing concerns that a wall would be built to keep them out, or that their loved ones could be deported at any moment. I also saw evidence of the Trump Effect in mixed-status families between 2016 and 2020 as they grew more anxious and lived with greater degrees of stress while at the same time finding fewer outlets for expression at school and in their neighborhood. Fears of detention and deportation rose, as did uncertainty about participating in the few social services to which they had access.[14] Parents like Jimena wondered whether the public charge rule that Trump expanded to include basic social services like nutritional benefits and health insurance would negatively affect them if they had the chance to apply for U.S. citizenship in the future.[15] All six families worried whether they would ever be able to reunite with family members still living in Mexico, El Salvador, and the Dominican Republic.

This sketch outlines just one view into the broader political rhythms that have formed the backdrop for my relationship with the girls from 2014 through the first years of the coronavirus pandemic and into the present. Although I could tell the story from other vantage points—the impact of the Black Lives Matter movement on their own identities and their sense of justice, for example—I have stayed close to a narrative focused on the explicit intersections between citizenship and schooling that I have witnessed over time. As the rest of this conclusion will show, I have gained this lifespan view through my ongoing acompañamiento as Pita, Hazel, Catalina, Aurora, Jenni, and Tere have found their way through high school and beyond. This has meant remaining in consistent touch after the formal period of data collection and continuing to listen to them and their families for nearly a decade. Together, we have continued to complicate traditional notions of study closure and exit from the field.

I now want to look at two recent moments in our ongoing relationship that echo many of the themes this book has explored and that offer snapshots of how they navigate the complexity of citizenship in the present. First, I will describe the process of helping Jenni obtain access to the technology she needed to participate in remote learning when schools were closed in spring 2020. Second, I will share conversations that I had with the group about their postsecondary options, along with excerpts from a meeting that I arranged with a public school teacher and DACA recipient. This will allow us to bring into relation the significance of citizenship for the girls at two important educational thresholds: their completing elementary school (chapters 2, 3, and 4) and their graduating from high school.

When the coronavirus pandemic hit the United States in March 2020, existing social and economic disparities became even more painfully visible. Since the pandemic began, immigrant families have been disproportionately affected in nearly every domain of life, including food and housing insecurity, unemployment, health insurance, and educational and digital access.[16] As New York City went into lockdown, I began hosting weekly Zoom meetings to bring the group—by then all of them were sixteen- and seventeen-year-old high school juniors—together in a virtual community of mutual aid based on our long-standing trust and openness in a time of upset and isolation. These virtual meetings were especially important to have in quarantine, when they were managing the shock of being more socially isolated than ever before while also having to take new kinds of risks to contribute to their family's survival.

Our meetings were meaningful for me, too; I benefited from seeing the group regularly at a time when I found myself severed from the social world beyond my home. During this period, I was homeschooling my two daughters (my eldest, Lucía, was born at the start of this study in 2013, and my youngest, Marcela, was born two years later), and they would often join us at the start of our Zoom meetings. Lucía and Marcela have always known Catalina, Aurora,

Pita, Hazel, Jenni, and Tere, and I've tended to refer to them all as my girls; it was joyous to see my girls chatting and laughing together. However, because the following pages are precisely about how I've followed the girls out of childhood and into young adulthood, I will refer to them as young women for the remainder of the book.

During the early days, all six of these young women were responsible for running family errands—picking up medicine for sick relatives, shopping for household groceries, retrieving packages from a UPS store because packages could not be reliably delivered to their buildings—at a time when leaving their homes was frightening. Catalina talked about not "feeling safe," while Aurora declared in one of our Zoom meetings that "being outside feels illegal." The mapping of their own preoccupations with immigration status onto the feelings they had being in public was indicative of their childhood experiences living in neighborhoods saturated with surveillance and policing.[17] These connections also mapped onto widely circulating discourses and policies related to migration at the time. Trump and the right-wing media that disseminated his views spread unfounded claims about migrants from Latin America being the ones who spread the coronavirus in the United States, using this misinformation to justify the increased detention and deportation of migrant children and to further militarize this country's southern border.[18] Over time, as institutions began to reopen, these young women also had to obtain and manage new forms of documentation—for example, vaccination cards and Covid-19 test results to attend in-person classes for those enrolled in college.

The pandemic lockdown was unprecedented, but many of the pandemic realities that the group shared on Zoom actually entailed a deepening of the already existing responsibilities they shouldered within their mixed-status families. Some of them had, for example, always played a significant role in helping family members treat long-term health problems, like Jenni's mother's diabetes and Aurora's younger sister's congenital birth conditions. But now frequent visits to the pharmacy and hospital had been become dangerous for high-risk family members attempting to avoid contagion, and it was increasingly difficult to attend medical appointments without regular public transportation services. They shared experiences of loss and illness exacerbated by unstable living conditions and unsafe working conditions. Jenni shared that "quarantine been a little stressed out, stressful. Like two weeks ago my friend's aunt died, the lady I used to be so close with, she died of coronavirus and it was really painful because I spent a lot of time with her in the summer when I used to be in the shelter and I had no place to be." Pita, whose undocumented uncle was hospitalized with Covid-19, commiserated: "I truly feel for people who had people pass away. A lot of my family from Long Island have been affected by it and one of my uncles was in the hospital and intubated. So it's tough. I don't like stressing all the time because it gets to me too much." They all described heightened levels of anxiety and depression as they mourned their losses and cared for vulnerable loved ones.

Gaining Access to Remote Learning

At the end of each weekly virtual check-in, I asked, "Do you have what you need for the coming week?" This is when I learned that Jenni lacked the hardware and wireless internet connection that she needed to participate in remote learning. Even though she could connect to our meetings, she often experienced unstable connections as she pirated service from neighboring apartments and businesses. She explained:

> I do have a tablet but the problem is I don't have internet. I was calling **la compañía** (the company) **y no me cogieron el teléfono** (and they didn't pick up the phone). I was going to get [a Department of Education iPad] **pero yo no sé** (but I don't know) if there was a certain date that you had to get it and I couldn't go. I been trying to finish certain works on the phone but it's hard because I don't understand it.

Jenni faced a number of intersecting challenges that were making it hard for her to get connected. She was an English language learner navigating an unfamiliar high school system; she lacked the money needed to purchase a device or pay the monthly fee for Wi-Fi; and she received little information from her school alerting her to the available resources. Accessing help had become more complicated for Jenni because the city had just relocated her and her mother from temporary transitional housing to an apartment in a public housing unit on Staten Island. This move meant leaving Brooklyn, living farther away from her high school, and losing proximity to neighbors, friends, and school staff whom she would have otherwise sought out for support.

I was determined to help Jenni get the technology she needed for virtual learning. This would ultimately require more than a dozen phone calls and several trips to Staten Island. The questions of exit that I explored above came to a head when I saw that I had a chance to leverage my knowledge of the public school system to help Jenni obtain the resources required to stay in school. This was an opportunity for me to live out the principle of beneficence even though I was no longer beholden to the IRB's regulations. This time, instead of offering Jenni an iPod, as I had back when she was in fifth grade, I was advocating for her to obtain the iPad that she needed to complete her junior year of high school.

Thankfully, Jenni attended Vista High School (which we visited in chapter 4), where Ms. Janet, the Dream Team faculty advisor, was still teaching. My first phone calls were to Ms. Janet, who put me in touch with Jenni's guidance counselors, who explained that she was indeed falling behind in school, in part because she lacked reliable digital access to school now that it was completely virtual. They redirected me to a district-wide office where staff were working to manage the distribution of devices to students. After one attempt to have the iPad delivered directly to Jenni, the device went missing; deliveries to her new home were unreliable. Several three-way phone calls later—Jenni and I contacted Department of Education staff together—I was able to arrange for the iPad to be sent to my house so I could drive it to Jenni and ensure that she received it. This process took over a month, so I lent her my personal iPad as a stopgap in the meantime.

Once we obtained the device, we faced the challenge of arranging for the internet service that Jenni needed to use it. After another round of phone calls, we were able to secure three months of free service because Jenni qualified for a student discount. On one of these calls, a service provider asked for Jenni's name, date of birth, address, and social security number. I distinctly recall Jenni's long silence in the wake of being asked for her social security number; I stepped in to ask why that information was necessary. The representative quickly explained that she did not need to provide a social security number to obtain the service and router, but that she would have to be accompanied by her mother, who would need to show a form of government-issued identification in order to activate it. After hanging up with the internet company, I called Jenni to ask about her silence and to see if she had any concerns. She explained: "Ohhh thank you, I got it it's just that I don't like to give that information. Even if it's a company or anything so yo le dije así (I just put it that way)." Jenni had obtained a green card in fifth grade, when we first met, and so had a social security number. She had recently informed me that her mom had also obtained a green card, meaning that they were more secure than before when it came to their juridical status—or, in her own words, she was "chilling with that." Still, her silence spoke to her sense of vulnerability, and Jenni implemented the lessons learned from her spiraling curriculum of citizenship: never disclose any information that could reveal your or a family member's citizenship status.

This exchange threw into relief the moments when students in mixed-status families face the risk of disclosure when trying to access basic resources. Even for Jenni—who was now a legal permanent resident but had lived for many years in a mixed-status household as her parents worked to obtain authorization—the request for her social security number gave her pause. Recall that in chapter 2 school lunch forms requiring Catalina's mother to enter in four Xs in lieu of a social security number also made her think twice about completing the application for much-needed nutritional resources. In both cases, institutional requests for a state-issued identification number produced a chilling effect—a quite different sense of "chilling" than Jenni's use above—which I helped to mitigate by redirecting the conversation (in the case of the phone call with the internet provider) and explaining the process (in the example of completing school paperwork). Even as school policymakers' guidance prohibits educators from asking families for this information when they enroll in school, there are many other moments in a child's schooling trajectory when they or their guardians are asked to furnish information that can point to their immigration status. As we have seen, these requests can instill fear in mixed-status family members and prompt them to take protective measures—measures like ending the exchange before they are able to access the resources that they need.[19]

Getting Help with College Applications

Against this backdrop of heightened anxiety and isolation, Catalina, Aurora, Pita, Hazel, Jenni, and Tere considered their postsecondary options. Let's turn now to a second example of how their knowledge of immigration status has continued to shape their schooling experiences from childhood through young adulthood. At the end of our first meeting in March 2020, Catalina brought up the subject of college, declaring, "I'm scared and I feel like I'm nine"—noting how old she had been just before this study began. Perhaps she was suggesting that I had a role to play in easing this transition now, just as I had back then. For all of us, their graduation from high school echoed that earlier transition from fifth grade to middle school, making vivid how far we'd traveled together and how their spiraling curriculum of citizenship continued to deepen across the lifespan.

Lockdown had brought their college preparatory activities to a halt, ending SAT classes, internship and volunteer-based programs, and the part-time jobs that had helped them to cover the fees associated with college entrance exams and applications. All six of them attended underresourced public high schools that were unable to provide their students with much-needed academic and mental health counseling services. It took months for any of these students to regain contact with their guidance counselors and homeroom teachers. Their sense of urgency about attending college despite these setbacks reflected a desire—a desire they'd had since elementary school—to make good on their parents' sacrifices by obtaining school documents (diplomas) that they hoped would lead to obtaining immigration status (papeles) in the future. It also reflects their ongoing focus on hyperdocumentation as a strategy for obtaining education-related papers that they could leverage to access more opportunities, or that could serve as a proxy for U.S. citizenship and belonging absent a change in their immigration status.

Our conversations led me to think that helping the group to apply for college was another form of beneficence that I could offer at a crucial educational moment. Drawing on my professional know-how and connections as a professor at the City University of New York—one of the schools they were applying to—I created a structure of support that included recurring check-ins, meetings with current CUNY students and alumnae, and meetings with professors and admissions officers. We also established a writing schedule focusing on their personal statements along with Zoom-based work sessions on topics like soliciting letters of recommendation and completing the online application. I answered many of their practical questions: What is the difference between a college and a university? Do I have to complete many different applications, or is there a common app? How do I format my résumé? We also broached the difficult subject of disclosure as it related to drafting their personal statements.

Pita and Catalina reported that their parents had begun narrating college access as the final point in their own immigration journey. Their parents believed that by obtaining a college diploma, their daughters would have more stable lives in the United States. As a result, the parents would become free to return to their countries of origin. Pita explained:

> I mean my mom like has always told me that my future is here. Like she- we- that she was like "Oh you know someday I just wanna like move back to El Salvador," because she likes it over there and she wants to like, I guess, age over there. And she's like. And it- it- it makes me like anxious. Like honestly it- it stresses me thinking about like growing up and you know, having so many responsibilities.

In chapter 3, we saw that these students' academic ambitions are inextricable from their sense of responsibility for the fate of their parents and siblings. Now, as they approached legal adulthood, their own schooling was once again linked to fears of separation. Catalina added:

> My parents also told me like later when my siblings grow up and they're like sustainable and they could take care of themselves they're gonna have to go because that's where they were born so they could like be with their parents and stuff. And it like makes me kinda anxious too. It's not like I depend on my parents, but I'm used to having my parents around me

and I just don't feel grown up enough to like separate from my parents.

Catalina talked about this potential for family separation in the future tense, but we know that she has been living with the fear of her and her parents' separation from deportation from a young age.

In addition to needing a space to share these feelings, the group enlisted me in sorting through the exclusionary policies, misinformation, and confusion that Donald Trump left in his wake. During one of our meetings, Catalina shared her concerns about answering questions regarding "immigration status" when she encountered it "in applications where it says you have to have a visa or be a resident." As they moved farther along in their applications and references to immigration status became more explicit, they faced new dilemmas surrounding disclosure and access. The more subtle—but still anxiety-producing—references to birthplace and nationality that we witnessed in elementary school were becoming increasingly overt in higher education. This prompted many conversations about college access for undocumented students. During one Zoom session Aurora said:

> I had questions about that. Mainly because um [my friend's mom] she's a teacher and she has DACA right now, right? And she's also like also been telling me about like colleges and like we speak about this together cuz I see her do whatever like her work and everything. And she asked me she's like um that are we- like if I would be allowed to be like going to college without like an active social security number and all of that. And I was like so there is a program in which it allows you to um go to college without an active social security number. But my question was because she said that for certain programs like going for hours or as a nurse just studying for certain- for a lot of, like, career paths you need your active social security number for them to even let you in. Not only for- she was like "I'm not even talking about like payment just like, just for you being inside?" So like that was my question, would like the program would help you with that?

It was clear that she and the other group members were unsure about what federal and local immigration policies might affect their educational opportunities, and that their concerns hinged on whether programs would grant them temporary authorization the way that DACA would (having what Aurora called an "active social security number"). The instability of the DACA program made the college application process infinitely harder to manage.

In one of our early college prep meetings in May 2020, when we began brainstorming topics for their personal statements, Pita, Aurora, Catalina, and I had the following exchange.

Ariana: If you had to write your essay RIGHT now::::, what would your instinct be? Would you ↓want to talk about something persona::l, a:::nd about your fa:::mily history, and your um immigration let's say? Or do you feel like that would ↓not be something you would wanna write about?

Pita: I feel like it should be. Like. Um. In like one way I _guess_ if you would write about it, it would like show others how even though you're _this_ even though you:: like were able to achie::ve ma::ny thi::ngs and. You know::. Being succe::ssful despite the fact that you're ↓undocumented or whatever. But at the ↑same time, you don't really know who::'s gonna to _read it_ and if they're gonna define you:: by like if you're ↓undocumented or not. Like I feel like I'd rather not to take like the risk of writing about it? Because I don't want to be like defined by it. It like depends on who it is that's gonna read it. Right?

Aurora: Yeah I agree with you. I feel like there's a lot of like stereotypes out there about like people that are undocumented. And it's. Like we never know who is actually reading it. Yeah. Yeah.

Catalina: I don't know- I don't know it's like. A difficult topic.

Ariana: What makes it hard?

Catalina: Cuz I mean if you say:: it . . . cuz you wanna go to college. You know? And like, I don't ↓know. Like Pita said. Depending on who reads it. Some people are >kinda crazy<. I don't know it's-

Pita: Would <u>you</u> write about it?

Catalina: I don't know::? Mmm::::

Aurora: I feel like it's a yeah and no. Not only because of like who's reading it but it'd be hard for them to try to- like a lot of people say "oh, I <u>under</u>stand." They actually really <u>don't</u> understand the pre:::ssure of like them being able to do so much stuff. ↑And they take >a lot of things for granted< that we <u>don't</u> because we know we don't have them. Um. And ↑I don't know. I feel like- I feel like some people don't <u>see</u> that and others <u>do</u>. But it ↓depends. I feel like a lot of things, like me personally a lot of things I do it's because I also wanna make my parents proud. And the fact that they did the <u>whole</u> pro:::cess of trying to come here. For a better future, not ↑like for them but for ↓me. And yeah. ᵒI don't know.

In some ways, these responses echoed concerns they have had about disclosure since they were children: proving their sense of self-worth through educational achievement, making their parents proud, and feeling a responsibility to represent their mixed-status communities. Their careful attention to questions of audience is also familiar; this was central in their decision-making about what stories to share in chapter 3 and in their preparation to interview the Dream Team in chapter 4. Their explicit mention of fear was striking. Pita talked about the "risk of writing," Catalina worried that "some people are kinda crazy," and Aurora was distrustful of people's ability to "understand the pressure" that she faced. After knowing them for a decade, I could see how the persistent—and now heightened—fear of disclosure made drafting a personal statement for a college application fraught and full of inquietud. At the same time, they believed—and were often told—that attending and graduating from college was a crucial step toward becoming U.S. citizens and experiencing a sense of belonging in the United States.

I wanted to connect them with a mentor who had firsthand experience attending college as an undocumented student. I had recently met an undocumented elementary school teacher and DACA recipient (whom some might colloquially refer to as being

DACAmented) named Claudia who I thought could serve as a role model. I met her through Ms. Daniela—who had left P.S. 432 and was now colleagues with Claudia at a different public elementary school—after Claudia had shared her immigration status with her colleagues at the school. After telling the group about Claudia and seeing their enthusiasm about meeting her, I invited her to join us in Zoom to talk about her experiences navigating access to schooling and her career before and after obtaining DACA. Our meeting with Claudia echoed the interview that Catalina, Aurora, Pita, Hazel, Jenni, and Tere conducted with the Dream Team members back when they were fifth graders, which I had also brokered by connecting Ms. Daniela and Ms. Janet, and which also involved explicit conversations about the metapragmatics of disclosure.

Claudia joined us on the first Sunday in June 2020. In advance of the meeting, I asked everyone in the group to choose an artwork to share during an icebreaker where they would introduce themselves to Claudia. Each of them had some creative practice—ranging from sketching to painting and fashion design—and I thought this would be a good way to prompt them to share something about themselves before we invited our guest to share her experiences with us. After their introductions, Claudia began by explaining that she had immigrated to the United States from Mexico while still an infant, grown up undocumented in Brooklyn, and faced many challenges pursuing a career in teaching. Even though she now had DACA, and while no one in our group had been able to apply for the program, they found common ground in their shared experiences of growing up in mixed-status families. Claudia's reminiscences were especially relatable for Aurora and Catalina, who immigrated to the United States as toddlers and remained undocumented.

The metalinguistic preoccupation with when and how to talk about their immigration status with others was central to this exchange, which Claudia had joined precisely to disclose the realities she faced as a person who now had DACA but who had grown up undocumented for most of her life. She reflected on the significance of recounting her story during the Zoom meeting:

> You know, I always wanted to talk to a group of young um ladies, you know, that are just like me,. You know, it makes me feel- I never you know did this to be honest. I've never spoken

to other people that are just like me. Um and any other, you know, adults either that are going through the same thing. So I always felt alone in so many ways.

In a way that will at this point be familiar, Claudia's personal decision about disclosure was inextricable from a broader sense of responsibility to a wider community that now included the six young women she was addressing in this meeting. She went on to explain, "You should always say to yourself that you are a big part of this community and this country, and we're the ones that are going to make a difference you know." She assumed the risks of disclosure in order to instill in others a sense of belonging.

After Claudia spoke, the group members took up the topic of the risks and responsibilities associated with disclosing immigration status. Commenting on Claudia's ideas without addressing her directly, Aurora shared:

I- I just wanted to say that it's like really um heartwarming to, like, see how, as she said, being like the only person seeing all this around her and not really having anybody that could relate to her. Cuz I feel like nobody could relate to me and, like they have everything, or like they don't care. And it's just like, hard because I don't tell them why I- why I care so much cuz I feel like, I don't know, I feel like that's just something that not everyone should know about me. Cuz like I don't know how people will react to that. Or like thinking "Oh!" or a lot people just make jokes about it. And it's just really annoying to me. And I know I will get pissed off. So I'd rather not say it.

In Aurora's mind, there were two kinds of students, echoing a phrase we heard in chapter 4, but with a different formulation. Here, there were those who are undocumented like her, and there were those who have U.S. citizenship and by extension have everything. Among the many risks involved in sharing her undocumented status, Aurora mentioned feeling disregarded, managing others' surprise ("Oh!"), and experiencing anger at being teased. This harked back to Aurora's early stories of children tauntingly saying, "I have papers and you don't. Na-na!" (chapter 1).

Claudia responded directly to Aurora, acknowledging the fear

that accompanies disclosure in the context of punitive immigration policies: "I totally get where you're coming from. And, you
know, I was younger, I thought the same way. Like, I never told
anyone." Fear of the threats associated with disclosure had prevented Claudia from speaking out because, as she explained, "I was
always scared that maybe I would tell the wrong person. And then
that person will always use that against me, whether it's only immigration, whether it's, you know, attacking my family, you know,
in some type of way." Over time, however, Claudia decided to share
her experiences as an undocumented person growing up and pursuing her career in the United States:

> Now like I always let them know who I am, like, "Yes, I'm an
> immigrant. Yes, I'm a person of color. I'm not like you." Um.
> They're never, I they're never going to understand the- the
> struggle and the hardship, even if they tell you, "Oh, I under-
> stand you." "You don't understand. You don't know where I
> came from, you don't know the hardship that we do, you don't
> know what our parents do to try to get us here." Um. So I don't
> feel like people will ever understand. But it's good to educate
> them to let them know . . . who we are.

Claudia not only modeled a conversation between herself and an
imaginary listener but also reframed the purpose of the disclosure. For her, disclosure was less about an opportunity to relate to
others and more aligned with her sense of responsibility to edu-
cate others about the intersections between immigration status,
racialization, and representation. She went on to model two other
modes of address: what she told herself and how she responded to
colleagues who may think less of her for being an undocumented
educator:

> You know, and I always said that to myself, and I kind of
> always uplifted me. In like "Okay, you got this far, because
> you were born here, and you um you know, you have all the
> benefits in the world to be a better person." But look,
>
> ((addressing an imaginary colleague))
>
> "I'm a teacher just like you, right. And that doesn't make us
> any different, I just work ten times harder. And, and, and for
> that, it's because I value my work ten times more."

Both Aurora and Claudia shared a preoccupation with the stigmas they had faced in the past as a result of not having papers. Yet Claudia insisted that disclosing being DACAmented could work against negative stereotypes and change people's beliefs. This too was something the group had considered at a young age. Recall that as early as fifth grade, Pita believed it was important for her to write and publish her personal memoir, "Frontera," in order to share the realities associated with being an undocumented immigrant and to help others view undocumented youth in light of their many strengths. A decade ago, when Pita imagined people reading "Frontera," she hoped that "when they go home they keep thinking ... and the phone rings and they say I heard a story about a girl, and people hear this and it spreads, so that other people know this well."

Of course, the dilemmas of disclosure were not resolved in one Zoom meeting, and Aurora remained concerned about the perils associated with sharing her loved ones' immigration status. She was torn between her desire to express her pride in her family and her worry about the risks she posed to them if she shared their undocumented status. She explained:

> I'm really proud of like where I'm coming from and what my family has done, like all of that. I'm really proud to even like mention it and um I feel like if I know it and the necessary people know it, then it doesn't matter who else knows it. I feel like it's just the people that are gonna influence in my life should know it. That's pretty much it. So that's how I try to keep it.

What it means to hold this knowledge—and whether they should withhold or disclose it—is a question that Aurora, Catalina, Pita, Hazel, Tere, and Jenni have lived with and continue to face. When we met them in fifth grade—at ages ten and eleven—we witnessed the many ways that the question of having or not having papers had already entered their consciousness and inflected their experience. Now, as they turned nineteen and twenty, they were still—anxiously, resourcefully—negotiating the realities and risks that attend citizenship status.

All of us listening to the voices of these six students over a span of ten years have broken with the myth of their innocence regarding citizenship status and its implications. But what about *our* innocence—the innocence of those of us working within education and its related fields? As educators, it's important that we acknowledge what we know and what we don't know about how immigration status shapes our students' everyday lives both within and beyond school. Such an acknowledgment is an important step toward affirming our shared responsibility for providing educational access and opportunity to all students, including those who are undocumented and growing up in mixed-status families.

As public schools serve as intensifying sites of debate over broader social policies of inclusion and exclusion, educators, school policymakers, professors, and researchers will need to develop more nuanced strategies of listening and responding to their students.[20] It is time for us to move away from being tongue-tied by existing guidance that leads to "don't ask, don't tell" policies in our schools.[21] Instead, we must become more conversant and fluent in the ways that children's educational experiences are saturated with an awareness of immigration status.[22] The numbers tell us that we should assume that all classrooms—from elementary school through college—are mixed-status classrooms.

Even though all K–12 schools must admit students regardless of their or their parents' or guardian's immigration status, there exists little to no institutional support for educators charged with serving undocumented students and those from mixed-status families. Rarely, if ever, do teachers have opportunities to consider, talk about, and prepare for teaching in mixed-status communities. The guidance issued to educators about how to uphold the *Plyler* ruling has focused attention on avoiding chilling effects at the time of enrollment, but there has been little discussion of moments that students and their parents may experience as chilling throughout their education. As we have seen, there are many instances where educators' actions may have unintended effects that instill fear or anxiety in undocumented students and parents, from everyday classroom activities that seek to be inclusive to sending home school forms that in essence require families to disclose their immigration status. In the absence of teacher preparation for mixed-status settings, the onus tends to fall on a select few staff members—usually the ESL teacher or a parent liaison—to advocate for the rights of undocumented students and those from mixed-status households.

All of this means that support for undocumented students is idiosyncratic at best.[23] In this book we have met teachers attuned to the intersections between immigration and education. Consider Ms. Janet's work as an ESL teacher and Dream Team faculty advisor, and Ms. Daniela's emails to me noting themes that emerged in her student writing and in classroom conversations. We have also seen teachers unaware of the complexities of broaching nationality in the classroom (remember the "stand up if you're from . . ." activity). I have also shared the ways that I, as a researcher, was able to provide some of the resources the schools lacked: college counseling for a mixed-status groups of peers and connecting students to DACAmented mentors. Too often, undocumented students and their peers from mixed-status families must depend on good fortune rather than good policy when navigating the school system.

We have had a "don't ask, don't tell" policy in place regarding immigration status in schools for the last forty years, but as this book demonstrates, we *have* been asking, and students *have* been telling. When a teacher asks students to interview a family member about their immigration experience for a social studies assignment and when the school sends home a form requiring that parents enter Xs in the absence of a social security number, we are asking them to disclose their immigration status. We have seen vivid examples of students choosing to explicitly share their understanding of citizenship in their schoolwork and conversation. But we have also seen how students tell us about citizenship with their knowing silences—their redirection, their encoding of immigration experience in writing, and their audible expressions of inquietud. My hope is that this book will help us listen.

Afterword

We Are Still Here

with Ruby Estrella Bonilla, Yazmin Montes Lopez,
Jennifer Magaly Portillo Rivera, and Lumari Sosa Garzón

After working together on this project for nearly a decade, we close
this book with an experiment in collective composition. This experiment involves an approach to authorship that allows us to
proudly identify ourselves while also mitigating the enduring risks
of disclosure traced throughout this book. Our challenge has been
to find a way of writing that allows us to reveal who we are without forcing any one of us to disclose our (or our family members')
immigration status. After many conversations among ourselves
and with our families about the wisdom of using our own names or
continuing with pseudonyms, we decided on a strategy that could
balance our desire to be visible with our need to protect the most
vulnerable among us. We list our real names in the table of con-
tents in recognition of our coauthorship, and we also shift between
"I," "she," "we," and "her" pronouns to anonymize any one individual's images or words. In order to move freely between speakers—
avoiding attributing experiences (and therefore immigration status) to any one of us—we have sometimes altered the subject–verb
agreement of our sentences throughout the prose. The result is a
choral, composite text in which we are all visible as writers but
also shielded from publicizing our immigration status.

We hope that this models a kind of expression beyond the "don't
ask, don't tell" policies following *Plyler* that have sought to uphold
our rights to schooling by rendering us invisible. We are inspired
here in part by the solidarity among documented and undocumented students on the Dream Team panel described in chapter 4—a solidarity that recognizes differences while building on
shared commitments. By finding creative ways of writing together,
we can talk back to the myth of ignorance while still working to

protect one another. This afterword extends our collective understanding of the ways in which immigration status has shaped our lives from childhood to young adulthood, and it also demonstrates that our commitment to this project and to one another has been equally long-lasting.

We present excerpts from four "lifemaps" that convey memories of our pasts and visions of our futures. We can call this a kind of pictorial prolepsis that underscores the use of visual methods to represent a moment in time that is laden with concerns about the future. Lifemaps, which are both approach and artifact, are a method used by researchers to elicit the narratives of immigrant children through drawing. We worked to create our lifemaps at two points in this project. In 2014, when we were ten and eleven years old in fifth grade, Ariana asked us to illustrate our experiences of coming to the United States, important events that took place before and after migration, and our goals for the future. Recently, in 2022, we revisited these documents together, and we added new imagery and text to our original drawings in order to bring our lifemaps up to date while imagining our future goals now that we are nineteen and twenty years old.[1] We also read and discussed work by Marjorie Faulstich Orellana and Inmaculada García-Sánchez, who use this approach with immigrant children. We wrote this afterword by analyzing our own lifemaps using sentence starters adapted from the scholarly literature that we completed in Google Docs. Ariana collaged images from our original and updated lifemap drawings as well as our written analyses into a draft that we then reviewed and further edited as a group.

Lifemaps are one way of "tapping into children's views of how their lives could unfold" by asking them to illustrate their experiences.[2] We think of lifemaps as "literary acts" or "pictorial narrations" that help us tell our stories by enlisting readers in meaning making beyond what is spoken out loud.[3] In this book about talk, where the transcripts represented in the preceding chapters hold so much information about us—based on what we have said and what we have chosen not to say—our lifemaps offer a different way to understand the unique and various situations we've found ourselves in, beginning at such young ages. The lifemaps that we share here make visible the connections between immigration and education across place and over time; they refer to geographic locations spanning national borders and educational programs that we have participated in over the last decade. In keeping with the themes of this book, they show how much we knew about the importance of having or not having papers from a very young age.

The term "lifemap" is, of course, metaphorical; it invites us to think of important life moments as destinations along a route.[4] The paths that we have drawn represent significant transitions in our lives and open onto futures that are still coming into view. For some of us, returning to our lifemaps felt like looking into a fog. It was hard to clearly name the emotions we were feeling in the moment. For others, revisiting our lifemaps and adding to them with new captions and additional drawings felt like entering a time machine or like seeing stars in the night sky, creating a connection with—a flashback to or a reflection of—what we were thinking and feeling when we first drew them. Some members of our group who participated in the original study have taken paths leading to more distance between us. The five of us have chosen to stay connected— avoiding taking the exit ramp—to continue the sustained inquiry that this project has become.

Our lifemaps display how even at young ages we were all, in our different ways, making sense of migration and raising questions about responsibility, sacrifice, belonging, and the importance of having papers. Figure 7 is a lifemap chronicling an intergenerational story that starts with a mother leaving her home in El Salvador via boat and continues with her U.S.-born daughter growing up in Brooklyn.

Figure 7. Original lifemap, drawn at age ten. Pregnant mother crossing the border.

Moving from left to right, this lifemap begins from the perspective of a mother who moved to the United States and then gave birth to one of us in New York City. We can see that she is taking this trip as a pregnant woman expecting to give birth, a mother on the move (the lady on the boat who then crosses the desert). This drawing represents a story of parental sacrifice coupled with a child's sense of responsibility for her family's well-being. As the path continues, the little U.S.-born girl with two ponytails grows taller and older. While the focus of the drawing is on the parent, this book has shown how the mother's experiences also affect the daughter. Looking back, I know that my childhood worries may not be considered normal or child-appropriate topics—border crossing, ICE, losing your parents—but they were very present for all of us with undocumented parents.

For those of us who crossed the border, those memories have always remained vivid, and they've shaped our lives ever since. Our early lifemaps show that this experience overshadowed other memories and even stifled our imaginations of the future. In Figure 8, one of us leaves a time stamp of crossing the border by noting how old I was when I experienced that defining moment that has shaped my interactions with people ever since.

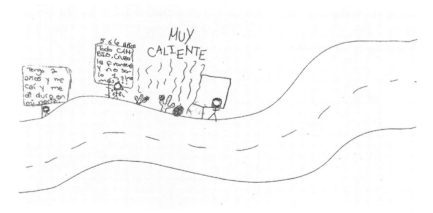

Figure 8. Original lifemap, drawn at age eleven.

This drawing focused on crossing borders—not just one, but several, which I had to pass through on the long trip from Central America to the United States. The road continues beyond the border without any additional detail, and I wonder whether those crossings were so formative that it was hard for me to imagine a future self at the time.

Despite the traumas we endured to come to the United States, we've never felt fully accepted here, and questions about our birthplace come up in everyday conversations with people. Even though we work to hide our immigration experiences from most people, we are often asked where we're from when we say our names in Spanish. It's common for people to express surprise when they hear us speak English fluently. Once, when I was just getting to know someone, he asked me to explain where I was from. Referring to how I spoke, he said, "Oh, you weren't born here?" When I answered no, he replied, "But your English is so good."

When this happens—when people ask us to say where we are from according to what we sound like—they are really telling us that to speak Spanish is to be from somewhere else, to not belong here. This is hard to hear for all of us, even though this kind of othering affects us differently if we are U.S. citizens born here or if we are born in Latin America and hold citizenship in our countries of origin.

Even though it was hard for some of us to leave our countries, we felt a sense of possibility in coming here, and it's been hard to face those moments when we cannot access opportunities because of our immigration status. In the illustration below (Figure 9), I represent sadness: being driven to the airport to leave my home in Mexico, where I was happy. That sense of loss is part of migration, and these sacrifices are justified by the idea leaving for the United States to pursue new opportunities. When I was younger, I drew New York City as a place with pretty, nice things. This was my way of making sense of the idea of leaving my country for the promise of a better life.

Figure 9. Original lifemap, drawn at age ten.

The promise of obtaining those nice things has always been tied up with the hard work that I knew I would need to put in to achieve my goals, even when the future remained uncertain. In my drawing, *"buena carrera"* (good career) and "future" are represented on a different road from my migration story, there is no transportation illustrated, and it is unclear how I would arrive there. At age ten, we just knew we wanted a good future for our older selves.

Over time, we've had to work to live with the contradiction of being told to be good students while still being denied certain chances. Updating my lifemap reminded me that I've missed out on opportunities to participate in schooling events because I didn't have a U.S. passport, and that I'm always making calculated choices about how to account for my realities without revealing my immigration status (Figure 10). It continues to be difficult to hide important parts of our lives from people we consider friends.

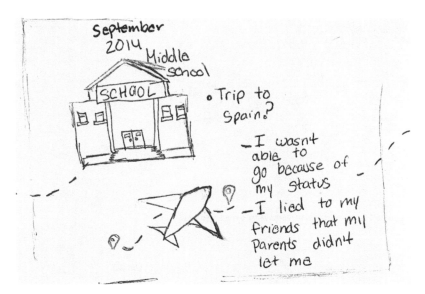

Figure 10. Excerpt from an updated lifemap, drawn at age nineteen.

Throughout a lifetime of living in our mixed-status communities, we have learned how to proudly assert who we are while always weighing the risks involved when we are asked about where we are from.

All of our stories convey the importance of travel as a symbol of possibility. For those of us living undocumented lives, travel by car has been the only way to visit family and places in other states throughout the country. Our lifemaps communicate our preoccupation with modes of transportation, beginning with childhood migrations to the United States, back when we were too young to choose, and continuing with travel to new destinations that, for us, symbolize independence. These drawings represent not only places but also the emotions we felt at ages ten and eleven when we thought about where we'd come from and tried to imagine where we might go next. In Figure 11, one of us travels by car from her birthplace in Mexico to a new home in Brooklyn. Rather than seeing it as a limitation, I've come to appreciate car travel because it deepens my sense of connection to each place, especially in that moment of leaving a town in Mexico for a city like New York.

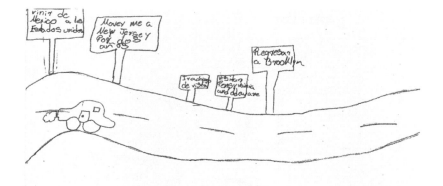

Figure 11. Original lifemap, drawn at age ten.

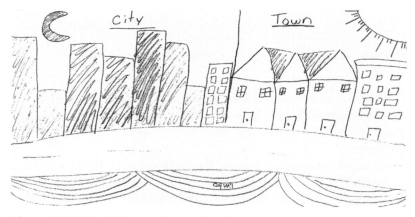

Figure 12. Original lifemap, drawn at age ten.

The lifemap in Figure 12 represents how much we were trying and how much we are still trying to figure out. The bottom arches on the left panel include the word "limbo," representing how much of life we felt unsure about. I knew that after elementary school there was middle school, and after middle it was high school. But now that I'm in college, I don't know what's next. There's not a set path for me, and I have questions. What is it that I can do and what is it that I cannot do as an undocumented student? I want to pursue a career in medicine, but I'm unsure about certain things—do I need to find a private institution that will accept me? Will my international taxpayer ID be enough, or will I need a social security number?

As I've grown up, moving around has remained important to me. When we revised our lifemaps recently, I chose to add new places that once seemed far away—like high school in Manhattan—before I could imagine traveling more than a few blocks away from home (Figure 13).

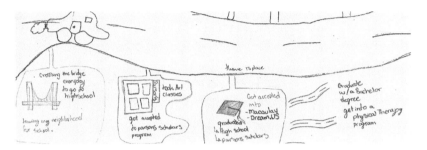

Figure 13. Updated lifemap, drawn at age twenty.

I also named the programs and places that we were able to apply for as non–U.S. citizens; I proudly included them as destinations on the map to show that I was accepted. When I applied to college, I started to see that I was more than just my good grades. I am also who I am because of the programs I've been a part of and because of the people I have connected with.

In spite of the difficult time of the pandemic—and the disappointment we experienced as we missed out on high school rituals like prom and graduation—all of us were admitted to college. One of us has taken a leave from college to work in a community-based organization, and three of us are juniors. The three of us felt a huge a sense of accomplishment on becoming the first people in our family to attend college. For two of us, being able to enroll in college while living undocumented has given way to new dreams of graduating, securing employment, and even obtaining a license (Figure 14 and Figure 15).

Figure 14. Excerpt from an updated lifemap, drawn at age twenty.

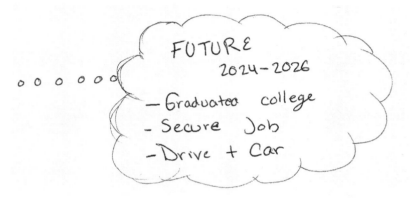

Figure 15. Excerpt from an updated lifemap, drawn at age twenty.

For several of us, driving a car is an important life goal; as of 2019, it is now a privilege that all of us can strive for regardless of immigration status.[5] This represents a step toward obtaining full membership in society that had previously been denied to people without social security numbers.

It's hard for us to disentangle the different forms of papers that remain important to us today. My updated lifemap and my new set of goals include getting my driver's license and also applying for citizenship. Even though I gained some sense of stability after getting my legal permanent resident status in elementary school, obtaining U.S. citizenship remains a major life goal. When I was younger, I knew about my immigration status and about the steps involved in obtaining a different set of papers, but back then, my mom managed decisions about schooling and paperwork. Ever since I entered high school, I've been in a position to establish my own goals and timeline, and the kinds of papers on my mind now include my driver's license, my citizenship, and my diploma (Figure 16).

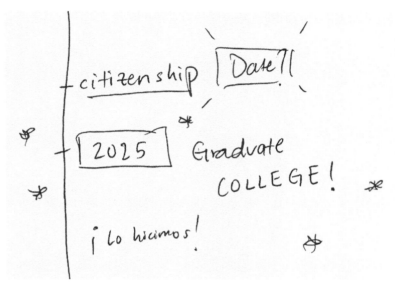

Figure 16. Excerpt from an updated lifemap, drawn at age twenty-one.

And for those of us born here, we continue to witness our parents, siblings, and friends pursuing the enduring and elusive goal of becoming U.S. citizens.

As we added new destinations to our lifemaps, the ongoing importance of migration and papers to our lives was clear. Our understanding of who we are is represented in these lifemaps and gives us a sense of footing as we continue our journeys into the future. Our work together over many years has had the stated of goal of helping educators and researchers to understand just how much we know; in the process, we have also come to see the importance of what we have experienced. We understand that our experiences growing up in mixed-status families link to the experiences of many other children in this country. We know how aware we have been of immigration status all these years, and we also see how much we have accomplished, not in spite of but because of our sense of responsibility to our loved ones. Our collaboration—which will continue beyond the borders of this book—fills us with a sense of possibility. Seeing our lifemaps now motivates us by connecting us again to those little girls who wanted a buena carrera. This process has encouraged us to keep on going with our goals. We are still here. We are still going strong.

Notes

Preface and Acknowledgments

1. El Barrio is the community name given to the neighborhood also known as East Harlem. A 2011 report, Center for Latin American, Caribbean, and Latino Studies, "Latino Population," details the residential demographics of Latinos living throughout New York City between 1990 and 2010. In 1990, the year that I attended fifth grade in one of El Barrio's public elementary schools, 49 percent of the city's Latino population was Puerto Rican.

2. Growing up bilingual, and continuing to live in both Spanish and English, I often switch between the two languages in my speaking and writing. In this study, I draw on my knowledge of both, in what Ofelia García calls "translanguaging": "the act performed by bilinguals of accessing different linguistic features or various modes of what are described as autonomous languages, in order to maximize communicative potential" ("Education, Multilingualism," 140). Throughout this book, I have sought to approximate this experience of translanguaging by representing both Spanish and English in similar ways without constantly marking one language as different from the other. Drawing inspiration from Mira Shimabukuro's way of representing Japanese—where switches between languages appear as fluidly in the text as they do in talk—I have chosen to italicize non-English words or phrases the first time that they appear, but not again. This way, once they are introduced, words and phrases in Spanish cease to be "set off by any further marks of difference" (Shimabukuro, *Relocating Authority,* xiii).

3. The City University of New York's Center for Puerto Rican Studies, also known as El Centro, was a place that I often visited throughout my adolescence and young adulthood as I learned more about my own Puerto Rican history. *Pa'lante* is the name of the bilingual newspaper published by the Young Lords Party between the years of 1970 and 1976. This became important reading for me when I was taking high school courses in U.S. history and the history of feminism and found works by Puerto Ricans and women of color to be largely missing from the curriculum.

4. One of the first books I was assigned as a master's student pursuing my teacher certification in bilingual education at the Bank Street College of Education was Ana Celia Zentella, *Growing Up Bilingual.* It was the first time that I saw a place and group of people whom I loved so dearly—Puerto Rican families living in El Barrio—represented in a book that emphasized

their social and cultural strengths. It was also the first published scholarship that I'd read examining the linguistic and cultural practices of living in both Spanish and English. Zentella—in both this book and her life's work—has been an inspiration to me ever since and continues to serve as a model for my own writing and research.

5. For demographic changes to the Latino population in New York City, disaggregated by neighborhood changes over time, see Center for Latin American, Caribbean, and Latino Studies, "Latino Population."

6. The early lessons I gained from studying at El Centro were central to the work of starting NYCoRE. The founding members and I returned to the issues of Pa'lante that I'd studied in high school, learning from both the Young Lords Party and the Black Panther Party as we drafted our own version of a ten-point program for teacher activists. In 2010, NYCoRE was granted a Union Square Award by the organization's director—and leading member of the Young Lords Party—Iris Morales. NYCoRE's work for educational justice and Morales's commitment to liberation continue to shape my work today.

7. New York City Department of City Planning, "NYC 2000 Results," shows that Puerto Ricans and Dominicans were the majority Latinx residents in the neighborhoods where I first worked as an ESL teacher.

8. For a critique of the deficit perspectives encoded in the demographic labels that we use in education to identify students acquiring English, see García, "Emergent Bilinguals," and Koyama and Menken, "Emergent Bilinguals." For a related and more recent decolonial analysis of language labels and deficit ideologies, see García et al., "Rejecting Abyssal Thinking."

9. In the early 2010s, when I began this study, immigration patterns changed as Mexican immigrants stopped frequently entering and leaving the United States, instead staying for long stretches of time. A 2019 Pew Research Center report chronicles this shift, noting that these "long-term residents" often stay to live in the United States for fifteen years or more (Passel and Cohn, "Mexicans Decline"). Several recent publications provide book-length treatments of the changes in immigration policy that have led to these demographic shifts. The introduction to Nancy Foner, *One Quarter of the Nation*, and the entirety of Ana Raquel Minian, *Undocumented Lives*, describe how the 1965 Immigration and Nationality Act was a turning point in immigration policy. It created new ways of constructing illegality while coupling them with exclusionary policies focused on border protection. A. Naomi Paik, *Bans, Walls, Raids, Sanctuary*, explains: "Border enforcement has also increased the undocumented population. The difficulty and expense of migrating across a militarized border has compelled many to stay once they make a successful crossing. Indeed a migrant *must* stay and work in the United States longer to recoup smuggling expenses and cannot afford the multiple crossings that once characterized long-standing patterns of seasonal labor migrations. Many

newer migrants thus settled permanently and brought their families to join them, rather than endure unending family separation" (68).

10. Elsewhere I have written about the ways that I, in partnership with colleagues at the City University of New York, have created ongoing research opportunities that helped to sustain these relationships far beyond the scope of the original study. See Mangual Figueroa and Fox, "Refusing Closure."

11. Turner and Mangual Figueroa, "Immigration Policy"; Mangual Figueroa, "Citizenship and Education."

12. Mangual Figueroa, "Fourteenth Amendment"; *Plyler v. Doe,* 457 U.S. 202.

13. A 2010 memo issued to district superintendents and school administrators explains, "While *Plyler* did not expressly address the issue of whether a school district may inquire about a student's immigration status at the time of enrollment, the decision is generally viewed as prohibiting any district actions that might 'chill' or discourage undocumented students from receiving a free public education. Accordingly, at the time of registration, schools should avoid asking questions related to immigration status or that may reveal a child's immigration status such as asking for a Social Security number" (New York State Education Department, "Student Registration Guidance," 1–2). This memo issues a statewide mandate that is based on the federal ruling issued in *Plyler.* Two things are particularly notable. First, the recommended approach to protecting the rights of undocumented students is to avoid any discussion of their status. Second, the focus is on the process of school enrollment and data collection, with no attention paid to the possibility of disclosure at other moments throughout the students' schooling experience.

14. School districts may violate the guidance issuing from *Plyler* by requesting documentation that—while not explicitly referencing immigration status—can implicitly reveal a family's noncitizen status. One example of this might be asking a parent or guardian to furnish a driver's license in a state where undocumented immigrants cannot obtain one. In most U.S. states, noncitizen residents cannot obtain a driver's license, so this can be akin to asking someone to reveal their immigration status. For evidence of such chilling effects that can deter students and families from obtaining a K–12 public education, see American Civil Liberties Union, "1 in 5 New York State School Districts." See also Pratt-Johnson, "Collision."

15. López and López, *Persistent Inequality.*

16. Jeffries and Dabach, "Breaking the Silence," 83.

17. 66.4 percent of children in New York State designated as limited English proficient between the years 2012 and 2016 were born in the United States. This mirrors the national average of 70.6 percent U.S.-born English learners enrolled in public schools. A higher percentage of U.S.-born students are enrolled in elementary school, whereas there were more

students labeled limited English proficient and born outside of the United States in grades six through twelve; more details are available in the fact sheet by Sugarman and Geary, "English Learners in New York State."

18. Jennifer Queenan, Paulette Andrade, Rebecca Lowenhaupt, and Ariana Mangual Figueroa, "Supporting Immigrants in School: Educators' Personal and Professional Identities in Context," unpublished paper.

19. Qualitative studies conducted at the secondary level have shown that teachers may conflate students' language proficiency or ethnicity with their juridical citizenship status and negatively impact students' self-perception and academic outcomes. Dafney B. Dabach, "You Can't Vote, Right?" observes the ways one social studies teacher mistakenly equated a perceived lack of English fluency with undocumented status. In a discussion about voting in presidential elections, the teacher explicitly states that students with limited English proficiency could not vote and would therefore be less motivated to participate in the lesson. Dabach argues that this kind of linguistic profiling undermines English learners' inclusion in school. In another example, Gonzales, Heredia, and Negrón-Gonzales, "Untangling *Plyler*'s Legacy," note that secondary teachers in California—some of whom state that their Latin-American origin students enrolled in ESL classes are destined for jail over graduation—influence undocumented students' exiting school before completing their degree.

20. Here I am thinking of pedagogical approaches like Funds of Knowledge, Culturally Relevant Pedagogy, and Culturally Sustaining Pedagogy. Each has a different emphasis, but all three approaches advocate for a "practice of asset pedagogies toward more explicitly pluralist outcomes" that pushes U.S. public schooling beyond its assimilationist goals (Paris and Alim, "What Are We Seeking," 87). The fundamental argument is that students' cultural and linguistic practices are inextricable from the structural exclusion that they and their communities experience and that school curricula and pedagogy should reflect these lived realities in order to support learning in historically marginalized communities (Vélez-Ibañez and Greenberg, "Formation and Transformation"). By taking a big-picture look at school inequality with a focus on structural failures instead of perceived student deficiencies, these approaches place the onus on educators and policymakers to change the practice of schooling to improve students' learning (Ladson-Billings, "But That's Just Good Teaching!"). See also Gallo and Link, "Diles la verdad," and Alvarez, "Multilingualism Beyond Walls."

21. I admire the work of scholars who make visible their choices regarding the terms they use when writing about the immigrant populations that they work alongside, even when I elect to use other terminology. See, for example, particularly thoughtful accounts of the politics of naming in Luis F. B. Plascencia, *Disenchanting Citizenship*, and Leisy Abrego, "On Silences."

22. Bloemraad, Korteweg, and Yurdakul, "Citizenship and Immigration."

23. For critical explorations of the ways in which the definitions and

criteria for U.S. citizenship—who is eligible for it and who is denied access to it—have shifted over time, see the following: Paik, *Bans, Walls, Raids, Sanctuary,* and Dunbar-Ortiz, *Not "A Nation of Immigrants."* Both trace the colonial origins of the U.S. nation-state into contemporary immigration policies that seek to uphold white supremacy while erasing, confining, and excluding nonwhite immigrants. Ngai, *Impossible Subjects,* and Chomsky, *Undocumented,* provide detailed analyses of the construction of the concept of illegality as it relates to citizenship, along with the development of policies and technologies used to reinforce state borders and punish those assigned this dehumanizing status at different points in time. As an ethnographer of immigrant children, I attend to the macro and micro dimensions of citizenship in order to denaturalize citizenship as a category and to draw attention to the social construction of the term. I am indebted to scholars who make explicit the links between state policy and everyday life in immigrant communities in the United States. Aihwa Ong, "Cultural Citizenship," warns that without attending to the power of the state, studies of citizenship may give "the erroneous impression that cultural citizenship can be unilaterally constructed and that immigrant or minority groups can escape the cultural inscription of state power and other forms of regulation that define the different modalities of belonging" (738). She calls for a view of citizenship as a "dual process of self-making and being-made within webs of power linked to the nation-state and civil society" that may be "at once specific and diffused" (738). For an autoethnographic examination of the intersections between changing conceptions of race and literacy—and the role that schools have played in the construction of citizens—see Ladson-Billings, "Through a Glass Darkly."

24. I thank Cynthia N. Carvajal, CUNY's inaugural director of undocumented and immigrant student programs at CUNY, for advising me to avoid using the phrase "legal citizenship" in this book because it would run the risk of assigning a legal/illegal designation to individuals and families. Leigh Patel, *Youth Held at the Border,* explains her choice not to use this phrasing: the "reductive dichotomy of *legal* and *illegal* obscures the complexity of the political, economic, and cultural factors that permeate the push and pull of human capital across borders" (6). In 2013, when Patel's book was published, mainstream news media outlets like the *New York Times* and the Associated Press still used the terms "legal" and "illegal" immigrant to refer to individuals who had entered the U.S. without authorization. After a public campaign called Drop the I-Word was organized that same year, the Associated Press revised its style book to use the term "illegal" to refer to actions instead of people. Activist anthropologists—including linguistic anthropologists Netta Avineri and Jonathan Rosa—played an important role in this campaign and helped make visible the cost of the linguistic and racial ideologies communicated in the term. For more on the Drop the I-Word campaign and the role of academics, see Race Forward, "Drop the I-Word," https://www.raceforward.org/sites

/default/files/DTIW_update_WhyDrop4.pdf, and Society for Linguistic Anthropology, "Public Outreach to Eliminate the I-Word," https://www.linguisticanthropology.org/i-word/.

25. Ngai, *Impossible Subjects*, xix.

26. More information about the New York State Youth Leadership Council is available at their website (https://www.nysylc.org/). Another good resource is a 2015 Public Broadcasting Station documentary entitled *Don't Tell Anyone* (No Le Digas a Nadie), which features one of the organization's codirectors, Angy Rivera, and her experiences of being undocumented and becoming active in the immigrant justice movement in the United States (https://www.pbs.org/pov/films/donttellanyone/).

27. Fix and Zimmerman, "All under One Roof," 397–98.

28. Rosaldo, "Social Justice," 243.

29. Flores, "Citizens vs. Citizenry."

30. Ngai, *Impossible Subjects*, 3.

31. Within the field of education, U.S. citizenship has tended to be viewed as a set of dispositions and actions that students can realize through political engagement (Westheimer and Kahne, "What Kind of Citizen?"). For an insightful view of the complexities of pledging allegiance, see vignettes in Rubin, *Making Citizens*. See also Westheimer, *Pledging Allegiance*. Each essay in Joel Westheimer's edited volume addresses important distinctions between citizenship, nationalism, patriotism, and dissent in periods of political extremism and war. Thea Abu El-Haj, *Unsettled Belonging*, details "the central role that everyday nationalism plays in drawing youth from im/migrant communities into the racialized social fabric of this country" (32). She examines how the discourses and curricula circulating in one public high school in Pennsylvania serve to reproduce a U.S. logic that treats American Muslim youth as outsiders and threats to the integrity of the nation-state. Going beyond the script provided within mainstream public schools, Abu El-Haj traces the ways high schoolers resist the dominant narrative that excludes them by developing transnational views of citizenship and belonging. Reva Jaffe-Walter, *Coercive Concern*, explores how educational policy and teachers' practices in Denmark shape educators' treatment of their Muslim immigrant students. Jaffe-Walter demonstrates the ways in which educational practices that are meant to celebrate diversity and promote inclusion are in fact based in exclusionary forms of nationalism.

32. For more ethnographic detail on the citizenship grade on the report card and how undocumented parents from Mexico interpreted the term citizenship grade to evoke their child's immigration status as well as their educational progress, see Mangual Figueroa, "Citizenship and Education." For a firsthand account of the significance of the citizenship grade, see Chang, "Undocumented Intelligence." The example of homework assignments evoking multiple meanings of citizenship that are visible on school bulletin boards is described more fully in chapter 2.

Introduction

1. "U.S. Citizen Children Impacted by Immigration Enforcement," American Immigration Council, June 24, 2021, https://www.american immigrationcouncil.org/research/us-citizen-children-impacted -immigration-enforcement#:~:text=Millions%20of%20U.S.%2Dcitizen %20children,family%20member%20as%20of%202018.

2 Ibid.

3. Chaudry et al., *Facing Our Future*; Passell and Cohn, *U.S. Unauthorized Immigrant Total Dips to Lowest Level in a Decade.*

4. The United States Citizen and Immigration Services website lists key terms in immigration policy, among them citizen and noncitizen. U.S. Citizenship and Immigration Services, "Glossary," https://www.uscis.gov /tools/glossary.

5. Taylor et al., "Unauthorized Immigrants."

6. Taylor et al., "Unauthorized Immigrants."

7. Pew Research Center, "Demographic and Family Characteristics."

8. New York City Department of City Planning, "Newest New Yorkers," provides a portrait of Dominican families that relocated in the years just before my starting this project.

9. Teachers' knowledge (or lack of knowledge) about undocumented students can affect their teaching, as Sophia Rodriguez and William McCorkle, "On the Educational Rights," find: "The data from this correlational study reveal that teachers' awareness of policies impacting undocumented students has a positive correlation with their attitudes toward educational rights for undocumented students. Similarly, teachers' awareness has a strong positive correlation with teachers' attitudes," 4.

10. MPI, "Profile."

11. MPI, "Profile."

12. New York City Department of City Planning, "Newest New Yorkers."

13. New York City Department of City Planning, "Newest New Yorkers."

14. All school-level information comes from publicly available New York City Department of Education reports; however, I do not cite them here in order to maintain anonymity at the school level.

15. Burawoy introduction to *Ethnography Unbound;* Marcus, "Ethnography."

16. Erica Meiners, *For the Children?*, offers a brief yet insightful discussion of coming out as the term relates to the "gay liberationists coming out and the outing tactics of the contemporary (youth) undocumented movement," 71. For an example of a Korean immigrant student openly declaring his undocumented status to push for immigration reform during one of Obama's presidential events, see https://www.nbcnews.com/news/asian-america /one-year-later-obamas-immigration-heckler-feels-vindicated-n258951.

17. Suárez-Orozco and Yoshikawa, "Shadow of Undocumented Status," 103.

18. The age range and developmental significance of the term "middle

childhood" varies. According to the book *Yardsticks*, a text commonly cited in resources developed by school districts around the country, children at age ten are highly concerned with classification and schematizing their world at the same time as they are concerned with fairness and rules. The girls in this study were no exception. However, if we consider the guidelines of more recent definitions of middle childhood, then they would not be included within the U.S. Centers for Disease Control and Prevention's age range, which goes from six to eight years old; see CDC, "Middle Childhood." Mah and Ford-Jones, "Spotlight on Middle Childhood: Rejuvenating the 'Forgotten Years,'" 81.

19. This view of children as innocent has a long history that did not begin with *Plyler*. Critical childhood scholars like Thorne, *Gender Play*, and Faulstich Orellana et al., "Transnational Childhoods," have debunked the social construction of the child as an innocent, passive subject. Rather than ascribing to a view of children as innocent, immature, and dependent, they have shown that children are agentic and astute. See also Luttrell, *Children Framing Childhoods;* Meiners, *For the Children?;* Woodhead, "Child Development."

20. López and López, *Persistent Inequality;* Mangual Figueroa, "Fourteenth Amendment"; *Plyler v. Doe*, 457 U.S. 202.

21. *Plyler v. Doe*, 457 U.S. 202 (1982), https://supreme.justia.com/cases/federal/us/457/202/, Powell at 236. See also Olivas, *No Undocumented Child Left Behind*.

22. *Plyler v. Doe*, 457 U.S. 202.

23. Olivas, *No Undocumented Child Left Behind*, 38.

24. Driver, *Schoolhouse Gate*. Pressure on state governments to issue this guidance has come in part from the important work that the ACLU has done to document the ways districts "chill" families by asking them to provide documents to prove residency that may inadvertently disclose legal status. One previously mentioned example is when school districts ask families to furnish a driver's license in states where undocumented individuals cannot apply for one. At the time of the study, this was the case in several New Jersey school districts (ACLU of New Jersey, "ACLU-NJ Sues 5 School Districts that Discriminate against Immigrant Students," press release, October 18, 2016, https://www.aclu.org/press-releases/aclu-nj-sues-5-school-districts-discriminate-against-immigrant-students) and in New York State (ACLU of New York, "Following NYCLU Advocacy, DOJ/DOE Affirm Immigrant Children's Right to Attend U.S. Public Schools," May 7, 2011, https://www.nyclu.org/en/press-releases/following-nyclu-advocacy-dojdoe-affirm-immigrant-childrens-right-attend-us-public).

25. Mangual Figueroa, "Speech or Silence." Parkhouse et al., "Teachers' Efforts," found that the guidance to adhere to a "don't ask, don't tell" policy regarding immigration status is commonplace in schools. However, the guidance on how to uphold this edict through everyday schooling practices is directed to school leaders; as a result, teachers learn of these guidelines

only secondhand and do not have the opportunity to decipher the policy and consider its implications for practice.

26. Interestingly, the New York State Department of Education lists immigration-related considerations regarding students on the portion of their website focused on English language instruction, thereby contributing to the conflation of language ability and immigration status. Parkhouse et al., "Teachers' Efforts," note that this is also directed to teachers.

27. Justin Driver, *Schoolhouse Gate*, discusses the case, concluding that it has had "broad applicability throughout the nation, and has served as a vital bulwark against widespread efforts to deprive unauthorized immigrants of access to education" (353–54). Yet threats to *Plyler* still exist. Isabela Dias describes recent attempts by Republican lawmakers and their advisers to revise the *Plyler* guidance by "giving states the option to deny undocumented students enrollment in K–12 schools" (Dias, "First *Roe*, Then *Plyler?* The GOP's 40-Year Fight to Keep Undocumented Kids Out of School," *Mother Jones*, June 15, 2002, https://www.motherjones.com/politics /2022/06/first-roe-then-plyler-the-gops-40-year-fight-to-keep -undocumented-kids-out-of-public-school/). From the start, *Plyler* has raised the question of how educational policy can be leveraged to deter immigrants from residing in the United States or include them in those institutions most fundamental to this country's well-being.

28. Olivas, *No Undocumented Child Left Behind*, 8.

29. *Plyler v. Doe*, 457 U.S. 202.

30. Gonzales, *Lives in Limbo*, 11.

31. Dias, "First *Roe*, Then *Plyler?*"; Driver, *Schoolhouse Gate;* Olivas, *No Undocumented Child Left Behind.*

32. Driver, *Schoolhouse Gate*, 316.

33. *Plyler v. Doe*, 457 U.S. 202.

34. Meiners, *For the Children?*

35. Jose Antonio Vargas, "My Life as an Undocumented Immigrant," *New York Times*, Sunday magazine, June 22, 2011, https://www.nytimes .com/2011/06/26/magazine/my-life-as-an-undocumented-immigrant .html.

36. Chomsky, *Undocumented*, 163.

37. Chomsky, *Undocumented*, 163. Vargas, foreword to Gonzales, *Lives in Limbo*, refers to childhood as a time when he was "buoyed by the blissful ignorance Gonzales writes about, an ignorance that envelops undocumented children at younger ages when neither they nor their teachers understand their status" (xii).

38. Suárez-Orozco and Yoshikawa, "Shadow of Undocumented Status," 104.

39. Suárez-Orozco et al., "Growing Up in the Shadows," 452.

40. Suárez-Orozco et al., "Growing Up in the Shadows," 453.

41. Suárez-Orozco and Yoshikawa, "Shadow of Undocumented Status,"

107. See also R. G. Gonzales and Leo R. Chavez, "Awakening to a Nightmare: Abjectivity and Illegality in the Lives of Undocumented 1.5-Generation Latino Immigrants in the United States," *Current Anthropology* 53, no. 3 (2012): 255–81.

42. Gonzales et al., "(Un)authorized Transitions."

43. This change in immigration policy accompanied the signing of the Patriot Act into law. This "sweeping law" resulted in expanded definitions of "terrorism," new levels of governance, and an unprecedented amount of funding dedicated to "homeland security" (Paik, *Bans, Walls, Raids, Sanctuary*, 36–37). To paraphrase Paik, those years marked a new approach to immigration enforcement that shifted from policing and militarizing a physical border between the United States and Mexico to instead surveilling and detaining immigrants that reside within the country, often far from the border.

44. Cornejo Villavicencio, *Undocumented Americans*, chronicles the stories of undocumented immigrants from Latin America living in New York City and throughout the country. In the chapters "Flint" and "Cleveland," she focuses on the experiences of children born to undocumented parents in the years after 2001. Her account, like the ethnographic one provided in this book, is evidence of the many ways children hold and manage their knowledge of the threat of detention and deportation. Growing up in an era of ICE has fundamentally altered the everyday life of children in mixed-status homes.

45. Catalina, Jenni, Aurora, and Pita's responses align with a proposal that Jocelyn Solis issued to educational researchers in 2008. "Illegality as an identity," Solis suggests, should be "theorized as the integration of societal and individual histories, rather than as separate, hierarchical, or linear progressions" (Solis, "No Human Being Is Illegal," 183). This view requires an understanding of child development as contingent on social factors, not just individual attributes. In mixed-status families, the disparities associated with an individual having or lacking U.S. citizenship shape the experiences of the entire family and can change over the course of a lifespan.

46. Thorne, *Gender Play*, 3. In this book, Barrie Thorne theorizes and models ethnographic approaches to the study of gender by asking not how gender makes boys and girls different but instead asking how children (or kids, to use the term preferred by the students in Thorne's studies) come to understand, challenge, and create gendered meaning in their lives. See also Marjorie Orellana's essay on Thorne's influence in her own life and career in her contribution to Oeur and Pascoe, *Gender Replay*.

47. Faulstich Orellana, *Immigrant Children*, 135.

48. Stephanie Condon, "Second Grader to Michelle Obama: 'My Mom Doesn't Have Any Papers,'" CBS News, video, May 19, 2010, https://www.cbsnews.com/news/second-grader-to-michelle-obama-my-mom-doesnt-have-any-papers-video/.

49. Bhimji, "Language Socialization."

50. Combs, González, and Moll, "U.S. Latinos."

51. Solis, Fernández, and Alcalá, "Mexican Immigrant Children."

52. Oliveira, *Motherhood across Borders*. For more on the strained relationships that negotiating differing immigration statuses can produce among siblings in a mixed-status family, see Dreby, *Everyday Illegal*; Beck and Stevenson, "Someday I'm Going to Have Papers!"; Zavella, *I'm Neither Here nor There*.

53. Mangual Figueroa, "Citizenship and Education."

54. Solis, "No Human Being Is Illegal." For a recent book-length exploration of children's drawings related to detention and deportation in the United States, see Rodriguez Vega, *Drawing Deportation*.

55. Gallo, *Mi Padre*.

56. Arnold, "Language Socialization."

57. Dreby et al., "Nací Allá."

58. Mangual Figueroa, "I Have Papers."

59. Mealtimes at home are one recurring family activity where socialization to speaking routines and norms for appropriate silences are explicitly taught. Ochs and Shohet, "Cultural Structuring."

60. Muriel Saville-Troike, "Place of Silence" (in Tannen and Saville-Troike, *Perspectives on Silence*), notes that "the time-spaces occupied by silence constitute an active presence (not absence) in communication" (10). This notion of silence as presence is a helpful formulation, although it only accounts for silences that are perceptible to others during an interaction. Other authors with essays in this volume argue that silence signifies by making an impact interactionally on the listeners. Deborah Tannen, "Silence," claims that silence "is always a joint production" (100), and Saville-Troike, "Place of Silence," explains that "silence 'means' what it conveys" (10). In this book, I draw on these claims while also examining instances of silence that may not be noticeable to others—and therefore do not affect them—but that are still meaningful to the individual withholding expression.

61. The strong influences of an ethnography of speaking approach is evident here; see Hymes, "On Communicative Competence." From this perspective, the study of an individual speaker's language use "must take as context a community, investigating its communicative habits as a whole, so that any given use of channel and code takes its place as but part of the resources upon which the members of the community draw" (3). Language use and withholding language are important in specific ways to particular groups of people, so observing when and why someone talks or remains silent teaches us something about the local norms governing communication itself. We might consider silence to be an integral part of competence, as Saville-Troike, "Place of Silence," explains: "an essential part of the acquisition of communicative competence, is how children learn when *not* to talk, and what silence means in their speech community" (11). Affirming the importance of silence in studies of communication, Keith Basso, "To Give Up on Words," writes that "knowledge of when *not* to speak may

be as basic to the production of culturally acceptable behavior as knowledge of what to say. It stands to reason, then, that an adequate ethnography of communication should not confine itself exclusively to the analysis
of choice within verbal repertoires." Basso suggests that ethnographers of
language should specify those conditions under which the "members of
the society regularly decide to refrain from verbal behavior altogether"
(215). Audra Simpson considers decisions to speak or remain silent to be a
twofold calculus: first, a "calculus of our predicaments" between ethnographer and "informant" regarding what topics to broach in the field, followed by a later calculation on the part of the researcher concerning what
to share once data have been collected (77).

62. Ochs, "Transcription as Theory," influentially argues for the need
to pay close attention to children's verbal and nonverbal communicative practices and to adapt our transcription methods to represent them.
Knowing how to talk—and when *not* to talk—is an important part of children's acquisition of competence in everyday conversations; see the early
work of Susan Philips *(Invisible Culture)*, Shirley Brice Heath *(Ways with
Words)*, and Norma Gonzalez *(I Am My Language)*, and others. In this way,
silence points to (or indexes) a set of concerns and beliefs that transcend
any particular conversation. The decision to remain silent or speak up in
any particular interaction is made against a broader sociopolitical backdrop that inflects and informs social life. In Ochs's words, "sociocultural
information is generally encoded in the organization of conversational
discourse and that discourse with children is no exception" ("Introduction," 3).

63. In order to understand the significance of speech or silence, we
have to go beyond an outside-researcher perspective on what counts as expression—or lack of expression. Hymes, "Introduction," calls this an "etic
grid"—what we might think of as a set of insider understandings regarding
what matters to speakers and how they have learned to address them (22).
Knowing when to be silent involves a sophisticated "ability to recognize/
interpret what social activity/event is taking place and to speak and act
in ways sensitive to the context" (Ochs, "Introduction," 3). By fine-tuning
our attention to children's speech and silence with close ethnographic evidence, insights are obtained into the etic grid of children growing up in
mixed-status families throughout the United States today.

64. In her study of Japanese American writing on mass incarceration
during World War II, *Relocating Authority*, Mira Shimabukuro traces the
changing meanings of the term *gaman:* a specific kind of silence resulting
from the suffering experienced in the internment camps. Shimabukuro
examines the governmental narratives that portray *gaman* as a kind of
suffering in silence that valorizes individual tolerance of injustice over
collective outrage. She juxtaposes this with the words of survivors—in
writing and through oral history—for whom *gaman* is a term that acknowledges a tangle of suppression and rage, silence and outcry, that can-

not be easily reconciled. Shimabukuro is relevant to this study because of her insistence on a study of speech and silence that addresses both talk and writing; also important in this context is her instructive claim that "while *gaman* is often discussed in terms of individual survivance, it has, as its base, an ethical commitment to a collective good" (82). Silence in schools is also often construed as an individual action or personal trait that reveals a broader community deficit (Cazden, *Classroom Discourse,* is a foundational book in this area), when it is in fact often better understood as a social practice adhered to by individuals in order to maximize their collective safety.

65. Early ethnographic studies of classroom interaction in the United States focus on comparative analyses of interactional patterns among different cultural and linguistic groups; examples include Cazden, *Classroom Discourse;* Philips, "Participant Structures" (a study conducted on the Warm Springs Indian Reservation in Oregon); and Kay M. Losey's study of Mexican American women in a community college in California. These studies examine what was at the time considered a mismatch between norms for communicative competence between mainstream schooling practices and assessments and those of historically marginalized students. These anthropologists seek both cultural and structural explanations for students' silences and discourse patterns in the classroom. These studies are rooted in questions about the power dynamics that become evident when educators negatively interpret speakers' silences in classrooms. See also Ron Scollon's analysis of the ways that institutions and outsiders—like schools and teachers—can pathologize the silences they perceive in students from nonwhite, racially minoritized discourse communities.

66. Pon, Goldstein, and Schecter, "Interrupted by Silences"; San Pedro, "Silence as Shields."

67. Gilmore, "Silence and Sulking."

68. San Pedro, "Silence as Weapons"; Schultz, "After the Blackbird Whistles."

69. O'Connor, "Language Out of Place"; Rampton and Charalambous, "Breaking Classroom Silences." Breaks in the normative flow of classroom interaction can produce opportunities for teachers and students to reexamine the underlying rules that guide school-based talk. Borrowing from Harold Garfinkel's approach to the study of interaction, I believe we can learn from observing breaches because a person's response reveals a set of tacit social norms that generally go unspoken. Breaches can be as revealing of children's unspoken beliefs as they can be of teachers' understandings of their students, as Baquedano-López, Solís, and Kattan, "Adaptation," show in their study of elementary school science classrooms in California. In the case of children from mixed-status families, who rarely explicitly report on the norms they have learned for disclosing or disguising their immigration status, a breach becomes an opportunity to witness the tacit knowledge they draw on when the topic of immigration arises. In

these moments, silence can serve as a resource to manage the risks that attend disclosure. For another examination of the relevance of breaches to undocumented communities, see Mangual Figueroa, "Embodying the Breach." See also Burruel-Stone, "Centering Place," which applies my framework to develop an anticolonial lens for analyzing schooling discourses regarding place and Latinx students in California. Garfinkel introduces the concept of breaches in *Studies in Ethnomethodology*.

70. Philips, "Interaction Structured," rightly notes that "talk and silence have been viewed largely in the context of interaction structured through talk. There is a need, then, to pay more attention to interaction structured through silence in our efforts to describe both the discourse structure of speech and the larger organization of communication in interaction as a whole" (212).

71. These all rely on what Agyekum, "Communicative Role of Silence," refers to as "eloquent silences" because they presume an audience that receives and assigns meaning to these signifying (and articulate) silences.

72. Mangual Figueroa, "Speech or Silence."

73. We can turn to an ethnographic study of language in a different historical and social context for a helpful heuristic of different kinds of silence. Richard Bauman, *Let Your Words Be Few*, distinguishes between two kinds of silence: literal silence, as in the "refraining from outward speaking" or the "curtailment of speaking"; and metaphorical silence, which involves "outward speaking" dictated by social norms governing divine speech that allows for some forms of speech while restraining others (21–22). Both kinds of silence involve restraint. In the literal sense, talk is completely withheld. In the metaphorical sense, specific forms of talk are permissible if they are considered appropriate for establishing a spiritual connection to God. This formulation provides a helpful schema for understanding the two kinds of verbal silences that appear in this study. There are moments in which children withhold speech, and there are other moments when children refrain from talking about immigration status in one way but replace it with another, more appropriate reference. In both cases, speakers are highly aware of the risks involved in talking, which include losing a connection to the divine or losing a sense of safety at school.

74. Take, as an example, Alberto Ledesma, "The Structure of My Undocumented Immigrant Writer's Block," which recounts his undocumented childhood in California. He chronicles the experience of withholding information at school as a protective stance his parents explicitly taught him. The vague or incomplete answers that he gives as a child on school assignments relating to family history, personal experiences, or ethnic identity lead to tensions that he feels throughout his education as he attempts to reconcile the inherent dilemma between completing assignments ("doing well in school") and the responsibility to keep his family safe. Ledesma's story points to the fact that teachers may perceive a

student's silence as a sign of deficiency when it can actually demonstrate maturity.

75. For a detailed analysis of two school documents that circulated between public schools and mixed-status homes in Pennsylvania—the report card with a "citizenship grade" and a letter to parents about student attendance that refers to "illegal absences"—see Mangual Figueroa, "Language Socialization Experiences," and Mangual Figueroa, "Citizenship and Education."

76. Kate Vieira, *American by Paper,* a study of the literacy practices of documented and undocumented Portuguese-speaking immigrants from Portugal and Brazil, examines the significance of papers that circulate in the lives of undocumented immigrants. Vieira finds that "the meanings attached to immigration documents also infused other papers," among them "diplomas, certificates, and time sheets" (3). Vieira learns that school documents issued in public elementary and secondary schools reproduce a hierarchy of access and belonging between students with U.S. citizenship and those without. As a result, "they often experience schools—public, authoritative, bureaucratic—as extensions of the very state that sought their expulsion" (119).

77. Anzaldúa, *Borderlands / La Frontera,* 42.

78. Anzaldúa, *Borderlands / La Frontera,* 100.

79. In their study of methodological considerations in the study of teen women's sexual desire—a subject shrouded in taboo, stigma, and repression in public schooling—Sara McClelland and Michelle Fine explore "the possibility that [the silence from young women] is not an absence, but perhaps something else: *an absence we know to be present.*" They go on to explain that amid the "stammering and the silence from young women"— sounds similar to those I heard throughout this study—one lesson we must continually remember is that the "presence or absence in young women's narratives" (in their case explicit mentions of desire, and in mine, talk about citizenship) "does not determine its existence" (McClelland and Fine, "Writing on Cellophane," 233, 245).

80. Ellen Basso, "Ordeals of Language," refers to the moments of dissonance that take place during social situations characterized by unequal power relations that can have high-stakes consequences. In these moments, Basso explains, a person may fall silent, suppressing the voice in a way that allows "the anxiety-producing event to be experienced as somewhat more manageable" (122). Basso's use of the word "suppressing" reminds me of Don Kulick's discussion of language, desire, and identity. Kulick, "Importance," calls on us to think beyond what is spoken in interaction and to consider the unspoken—perhaps unspeakable—dimensions of our social identities as well. As he puts it, "To the extent that our goal in thinking about language, interaction and culture is to make claims about how and why speakers use linguistic resources, and how and why those linguistic resources both constrain and enable subjectivity and action,

then it seems crucial to recognize that subjectivity and action ought not to be reduced to literal performance—the 'there' in an interaction. Subjectivity and action should also be understood in relation to what is barred from performance, what is not or cannot be performed—the not-there, the unsaid traces, the absent presences, that structure the said and the done" (616). For Kulick, social identity is not merely something that one consciously wills into being and actively performs or asserts, because in order to portray one particular self, there may be other aspects of the self that must be suppressed. In my study, students may feel that they need to suppress—hide or deny—what they know about their undocumented status in order to outwardly project an image of being a good or successful student to their teachers and peers. To take another example: in a study of indigenous activism, Sherina Feliciano-Santos and Barbra Meek, "Interactional Surveillance," argue that suppression can be a political strategy to advance a collective goal. In their analysis of the assertions and silences of Taíno activists in southeastern Puerto Rico, they "highlight self-suppression as an active technique involved in many linguistic interactions, the interactional outcomes of which then depend on the local contexts, histories, and social relationships presupposed and desired" (375). They study communication between members of the Taíno grassroots community and the colonial Puerto Rican government, finding that "self-suppression and silence became, within the limitations of this particular context, strategic techniques of empowerment" (388). Silence here is a politically savvy choice when communicating with state officials, who could not be trusted to act on behalf of the community's expressed desires.

81. My hope is to integrate the many dimensions of children's communicative practices here—to render visible what William Hanks, "Joint Commitment," calls "the various dimensions of context" needed to "arrive at a joint understanding" (300, 301). For Hanks, "integration is produced through a combination of linguistic, semiotic, and perceptual resources" that include "intersubjective relevance (perceived or inferred), the history of interactions between the parties, the nonverbal setting and other features of context that appear nowhere in a transcript, no matter how exacting or comprehensive it is" (300, 302). This challenge—to represent the anxiety and fear, strength and resolve of children—is part of what I am taking on by presenting a transcript that integrates the aural and physical resources that they use to communicate with one another, with me, and with their teachers.

82. Katherine Schultz, "Interrogating Students' Silences," calls on teachers "to listen deeply to both talk and silence. Above all, inquiring into silence might lead to classrooms where engaged and equitable participation are defined as broadly as possible" (221).

83. Michelle Fine and Lois Weis, *Silenced Voices,* note: "Silence is not simply the absence of exported marginalized voices; it is the simultaneous

and parasitic invitation to voices that dominate and 'other'" (7). That is to say, beliefs and ideologies circulate even—or especially—in the status quo silences of schools, and they communicate who is believed to be smart, moral, or worthy. Classroom practices reinforce these beliefs as students are given opportunities to speak and their contributions are accepted, refuted, or silenced. Rick Ayers and William Ayers, *Teaching the Taboo*, invite us to explore the "taken-for-granted in teaching" and to "open our eyes to a deeper reality through a pedagogy of questioning" (1). They explore the detrimental consequences for democratic learning when so many school topics are labeled as untouchable. They describe a situation that resonates with this study: "Schools routinely suppress or deny the experiences of young people—they know terrible things, but they mustn't let the adults know that they know, and the adults are living in deep denial. Student voices are silenced, their insights ignored, their feelings patronized, their integrity undone, and sometimes, especially in high schools, enormous energy and resources are expended in a project of enforced ignorance" (72). Indeed, teacher education programs that prepare candidates to teach in public schools often sanction professional silences by not raising pressing social issues and making explicit connections to education. For example, few, if any, teacher education programs offer courses or even opportunities to discuss the intersections between immigration and education. In their exploration of models of teacher activism that explicitly discuss the intersections between racism and schooling, Valdez et al., "We Are Victorious," find that teachers and teacher candidates often look outside of schools (that is, their own institutions of higher education and the schools where they teach) to engage in a pedagogy of questioning and to challenge systemic silence. These teachers discover that teacher-sanctioned talk in schools is complicit in the silencing and erasure of the complexities of their own and their students' lives. As one future teacher, Nelly, puts it— referencing Audre Lorde's phrase "your silence will not protect you"—it is important that we have shared professional experiences that "expose our quietness on topics we thought we had raised our voice for" (253).

84. In their interview study of eighteen teachers serving undocumented students in Virginia public schools, Parkhouse et al., "Teachers' Efforts," report that "teachers' capacity for supporting their undocumented students was greatly constrained by unclear policy contexts, chilling school climates, and concerns about restrictions on political speech" (534). As a result, their respondents are caught in a paradox: "they had an ethical obligation to support students' specific needs, but they could not inquire about those needs if they pertained to immigration status. Whereas *Plyler* established a system in which status is withheld from schools, the reality is that concealment is not always possible or even desirable, as knowledge of status often helps teachers better support their students" (535). Sarah Gallo and Holly Link, "Exploring the Borderlands,"

examine the ways teachers respond to their immigrant-origin students from mixed-status families when they learn about their lived experiences. Gallo and Link place teachers on a continuum from acknowledgment to avoidance and call on educational researchers and teacher educators to go beyond a "don't ask, don't tell" approach and to support teachers in their development as advocates by raising the topic of immigration status and educational experiences throughout their training.

85. Mangual Figueroa and García-Sánchez, "New Horizons." See also Menjívar, "Liminal Legality."

86. I draw inspiration for the idea of writing collaboratively from Saavedra et al., *Eclipse of Dreams*, written and edited by a mixed-status "collective of documented and undocumented activists" that includes both university professors and their students.

1. "Recording Everything I Say"

1. Abu El-Haj, *Unsettled Belonging*; Oliveira, *Motherhood across Borders*; Ong, "Cultural Citizenship"; Ramanathan, "Language Policies."

2. Gonzales and Chavez, "Awakening to a Nightmare"; Sassen, "Repositioning."

3. Marks, Ejesi, and García Coll, "Understanding the U.S. Immigrant Paradox"; Suárez-Orozco, Suárez-Orozco, and Todorova, *Learning a New Land*.

4. Smith, *Mexican New York*.

5. Suárez-Orozco, Suárez-Orozco, and Todorova, *Learning a New Land*, 8.

6. Garrett and Baquedano-López, "Language Socialization."

7. Mangual Figueroa, "I Have Papers So I Can Go Anywhere!"

8. See Slobin et al., *Field Manual*, published by the University of California, Berkeley. This manual was meant to guide fieldwork on language use among young children and is significant because it constituted "the first systematic initiative to bridge academic divisions" between psychology, anthropology, and sociology in order to develop a research program for the study of children's language acquisition and socialization (3). Like the authors of the original field manual, I believe it is important to provide details regarding the recording tools and approaches that I used throughout this study. However, in a departure, I will also detail the significant ways that the children themselves shaped this methodology. Ochs and Schieffelin, "Language Socialization."

9. The number of foreign-born and Spanish-language-dominant Latinos who acquired cellphones and smartphones increased dramatically between 2009 and 2012; see Lopez, Gonzalez-Barrera, and Patten, *Closing the Digital Divide*.

10. Mangual Figueroa, "Speech or Silence."

11. I explore this question in a series of publications issuing from an ethnographic study of mixed-status families living in Pennsylvania:

Mangual Figueroa, "Citizenship, Beneficence"; Mangual Figueroa, "La carta de responsabilidad."

12. Tuck and Guishard, "Uncollapsing Ethics," 7.

13. Over the length of the project, the girls began to describe wearing the iPods and having their words recorded as a kind of benefit. As they went on to middle school and high school, they reflected on the way their study participation made them believe that they had something valuable to say. There is no question that being in the study involved moments of discomfort, but there were also many moments in which Jenni, Tere, Hazel, Pita, Catalina, and Aurora developed a sense of confidence. This is expressed in this book's afterword, collectively authored by four of the six original participants.

14. Like the children described in Dreby, *Everyday Illegal,* and those in Mangual Figueroa, "I Have Papers," the children in my study expressed their belief that juridical citizenship—having or lacking papers—is linked to questions of self-worth and fairness.

15. Hill, "Mock Spanish."

16. See Thorne, *Gender Play,* for an insightful discussion of "the underground economy of food and objects" (20)—much like the economy made visible to us when Tere secretly asked Aurora to bring her a pencil that she was forbidden to carry in the lunchroom and schoolyard.

17. The 2016 special issue of *Anthropology and Education Quarterly* provides a longer treatment of the intersections between qualitative research and surveillance. Its articles offer critical ethnographic accounts of students' perceptions of researchers' recording techniques.

18. Rethinking accountability as a central part of our research involves relinquishing the expert role traditionally associated with being a researcher, instituting what Fox and Fine, "Accountable to Whom?," refer to as systems of "collective accountability" issuing from redistributing power among those involved.

2. A Spiraling Curriculum of Citizenship

1. Mangual Figueroa, "I Have Papers"; Mangual Figueroa, "Citizenship and Education."

2. Vieira, *American by Paper,* 3.

3. Vieira, *American by Paper,* 3.

4. Chang, *Struggles of Identity,* 3.

5. Chang, *Struggles of Identity,* 14.

6. Mangual Figueroa, "Citizenship and Education."

7. Mangual Figueroa, "Citizenship and Education."

8. Another case of a school form producing fear in an undocumented parent was a "Notice of Illegal Absence," issued by a Pennsylvania public school district. This mother received the notice in the mail after her son was absent several times without being excused. Her husband had just been detained and deported to Mexico, and amid this crisis, the mother

had to suddenly change residences and jobs. As a result of this sudden instability, her three children missed a lot of school. Instead of opening a
line of communication between her and her children's teachers, the notice scared her, and she refused to visit the school. She called on me to
help restore a clean attendance record without revealing the reason behind the absences. Mangual Figueroa, "Language Socialization Experiences." Parkhouse et al., "Teachers' Efforts," note a similar phenomenon
recounted by a teacher describing something she had heard from the parent of a student in her classroom: "an undocumented mother afraid to sign
forms or come to school to sign those [forms] needed to get her son free
eyeglasses" (537).

9. Mangual Figueroa, "Citizenship and Language." In eighteen qualitative interviews with public school teachers conducted in a "new Latino
destination" in Virginia, Parkhouse et al., "Teachers' Efforts," report that
teachers expressed concerns about how school documents could reveal
family members' immigration status to educators (527). One teacher reported "instances in which she could infer students' status, such as by noticing missing Social Security numbers on forms" (535).

10. Jerome Bruner, *Process of Education*, theorizes that students learn
best when given the opportunity to learn the guiding principles relevant
to a particular subject matter and then apply them to increasingly complex problems within that discipline. Referring to the sciences and humanities, he argues that educators should teach students ideas fundamental to each content area, noting, "A curriculum as it develops should
revisit these basic ideas repeatedly, building upon them until the student
has grasped the full formal apparatus that goes with them. Fourth-grade
children can play absorbing games governed by the principles of topology
and set theory, even discovering new 'moves' or theorems. They can grasp
the idea of tragedy and the basic human plights represented in myth. But
they cannot put these ideas into formal language or manipulate them as
grown-ups can. There is much still to be learned about the 'spiral curriculum,' that turns back on itself at higher levels" (13). Bruner theorizes that
with practice, those principles become heuristics that learners refer back
to and build on as they apply them over time. The idea that these ideas are
forming even if children cannot express them directly is important to our
adapting the notion of the spiraling curriculum to children's understanding of citizenship.

11. Pew Hispanic Center, "Mexican-American Boom."

12. For an example of how show-and-tell is connected to state learning standards and student developmental outcomes in schools today, see
the following guide developed for early childhood educators, guardians,
and parents: New York State Education Department, "New York State Pre-
kindergarten Foundation for the Common Core," Early Childhood Advisory
Council, 2006, https://www.ccf.ny.gov/files/5813/9145/7002/PreK_Common
_Core_2013-10-28.pdf.

13. Joanna Dreby, *Everyday Illegal,* describes a sibling "pecking order" (129) that is based on immigration status. In her book chronicling the impact of restrictive immigration policies on mixed-status families, Dreby finds a pattern in which undocumented siblings are expected to shoulder a greater share of the household chores than their U.S.-born counterparts. Scott Beck and Alma Stevenson, "Someday I'm Going to Have Papers!," found that U.S.-born siblings in mixed-status families displayed signs of the "immigrant paradox" (127): the children and youth in their study felt a kind of apathy and disregard for schooling that ran counter to their parents' insistence that they do well in school. This contrasted with the life experiences of undocumented siblings who worked hard to achieve mainstream success in schooling because they were acutely aware that they could not rely on birthright citizenship to grant them access to higher education or social services.

14. Dell Hymes, "On Communicative Competence," notes that a "confrontation between different systems of competency" (68) permits the ethnographer to observe the ways in which people learn, resist, and even redefine the agreed-on social norms of a particular community. During points of contact between private systems (domestic) and public systems (schooling, travel, or health care), mixed-status family members confronted varying norms about competence related to their experiences as U.S.-born or undocumented individuals. In these moments, parents and children demonstrated their understandings of the specific behaviors expected of citizens, the forms of participation available to those who have citizenship, and the appropriate ways to talk about citizenship status.

15. Alulema and Pavilon, "Immigrants' Use."

16. Cory Turner, "Food Fight: How 2 Trump Proposals Could Bite into School Lunch," NPR News, February 19, 2020, https://www.npr.org/2020/02/19/806155521/food-fight-how-2-trump-proposals-could-bite-into-school-lunch.

17. Mary Romero, "Foreword," writes that "the current anti-immigrant sentiment and high deportation numbers have created a 'chilling effect' in accessing social services and exercising citizenship rights that might place noncitizen family members at risk. Parents are hesitant to use benefits their children are eligible for, like school lunch programs, for fear of jeopardizing future chances for citizenship because they might be perceived as a 'public charge.'" (xvi).

18. Kate Vieira, *American by Paper,* describes moments in which school forms sent home evoked fear in undocumented students and their parents (119). For undocumented high school students from Brazil, submitting forms in order to access internship opportunities or employment, or to prepare to graduate and seek admission to college, produced anxiety about disclosing their undocumented status. She bore witness as students and their parents worried whether the information they were asked to provide on these routine forms could upend their lives in the United States if

they ended up in the hands of the wrong person. Vieira explains: "Perhaps educational institutions were the only sites in which to pursue social mobility, but they were also closely enough aligned with the state that they could plausibly demand papers" (123).

19. Meredith Byrnes, "Learning," demonstrates how school-based assessments that label Spanish-speaking children attending U.S. public schools as in need of remediation affect Mexican-born parents' perceptions of their children's progress. She details the moments in which parents call on their children to "echarle ganas," or put in effort, where effort is equated with achieving good grades and showing progress by the school's monolingual English standard.

20. Roxanne Dunbar-Ortiz, Not "A Nation of Immigrants," notes that discourses that universalize the immigrant experience in the United States operate on two simultaneous ideological levels. On the one hand, this discourse serves to galvanize and unify a national identity integral to maintaining an exploitative capitalist system that depends on the belief in a meritocracy where hard work and sacrifice can result in social mobility, as in the American dream. On the other hand, this view of a universal immigrant experience erases the history of Native American genocide and the enslavement of African people on which this country is founded, leaving no room for understanding the shifting racial and legal classifications that have shaped immigration policy over the last four hundred years into the present. In both cases, the "we are all immigrants" narrative ignores the structural inequalities that facilitate or prohibit assimilation into a U.S. mainstream.

21. The "sample writing" provided by the teacher reads: "Barack Obama, Kenya, U.S.A.," followed by a sentence starter: "My family came to the U.S.A. because . . ." The assignment's evocation of Barack Obama's family connection to Kenya is particularly fraught in this context. It both links questions of immigration to legality (the president represents state power) and summons the birther discourse in which Obama's own birthright citizenship—and thus his right to hold office—was disputed.

22. As David Howard, Coloring the Nation, explains: "The concept of residency is an important issue in Dominican society. La residencia is a term frequently used in the context of Dominicans attaining residential rights and citizenship in the United States. As such, it is a much sought-after status and a significant sign of prestige" (35). Here we see how a term denoting immigration status shaped a child's view of educational documents she encountered at school.

23. The 2011 special issue of the Harvard Educational Review includes a "collection of autobiographical stories" authored by student members of the nonprofit organization Educators for Fair Consideration. One of the stories recounted by Fermín Mendoza echoes Aurora's response to this social studies assignment. The parallels are so significant I will reproduce

the narrative here. Fermín Mendoza recalls a classroom activity on the first day of geography class during freshman year of high school: "One at a time, everyone will reveal their birthplaces. I stare off into the whiteboard, scared. No one in the room knows I was born in Mexico. People start giving simple answers I wish I could use: Houston, San Antonio. Someone says Matamoros, a Mexican City, but I can tell he has papers—he is confident, popular, and I think his parents speak English. I think about the name of my birthplace: Gustavo Diaz Ordaz, Tamaulipas, 'Where-the-roads-were-made-of-dirt-and-family-hens-made-family-meals,' Mexico. I am sure this humble name will give me away. I look at the world map. I don't even know where my hometown is. It's my turn to share now. *Diaz Ordaz, Tamaulipas,* I tell Mr. Giordano. *Is that a big city?* He asks. *Yes,* I lie. *I've never heard of it,* he replies. The next student speaks. I wonder if the class knows I'm illegal" (502). This account provides a rare glimpse—along the lines of the ethnographic accounts that I provide throughout this book—of the moments in which routine schooling exercises that teachers imagine will instill pride in their students and foster connection in fact motivate fear in their undocumented students. Like Aurora, Fermín wished for a simple answer to the question "where are you from?," and like Fermín, Aurora experienced the anxiety associated with wondering whether sharing the real name of the country, region, or town where she was born could put her or her family at risk.

24. Mangual Figueroa, "Speech or Silence"; Mangual Figueroa, "I Have Papers."

3. Speech or Silence at School

1. Ochs and Capps, *Living Narrative,* 2.

2. Two book-length studies address this color-blind ideology and how it shapes contemporary public schooling: Turner, *Suddenly Diverse,* and Castagno, *Educated in Whiteness.* The first focuses on district-level policymaking by educational leaders and how they use a style of "color-blind managerialism" that acknowledges diversity while evading questions about structural inequality and power differences among stakeholders. The second takes a close look at teacher–student interactions in two high schools in a single school district. Castagno traces what she calls an ideology of "powerblind sameness" to show how school conversations about diversity reify a belief that the status quo is acceptable by acknowledging student differences (such as race, ethnicity, language, and immigration) in a celebratory way without engaging in potentially challenging conversations about the structural inequality that often attends such differences.

3. Ochs and Capps, *Living Narrative,* 102.

4. Pita's father, who had been living in Brooklyn for many years before Pita and her mother migrated, was granted amnesty following the

1986 passing of the Immigration Reform and Control Act. As a naturalized U.S. citizen, he was able to petition for a status change for Pita and her mother in 2013. When I met them, they were already several years into the application process.

4. An Interview with the Dream Team

1. Wides-Muñoz, *The Making of a Dream,* a chronicles the genesis of the federal Dream Act legislation, the political debates that resulted, and the nationwide activism that ensued.

2. See Abrego and Negrón-Gonzales, introduction to *We Are Not Dreamers,* for a discussion of the critique of the term Dreamers. They explain that for the volume's authors, "there is deep resistance to the DREAMer narrative and a call for a nuanced understanding of how this critique aims to shift conceptions of deservingness but also of how undocumented subjectivities are negotiated and crafted" (16).

3. Davidson, "New York State Just Passed the Dream Act"; Fernández, "Unfinished Business."

4. Christina Goldbaum, "Dream Act Is Approved in N.Y. to Aid Undocumented Students, in Rebuke to Trump," *New York Times,* January 23, 2019, https://www.nytimes.com/2019/01/23/nyregion/dream-act-bill-passed .html.

5. See the New York State Youth Leadership Council (NYSYLC) definition of a Dream Team at https://www.nysylc.org/dtn. Guadalupe Ambrosio, former Executive Director of the NYSYLC, has been a leader in developing a Dream Team Network throughout New York City high schools and college campuses. For more on the history of Dream Teams in New York City, see Initiative on Immigration and Education, "Comprehensive Educator Modules," https://www.cuny-iie.org/comprehensive-educator-modules.

6. Linguistic anthropologists are especially attuned to the significance of the interview as a highly metalinguistic act in which the social conventions and power hierarchies are on display, including the dynamics of posing questions, negotiating turn taking, and reckoning with the roles of expert or novice. See, for example, Briggs, "Learning How to Ask," which has been influential in my thinking about the metapragmatic significance of the interview.

7. Mangual Figueroa, "Speech or Silence."

8. Chang, *Struggles of Identity.*

9. Brett McDonald, "Pushing the Dream," *New York Times,* November 30, 2012, https://www.nytimes.com/video/us/100000001929737/pushing -the-dream.html.

10. For an examination of cultural-deficit framing, see Baquedano-López, Alexander, and Hernández, "Equity Issues." Dabach et al., "Future Perfect?," is a more recent empirical study of how these deficit beliefs take hold in teachers' perceptions of their students.

11. *Plyler v. Doe,* 457 U.S. 202.

12. *Plyler v. Doe*, 457 U.S. 202.

13. Negrón-Gonzales, "Undocumented," 271–72.

14. See the film *Don't Tell Anyone* (No le digas a nadie), PBS, 2015, https://www.pbs.org/pov/films/donttellanyone/.

15. For more information on traffic checkpoints and immigrants' rights, see ACLU, "Know Your Rights: 100 Mile Border Zone," https://www.aclu.org/know-your-rights/border-zone.

16. For a history of school safety agents (SSAs) in New York City, see the police-free tool kit, "Sustaining Police-Free Schools through Practice," published by the New York City–based nonprofit organization Girls and Gender Equity in 2020 (https://ggenyc.org/police-free-schools-toolkit/), which details the long history of police presence in public schools—both in New York City and around the country—and which notes that SSAs have been under the jurisdiction of the New York City Police Department since 1998. SSAs "are certified New York City Special Patrolmen, and granted New York State peace officer authority—meaning, among other authorities, the power to use physical force and deadly physical force."

17. I have assigned these two Dream Team members pseudonyms for confidentiality.

18. Here Ms. Janet also added more detail about the Dream Team's work with the YLC and explained the YLC's role in shaping immigration policy at the state and school levels: "So the high school . . . after school class has done a lot of work with the group called the New York State Youth Leadership Council, which is a group of undocumented mostly college students and in the protests we saw. . . . Most of the people there were high school students but it was planned by this organization. And they do a lot of really cool work in New York trying to get more rights for undocumented people; especially undocumented students. So like they actually wrote the New York Dream Act. They wrote it and they met with their senators and they talked to them and they said, 'We want to pass this.' And even though it didn't pass, that law was basically written by college students."

Conclusion

1. According to a 2017 report from the Center for American Progress, 16.7 million people "in the country have at least one unauthorized family member living with them in the same household." Mathema, "Keeping Families Together."

2. Dias, "First *Roe,* Then *Plyler?*"; Olivas, *No Undocumented Child Left Behind.*

3. This approach to protecting undocumented students' rights to schooling by shrouding them in invisibility seems to run counter to the spirit of the *Plyler* decision. The justices writing for the majority believed that their decision to grant undocumented students protection under the Fourteenth Amendment would avoid creating what they call a "shadow

population" of immigrant children by integrating undocumented students into primary and secondary schooling. However, federal and state guidance on how to interpret the ruling has de facto pushed students who are undocumented or from mixed-status families into those very shadows, placing the onus on the most vulnerable to disclose their undocumented status to educators when they are seeking out educational opportunities.

4. Mangual Figueroa, "Citizenship, Beneficence"; Mangual Figueroa, "La carta de responsabilidad."

5. Belmont Report, 5.

6. Dyrness and Sepúlveda III, *Border Thinking,* 28; Dyrness and Sepúlveda III, "How Not to Think Like a State."

7. Alfonso Serrano, "Obama Faces Immigration Protests in 40 U.S. Cities," *Aljazeera America,* April 4, 2014, http://america.aljazeera.com/articles/2014/4/4/immigration-advocatespressureobamaondeportations.html; Chishti, Pierce, and Bolter, "Obama Record."

8. For a helpful analysis of the changes and legal battles surrounding DACA—as well as a detailed discussion of the efforts that students, community organizers, and higher education staff and leadership have made to support undocumented students directly affected by these changes—see Wides-Muñoz, *The Making of a Dream.*

9. Chishti and Gelatt, "At Its 10th Anniversary."

10. Nina Totenberg, "Supreme Court Rules for Dreamers, against Trump," National Public Radio, June 18, 2020, https://www.npr.org/2020/06/18/829858289/supreme-court-upholds-daca-in-blow-to-trump-administration.

11. Chishti and Gelatt, "At Its 10th Anniversary." DACA's ongoing "legal limbo" has continued through the program's eleventh anniversary (https://www.fwd.us/news/daca-court-case/#posts).

12. For more on the impact of Trump-era enforcement policies and political discourse on teachers, students, and schools, see the two-part City University of New York TV episode entitled "I Am a Dreamer Special: Beyond DACA," facilitated by Cynthia N. Carvajal, CUNY's inaugural director of undocumented and immigrant student programs, available at https://tv.cuny.edu/show/iamadreamer/PR2010779. Ee and Gándara, "Impact of Immigration Enforcement"; Rogers et al., *Teaching and Learning.*

13. Costello, "Trump Effect."

14. KBI, CMS, and OJE. "Communities in Crisis."

15. In 1982, one of the dissenting Supreme Court justices called undocumented immigrants "wetbacks" during the deliberations over the *Plyler* ruling (Driver, *Schoolhouse Gate,* 354). Trump, who in 2019 called Central American immigrants by the same derogatory name, attempted to revise the *Plyler* guidance by "giving states the option to deny undocumented students enrollment in K-12 schools" (Dias, "First *Roe,* Then *Plyler?*"). From the start, *Plyler* has raised the question of how educational policy can be leveraged to deter immigrants from residing in the United

States or include them in those institutions most fundamental to this country's well-being.

16. Clark et al., "Disproportionate Impact"; Gomez and Meraz, "Immigrant Families."

17. This sense of "feeling illegal" is not surprising, given the dramatic increase in ICE's presence throughout Brooklyn in the early days of the pandemic. One of the undocumented mothers in this study recounted to me the daunting presence of local police and federal immigration officers during lockdown, raising community fears of detention and deportation even as they were counted on to fill the role of essential service workers throughout the city. She also told me about citizens' watches being organized at the grassroots level, so community members could warn one another about neighborhood checkpoints. For more on how this played out throughout New York City and in Brooklyn, see IDF and CCR, "ICE Policing." For additional book-length treatments on the everyday experiences of undocumented immigrants living with surveillance and policing, see Asad, *Engage and Evade;* García, *Legal Passing.*

18. Cynthia Miller-Idriss, "Republicans Blaming Covid on Immigrants Threatens Public Health and Our Democracy," MSNBC, October 2, 2021, https://www.msnbc.com/opinion/republicans-blaming-covid-immigrants -threatens-public-health-our-democracy-n1280599; Camilo Montoya-Galvez, "How Trump Officials Used Covid-19 to Shut U.S. Borders to Migrant Children," CBS News, November 2, 2020, https://www.cbsnews.com /news/trump-administration-closed-borders-migrant-children-covid-19/.

19. Mangual Figueroa, "Citizenship and Education"; Mangual Figueroa, "Citizenship and Language."

20. Public schooling is a site where broader national debates over immigration policy, race, and patriotism are played out. As one example at the federal level, Republican state leaders have threatened to take *Plyler* back to court in hopes of repealing the ruling and discouraging immigrants from coming to the United States. More recently, in 2022, Mexican American Legal Defense and Education Fund issued a statement condemning Texas governor Greg Abbott for threatening to revisit *Plyler* in the hopes of repealing it; this is the same governor who fueled anti-immigrant sentiment by referring to an invasion at the border between the United States and Mexico. Heidi Pérez-Moreno and James Barragán, "Critics Denounce Greg Abbott and Dan Patrick's 'Invasion' Rhetoric on Immigration, Saying It Will Incite Violence," *Texas Tribune,* June 17, 2021, https:// www.texastribune.org/2021/06/17/greg-abbott-dan-patrick-el-paso -invasion-immigration/amp/. The increasing political polarization in this country has made it harder than ever for teachers to broach topics considered controversial—specifically those related to race and immigration— because they fear retribution from their colleagues. At the school district level, Turner, "Districts' Responses," reports that school board members must contend with local residents who express anti-immigrant and

anti-Spanish sentiment, calling for school policymakers to exclude non-citizen students and eliminate bilingual programming. In her study of district leaders' responses to demographic change in two Wisconsin school districts, Turner finds that "these district leaders said the opposition did not impede their efforts to meet the educational needs" of English learners (23). We can see here evidence of conflation of student designation as language learners and their immigration status, perhaps as a precautionary measure to return local anti-immigrant discourse to matters of school language policy that are more easily discussed and managed. This is an indication of how hard it is for school leaders to respond to explicit threats to *Plyler* that take place among their constituents.

21. Through our collaborative research across six U.S. school districts, we found that teachers were scared to broach subjects considered political (Lowenhaupt, Dabach, and Mangual Figueroa, "Safety and Belonging"). Given the national polarization over immigration policy and border enforcement, the subject of immigration has become harder to teach and harder to discuss in school, reinforcing the "don't ask, don't tell" dynamic already in place.

22. Kleyn, *Living, Learning,* calls for "integrating immigration issues into teacher certification" (155); Parkhouse et al., "Teachers' Efforts," advocate for teachers to develop "status consciousness" in order to become more informed advocates who "can counter school climates and societal discourses that can marginalize and dehumanize" (545).

23. Jeffries and Dabach, "Breaking the Silence." As Parkhouse et al., "Teachers' Efforts," surmise from the interviews with public school teachers in the state of Virginia, "because political contexts were always in flux and ambiguous, their [teachers'] actions were often spontaneous and improvised responses to particular incidents. And while they found creative ways to support students, they lacked an understanding of what the law required of them" (538). A lack of clear guidance or professional conversation involving practicing educators has resulted in an ad hoc approach to advocating for undocumented students.

Afterword

1. Most of us added new drawings to our original lifemaps; one of us shifted from sketching to creating a timeline. Creating a timeline was one way of representing continuity while also representing new ways of thinking about my own life that I was grappling with at this time.

2. Faulstich Orellana, "Work Kids Do," 373.

3. Faulstich Orellana, "Work Kids Do," 373; García-Sánchez, *Language,* 10.

4. Metaphors can help us to understand our own thinking about lifemaps and what they represent thematically and relationally for us as researchers. Faulstich Orellana, "Work Kids Do," writes of the lifemaps she cocreated: "I find the metaphor of a camera helpful here. By moving back

and forth between a wide-angle lens and a zoom lens, we may see things that we might not see with a more fixed gaze." We used Faulstich Orellana's work as a model when drafting our own metaphors about the process. Given our long-standing connections to this inquiry and to one another, we believe that these longitudinal lifemaps go beyond a snapshot of immigrant-origin children's lives to provide a panoramic view of how, when, and which kinds of papers become prominent for us throughout a lifetime of growing up in mixed-status families.

5. As of March 13, 2023, nineteen states and the District of Columbia have passed laws that allow undocumented immigrants to apply for a driver's license; National Conference of State Legislators, "States Offering Driver's Licenses to Immigrants," https://www.ncsl.org/immigration/states-offering-drivers-licenses-to-immigrants.

Bibliography

Abrego, Leisy J. "On Silences: Salvadoran Refugees Then and Now." *Latino Studies* 15, no. 1 (2017): 73–85. https://doi.org/10.1057/s41276-017-0044-4.

Abrego, Leisy J., and Genevieve Negrón-Gonzales. Introduction to *We Are Not Dreamers: Undocumented Scholars Theorize Undocumented Life in the United States,* 1–22. Durham, N.C.: Duke University Press, 2020.

Abu El-Haj, Thea Renda. *Unsettled Belonging: Educating Palestinian American Youth after 9/11.* Chicago: University of Chicago Press, 2015.

Agyekum, Kofi. "The Communicative Role of Silence in Akan." *Pragmatics* 12, no. 1 (2002): 31–51. https://doi.org/10.1075/prag.12.1.03agy.

Alulema, Daniela, and Jacquelyn Pavilon. "Immigrants' Use of New York City Programs, Services, and Benefits: Examining the Impact of Fear and Other Barriers to Access." Center for Migration Studies, January 2022. https://cmsny.org/wp-content/uploads/2022/01/immigrants-use-of-new-york-city-programs-services-and-benefits-cms-report-013122-final-1.pdf.

Alvarez, Sara P. "Multilingualism Beyond Walls: Undocumented Young Adults Subverting Writing Education." In *Writing on the Wall: Literacy Education and the Resurgence of Nationalism,* edited by David S. Martins, Brooke R. Schrieber, and Xiaoye You, 106–28. Denver: University Press of Colorado, 2023.

American Civil Liberties Union. "1 in 5 New York State School Districts Puts Up Illegal Barriers for Immigrant Children." July 23, 2010. https://www.nyclu.org/en/press-releases/nyclu-analysis-1-5-new-york-state-school-districts-puts-illegal-barriers-immigrant.

American Immigration Council. "U.S. Citizen Children Impacted by Immigration Enforcement." June 24, 2021. https://www.american immigrationcouncil.org/research/us-citizen-children-impacted-immigration-enforcement#:~:text=Millions%20of%20U.S.%2Dcitizen%20children,family%20member%20as%20of%202018.

Anzaldúa, Gloria. *Borderlands / La Frontera: The New Mestiza.* San Francisco, Calif.: Aunt Lute, 2007.

Arnold, Lynnette. "Language Socialization across Borders: Producing Scalar Subjectivities through Material-Affective Semiosis." *Pragmatics* 29, no. 3 (2019): 332–56. https://doi.org/10.1075/prag.18013.arn.

Asad, Asad L. *Engage and Evade: How Latino Immigrant Families Manage Surveillance in Everyday Life.* Princeton, N.J.: Princeton University Press, 2023.

Ayers, Rick, and William Ayers. *Teaching the Taboo: Courage and Imagination in the Classroom*. New York: Teachers' College, 2011.

Baquedano-López, Patricia, Rebecca Anne Alexander, and Sera J. Hernández. "Equity Issues in Parental and Community Involvement in Schools: What Teacher Educators Need to Know." *Review of Research in Education* 37, no. 1 (2013): 161–94. https://doi.org/10.3102/0091732X12459718.

Baquedano-López, Patricia, Jorge L. Solís, and Shlomy Kattan. "Adaptation: The Language of Classroom Learning." *Linguistics and Education* 16, no. 1 (2005): 1–26. https://doi.org/10.1016/j.linged.2005.11.001.

Basso, Ellen B. "Ordeals of Language." In *Culture, Rhetoric, and the Vicissitudes of Life,* edited by Michael Carrithers, 121–37. New York: Berghahn, 2009.

Basso, Keith H. "'To Give Up on Words': Silence in Western Apache Culture." *Southwestern Journal of Anthropology* 26, no. 3 (1970): 213–30.

Bauman, Richard. *Let Your Words Be Few: Symbolism of Speaking and Silence among Seventeenth-Century Quakers*. Cambridge: Cambridge University Press, 1983.

Beck, Scott, and Alma Stevenson. "'Someday I'm Going to Have Papers!' (¡Algún día yo voy a tener papeles!): Mixed-Status Families in the Rural South." In *Living Together, Living Apart: Mixed Status Families and U.S. Immigration Policy,* edited by April Schueths and Jodie Lawston, 119–36. Seattle: University of Washington Press, 2015.

The Belmont Report. April 18, 1979. https://www.hhs.gov/ohrp/sites/default/files/the-belmont-report-508c_FINAL.pdf.

Bhimji, Fazila. "Language Socialization with Directives in Two Mexican Immigrant Families in South Central Los Angeles." In *Building on Strength: Language and Literacy in Latino Families and Communities,* edited by Ana Celia Zentella, 60–76. New York: Teachers College Press, 2005.

Bloemraad, Irene, Anna Korteweg, and Gökçe Yurdakul. "Citizenship and Immigration: Multiculturalism, Assimilation, and Challenges to the Nation-State." *Annual Review of Sociology* 34 (2008): 1–27. https://doi.org/10.1146/annurev.soc.34.040507.134608.

Briggs, Charles. "Learning How to Ask: Native Metacommunicative Competence and the Incompetence of Fieldworkers." *Language and Society* 13, no. 1 (1984): 1–28. https://doi.org/10.1017/S0047404500015876.

Bruner, Jerome. *The Process of Education*. Cambridge, Mass.: Harvard University Press, 1960.

Burawoy, Michael. Introduction to *Ethnography Unbound: Power and Resistance in the Modern Metropolis,* edited by Michael Burawoy, Alice Burton, Ann Arnett Ferguson, Kathryn J. Fox, Joshua Gamson, Leslie Hurst, Nadine G. Julius, Charles Kurzman, Leslie Salzinger, Josepha Schiffman, and Shiori Ui, 1–7. Berkeley: University of California Press, 1991.

Burruel Stone, T. "Centering Place in Ethnographies of 'Latinx' Schooling: The Utility of a Multi-sited Place Project for Revealing Emplaced Narratives." *International Review of Qualitative Research* 15, no. 3 (2022): 1–27. https://doi.org/10.1177/19408447211068195.

Byrnes, Meredith. "Learning to 'Echar Ganas en la Escuela' (Try Hard in School)." *Texas Linguistics Forum* 59 (2016): 1–11.

Castagno, Angelina E. *Educated in Whiteness: Good Intentions and Diversity in Schools*. Minneapolis: University of Minnesota Press, 2014.

Cazden, Courtney B. *Classroom Discourse: The Language of Teaching and Learning*. Portsmouth, N.H.: Heinemann: Pearson Education, 1988.

CDC. "Middle Childhood (6–8 Years of Age)." U.S. Centers for Disease Control and Prevention (CDC). https://www.cdc.gov/ncbddd /childdevelopment/positiveparenting/middle.html.

Center for Latin American, Caribbean, and Latino Studies. "The Latino Population of New York City, 1990–2010." Latino Data Project, November 2011, 44. https://academicworks.cuny.edu/cgi/viewcontent.cgi ?article=1018&context=clacls_pubs.

Chang, Aurora. *The Struggles of Identity, Education, and Agency in the Lives of Undocumented Students: The Burden of Hyperdocumentation*. London: Palgrave Macmillan, 2018.

Chang, Aurora. "Undocumented Intelligence: Laying Low by Achieving High—An 'Illegal Alien's' Co-option of School and Citizenship." *Race Ethnicity and Education* 15, no. 6 (2016): 1164–76. https://doi.org/10 .1080/13613324.2016.1168539.

Chaudry, Ajay, Randolph Capps, Juan Pedroza, Rosa Maria Castañeda, Robert Santos, and Molly M. Scott. *Facing Our Future: Children in the Aftermath of Immigration Enforcement*. Washington, D.C.: Urban Institute, 2010.

Chishti, Muzaffar, and Julia Gelatt. "At Its 10th Anniversary, DACA Faces a Tenuous Future Despite Societal Benefits." Migration Policy Institute, June 9, 2002. https://www.migrationpolicy.org/article/daca -10th-anniversary.

Chishti, Muzaffar, Sarah Pierce, and Jessica Bolter. "The Obama Record on Deportations: Deporter in Chief or Not?" Migration Information Source, January 26, 2017. https://www.migrationpolicy.org/article /obama-record-deportations-deporter-chief-or-not.

Chomsky, Aviva. *Undocumented: How Immigration Became Illegal*. Boston: Beacon, 2014.

Clar, Eva, Karla Fredericks, Laila Woc-Colburn, Maria Elena Bottazzi, and Jill Wheatherhead. "Disproportionate Impact of the Covid-19 Pandemic on Immigrant Communities in the United States." *PLoS Neglected Tropical Diseases* 14, no. 7 (2020): 185–204. https://doi.org /10.1371/journal.pntd.0008484.

Combs, Mary Carol, Norma González, and Luis C. Moll. "U.S. Latinos and the Learning of English: The Metonymy of Language Policy."

In *Ethnography and Language Policy,* edited by Teresa L. McCarty, 185–204. New York: Routledge, 2011.

Cornejo Villavicencio, Karla. *The Undocumented Americans.* New York: Penguin Random House, 2021.

Costello, Maureen B. "The Trump Effect: The Impact of the Presidential Campaign on Our Nation's Schools." Southern Poverty Law Center. https://www.splcenter.org/sites/default/files/splc_the_trump_effect.pdf.

Dabach, Dafney Blanca. "'You Can't Vote, Right?': When Language Proficiency Is a Proxy for Citizenship in a Civics Classroom." *Journal of International Social Studies* 4, no. 2 (2014): 37–56. https://www.iajiss.org/index.php/iajiss/article/view/149.

Dabach, Dafney Blanca, Carola Suárez-Orozco, Sera J. Hernández, and Maneka Deanna Brooks. "Future Perfect? Teachers' Expectations and Explanations of Their Latino Immigrant Students' Postsecondary Futures." *Journal of Latinos and Education* 17, no. 1 (2017): 38–52. https://doi.org/10.1080/15348431.2017.1281809.

Davidson, Lauren. "New York State Just Passed the Dream Act. Here's What That Means." Women's Media Center, February 7, 2019. https://womensmediacenter.com/fbomb/new-york-state-just-passed-the-dream-act-heres-what-that-means.

"Dear Colleague Letter: School Enrollment Procedures." U.S. Department of Justice, Civil Rights Division, and U.S. Department of Education, Office for Civil Rights, Office of the General Counsel, May 8, 2014. https://www2.ed.gov/about/offices/list/ocr/letters/colleague-201405.pdf.

Dreby, Joanna. *Everyday Illegal: When Policies Undermine Immigrant Families.* Berkeley: University of California Press, 2015.

Dreby, Joanna, Sarah Gallo, Florencia Silveira, and Melissa Adams-Corral. "Nací Allá: Meanings of U.S. Citizenship for Young Children of Return Migrants to Mexico." *Harvard Educational Review* 90, no. 4 (2020): 573–97. https://doi.org/10.17763/1943-5045-90.4.573.

Driver, Justin. *The Schoolhouse Gate: Public Education, the Supreme Court, and the Battle for the American Mind.* New York: Pantheon, 2018.

Dunbar-Ortiz, Roxanne. *Not "A Nation of Immigrants": Settler Colonialism, White Supremacy, and a History of Erasure and Exclusion.* Boston: Beacon, 2021.

Dyrness, Andrea, and Enrique Sepúlveda III. *Border Thinking: Latinx Youth Decolonizing Citizenship.* Minneapolis: University of Minnesota Press, 2020.

Dyrness, Andrea, and Enrique Sepúlveda III. "How Not to Think Like a State." *Anthropology News,* July 19, 2021. https://www.anthropology-news.org/articles/how-not-to-think-like-a-state/.

Ee, Jongyeon, and Patricia Gándara. "The Impact of Immigration Enforcement on the Nation's Schools." *American Educational Research Journal* 57, no. 2 (2019): 840–71. https://doi.org/10.3102/0002831219862998.

Faulstich Orellana, Marjorie. *Immigrant Children in Transcultural Spaces: Language, Learning, and Love.* New York: Routledge, 2016.

Faulstich Orellana, Marjorie. "With Love and Respect for Young People: Learning with and from Barrie Thorne in the Ethnography of Childhood." In *Gender Replay: Reflections on Youth, Feminism, and Schools,* edited by Oeur Freeden Blume and C. J. Pascoe, 36–50. New York: New York University Press, 2023.

Faulstich Orellana, Marjorie. "The Work Kids Do: Mexican and Central American Immigrant Children's Contributions to Households and Schools in California." *Harvard Educational Review* 71, no. 3 (2001): 366–89. https://doi.org/10.17763/haer.71.3.52320g7n21922hw4.

Faulstich Orellana, Marjorie, Barrie Thorne, Anna Chee, and Wan Shun Eva Lam. "Transnational Childhoods: The Participation of Children in Processes of Family Migration." *Social Problems* 48, no. 1 (2001): 572–91. https://doi.org/10.1525/sp.2001.48.4.572.

Feliciano-Santos, Sherina, and Barbara A. Meek. "Interactional Surveillance and Self-Censorship in Encounters of Dominion." *Journal of Anthropological Research* 68, no. 3 (2012): 373–97.

Fernández, Marlen. "Unfinished Business: The New York State Dream Act." North American Congress on Latin America, February 19, 2019. https://nacla.org/news/2019/02/26/unfinished-business-new-york-state-dream-act.

Fine, Michelle, and Lois Weis. *Silenced Voices and Extraordinary Conversations: Re-imagining Schools.* New York: Teachers' College, 2003.

Fix, Michael, and Wendy Zimmerman. "All under One Roof: Mixed-Status Families in an Era of Reform." *International Migration Review* 35, no. 2 (2001): 397–419. https://doi.org/10.1111/j.1747-7379.2001.tb00023.x.

Flores, William Vincent. "Citizens vs. Citizenry: Undocumented Immigrants and Latino Cultural Citizenship." In *Latino Cultural Citizenship: Claiming Identity, Space, and Rights,* edited by William Vincent Flores and Rina Benmayor, 255–78. Boston: Beacon, 1998.

Foner, Nancy. *One Quarter of the Nation: Immigration and the Transformation of America.* Princeton, N.J.: Princeton University Press, 2022.

Fox, Madeline, and Michelle Fine. "Accountable to Whom? A Critical Science Counter-story about a City that Stopped Caring for Its Young." *Children and Society* 27, no. 4 (2013): 321–35. https://doi.org/10.1111/chso.12031.

Gallo, Sarah. *Mi Padre: Mexican Immigrant Fathers and Their Children's Education.* New York: Teacher's College, 2017.

Gallo, Sarah, and Holly Link. "'Diles la verdad': Deportation Policies, Politicized Funds of Knowledge, and Schooling in Middle Childhood." *Harvard Educational Review* 85, no. 3 (2015): 357–82. https://doi.org/10.17763/0017-8055.85.3.357.

Gallo, Sarah, and Holly Link. "Exploring the Borderlands: Elementary School Teachers' Navigation of Immigration Practices in a New Latino

Diaspora Community." *Journal of Latinos and Education* 15, no. 3 (2016): 180–96. https://doi.org/10.1080/15348431.2015.1099531.

García, Angela S. *Legal Passing: Navigating Undocumented Life and Local Immigration Law.* Berkeley: University of California Press, 2019.

García, Ofelia. "Education, Multilingualism and Translanguaging in the 21st Century." In *Multilingual Education for Social Justice: Globalising the Local,* edited by Ajit Mohanty, Minati Panda, Robert Phillipson, and Tove Skutnabb-Kangas, 128–45. New Delhi: Orient Blackswan, 2009.

García, Ofelia. "Emergent Bilinguals and TESOL: What's in a Name?" *TESOL Quarterly* 43, no. 2 (2009): 322–26.

García, Ofelia, Nelson Flores, Kate Seltzer, Li Wei, Ricardo Otheguy, and Jonathan Rosa. "Rejecting Abyssal Thinking in the Language and Education of Racialized Bilinguals: A Manifesto." *Critical Inquiry in Language Studies* 18, no. 3 (2021): 203–28. https://doi.org/10.1080/15427587.2021.1935957.

García-Sánchez, Inmaculada Ma. *Language and Muslim Immigrant Childhoods: The Politics of Belonging.* Oxford: Wiley-Blackwell, 2014.

Garfinkel, Harold. *Studies in Ethnomethodology.* Englewood Cliffs, N.J.: Prentice-Hall, 1967.

Garrett, Paul B., and Patricia Baquedano-López. "Language Socialization: Reproduction and Continuity, Transformation and Change." *Annual Review of Anthropology* 31 (2002): 339–61. https://doi.org/10.1146/annurev.anthro.31.040402.085352.

Gilmore, Perry. "Silence and Sulking: Emotional Displays in the Classroom." In *Perspectives on Silence,* edited by Deborah Tannen and Muriel Saville-Troike, 139–62. New York: Ablex, 1985.

Gomez, Juan Carlos, and Vanessa Meraz. "Immigrant Families during the Pandemic: On the Frontlines but Left Behind." Center for Law and Social Policy, February 2021. https://www.clasp.org/wp-content/uploads/2022/01/immigrantfamiliesduringpandemic_02122021_final.pdf.

González, Norma. *I Am My Language: Discourses of Women and Children in the Borderlands.* Tucson: University of Arizona Press, 2006.

Gonzales, Roberto G. *Lives in Limbo: Undocumented and Coming of Age in America.* Foreword by Jose Antonio Vargas. Berkeley: University of California Press, 2016.

Gonzales, Roberto G., and Leo R. Chavez. "'Awakening to a Nightmare': Abjectivity and Illegality in the Lives of Undocumented 1.5-Generation Latino Immigrants in the United States." *Current Anthropology* 53, no. 3 (2012): 255–81. https://doi.org/10.1086/665414.

Gonzales, Roberto G., Basia Ellis, Sarah A. Rendon-García, and Kristina Brant. "(Un)authorized Transitions: Illegality, DACA, and the Life Course." *Research in Human Development* 15, no. 3–4 (2018): 345–59. https://doi.org/10.1080/15427609.2018.1502543.

Gonzales, Roberto G., Luisa L. Heredia, and Genevieve Negrón-Gonzales. "Untangling *Plyler*'s Legacy: Undocumented Students, Schools, and

Citizenship." *Harvard Educational Review* 85, no. 3 (2015): 318–41. https://doi.org/10.17763/0017-8055.85.3.318.

Hanks, William F. "Joint Commitment and Common Ground in a Ritual Event." In *Roots of Human Sociality: Culture, Cognition and Interaction,* edited by Stephen C. Levinson and Nicholas J. Enfield, 299–328. Oxford: Berg, 2006.

Heath, Shirley Brice. *Ways with Words: Language, Life, and Work in Communities and Classrooms.* Cambridge: Cambridge University Press, 1983.

Hernandez, Ingrid, Fermín Mendoza, Mario Lio, Jirayut Latthi, and Catherine Eusebio. "Things I'll Never Say: Stories of Growing Up Undocumented in the United States." *Harvard Educational Review* 81, no. 3 (2011): 500–507. https://doi.org/10.17763/haer.81.3.50825835358484u6.

Hill, Jane. "Mock Spanish, Covert Racism, and the Leaky Boundary between Public and Private Spheres." In *Languages and Publics: The Making of Authority,* edited by Susan Gal and Kathryn Woolard, 83–102. Manchester: St. Jerome, 2001.

Howard, David. *Coloring the Nation: Race and Ethnicity in the Dominican Republic.* Oxford: Signal, 2001.

Hymes, Dell. "Introduction: Toward Ethnographies of Communication." *American Anthropologist* 66, no. 6 (1964): 1–34. https://doi.org/10.1525/aa.1964.66.suppl_3.02a00010.

Hymes, Dell. "On Communicative Competence." In *Linguistic Anthropology: A Reader,* edited by Alexander Duranti, 53–74. Malden, Mass.: Blackwell, 2001.

IDF and CCR. "ICE Policing throughout the Pandemic." Immigrant Defense Project (IDF) and Center for Constitutional Rights (CCR), December 17, 2020. https://ccrjustice.org/home/blog/2020/12/17/ice-policing-through-pandemic.

Jaffe-Walter, Reva. *Coercive Concern: Nationalism, Liberalism, and the Schooling of Muslim Youth.* Redwood City, Calif.: Stanford University Press, 2016.

Jeffries, Julián, and Dafney Blanca Dabach. "Breaking the Silence: Facing Undocumented Issues in Teacher Practice." *Association of Mexican-American Educators* 8, no. 1 (2014): 83–93.

KBI, CMS, and OJE. "Communities in Crisis: Interior Removals and Their Human Consequences." Kino Border Initiative (KBI), Center for Migration Studies of New York (CMS), and Office of Justice and Ecology (OJE) of the Jesuit Conference of Canada and the United States, 2018. https://cmsny.org/wp-content/uploads/2018/11/FINAL-Communities-in-Crisis-Report-ver-5.pdf.

Kleyn, Tatyana. *Living, Learning, and Languaging across Borders: Students between the U.S. and Mexico.* New York: Routledge, 2021.

Koyama, Jill, and Kate Menken. "Emergent Bilinguals: Framing Students as Statistical Data?" *Bilingual Research Journal* no. 36 (2013): 82–99. https://doi.org/10.1080/15235882.2013.778223.

Kulick, Don. "The Importance of What Gets Left Out." *Discourse Studies* 7, no. 4–5 (2005): 615–24. https://doi.org/10.1177/1461445605054408.

Ladson-Billings, Gloria. "But That's Just Good Teaching! The Case for Culturally Relevant Pedagogy." *Theory into Practice* 34, no. 3 (1995): 159–65. https://doi.org/10.1080/00405849509543675.

Ladson-Billings, Gloria. "Through a Glass Darkly: The Persistence of Race in Education Research and Scholarship." *Educational Researcher* 41, no. 4 (2012): 115–20. https://doi.org/10.3102/0013189X12440743.

Ledesma, Alberto. "On the Grammar of Silence: The Structure of My Undocumented Immigrant Writer's Block." *Harvard Educational Review* 85, no. 3 (2015): 415–26. https://doi.org/10.17763/0017-8055.85.3.415.

López, Maria Pabon, and Gerardo R. López. *Persistent Inequality: Contemporary Realities in the Education of Undocumented Latina/o Students.* New York: Routledge, 2010.

Lopez, Mark Hugo, Ana Gonzalez-Barrera, and Eileen Patten. *Closing the Digital Divide: Latinos and Technology Adoption.* Washington, D.C.: Pew Research Center, 2013.

Losey, Kay M. *Listen to the Silences: Mexican American Interaction in the Composition Classroom and the Community.* New York: Bloomsbury, 1997.

Lowenhaupt, Rebecca, Dafney Blanca Dabach, and Ariana Mangual Figueroa. "Safety and Belonging in Immigrant-Serving Districts: Domains of Educator Practice in a Charged Political Landscape." *American Educational Research Journal Open* 7 (2021). https://doi.org/10.1177/23328584211040084.

Luttrell, Wendy. *Children Framing Childhoods: Working-Class Kids' Vision of Care.* Bristol: Policy, 2020.

Mah, V. Kandice, and E. Lee Ford-Jones. "Spotlight on Middle Childhood: Rejuvenating the 'Forgotten Years.'" *Paediatr Child Health* 17, no. 2 (2012): 81–83. doi: 10.1093/pch/17.2.81.

Mangual Figueroa, Ariana. "Citizenship and Education in the Homework Completion Routine." *Anthropology and Education Quarterly* 42, no. 2 (2011): 263–80. https://doi.org/10.1111/j.1548-1492.2011.01131.x.

Mangual Figueroa, Ariana. "Citizenship and Language Education Policy in an Emerging Latino Community in the United States." *Language Policy* 12 (2013): 333–54. https://doi.org/10.1007/s10993-013-9275-x. Erratum, April 24, 2014.

Mangual Figueroa, Ariana. "Citizenship, Beneficence, and Informed Consent: The Ethics of Working in Mixed-Status Families." *International Journal of Qualitative Studies in Education* 29, no. 10 (2016): 66–85. https://doi.org/10.1080/09518398.2014.974722.

Mangual Figueroa, Ariana. "Embodying the Breach: (In)securitization and Ethnographic Engagement in the U.S." *Journal of Sociolinguistics* 24, no. 1 (2020): 96–102. https://doi.org/10.1111/josl.12406.

Mangual Figueroa, Ariana. "The Fourteenth Amendment." In *Undocumented Immigrants in the United States: An Encyclopedia of Their Ex-*

perience, edited by Anna Ochoa O'Leary, 274–76. Santa Barbara, Calif.: ABC-CLIO, 2014.

Mangual Figueroa, Ariana. "'I Have Papers So I Can Go Anywhere!': Everyday Talk about Citizenship in a Mixed-Status Mexican Family." *Journal of Language, Identity, and Education* 11, no. 5 (2012): 291–311. https://doi.org/10.1080/15348458.2012.722894.

Mangual Figueroa, Ariana. "La carta de responsabilidad: The Problem of Departure." In *Humanizing Research: Decolonizing Qualitative Inquiry with Youth and Communities,* edited by Django Paris and Maisha T. Winn, 129–46. Thousand Oaks, Calif.: Sage, 2014.

Mangual Figueroa, Ariana. "Language Socialization Experiences of Mixed-Status Mexican Families Living in the New Latino Diaspora." PhD diss., University of California, Berkeley, 2010. https://escholarship.org/uc/item/2s04f6sd.

Mangual Figueroa, Ariana. "Speech or Silence: Undocumented Students' Decisions to Reveal Their Citizenship Status in School." *American Educational Research Journal* 54, no. 3 (2017): 485–523. https://doi.org/10.3102/0002831217693937.

Mangual Figueroa, Ariana, and Madeline Fox. "Refusing Closure through Critical Care." In *Critical Youth Research in Education,* edited by Arshad Imitiaz Ali and Teresa L. McCarty, 227–42. New York: Routledge, 2020.

Mangual Figueroa, Ariana, and Inmaculada García-Sánchez. "New Horizons in the Study of Language and Liminality: An Introduction." *International Journal of the Sociology of Language* 279 (2023): 1–18. https://doi.org/10.1515/ijsl-2022-0097.

Marcus, George E. "Ethnography in/of the World System: The Emergence of Multi-sited Ethnography." *Annual Review of Anthropology* 24 (1995): 95–117. https://doi.org/10.1146/annurev.an.24.100195.000523.

Marks, Amy K., Kida Ejesi, and Cynthia García Coll. "Understanding the U.S. Immigrant Paradox in Childhood and Adolescence." *Child Development Perspectives* 8, no. 2 (2014): 59–64. https://doi.org/10.1111/cdep.12071.

Mathema, Silva. "Keeping Families Together: Why All Americans Should Care about What Happens to Unauthorized Immigrants." Center for American Progress, March 16, 2017. https://www.americanprogress.org/article/keeping-families-together/.

McClelland, Sara, and Michelle Fine. "Writing on Cellophane: Studying Teen Women's Sexual Desires, Inventing Methodological Release Points." In *The Methodological Dilemma: Creative, Critical, and Collaborative Approaches to Qualitative Research,* edited by Kathleen Gallagher, 232–60. New York: Routledge, 2008.

Meiners, Erica R. *For the Children? Protecting Innocence in a Carceral State.* Minneapolis: University of Minnesota Press, 2016.

Menjívar, Cecilia. "Liminal Legality: Salvadoran and Guatemalan Immigrants' Lives in the United States." *American Journal of Sociology* 111, no. 4 (2006): 999–1037.

Minian, Ana Raquel. *Undocumented Lives: The Untold Story of Mexican Migration.* Cambridge, Mass.: Harvard University Press, 2018.

MPI. "Profile of the Unauthorized Population: New York." Migration Policy Institute (MPI). https://www.migrationpolicy.org/data/unauthorized -immigrant-population/state/NY.

NBC News. "One Year Later, Obama's Immigration Heckler Feels Vindicated." December 2, 2014. https://www.nbcnews.com/news/asian -america/one-year-later-obamas-immigration-heckler-feels -vindicated-n258951.

Negrón-Gonzales, Genevieve. "Undocumented, Unafraid and Unapologetic: Re-articulatory Practices and Migrant Youth Illegality.'" *Latino Studies* 12 (2014): 259–78. https://doi.org/10.1057/lst.2014.20.

New York City Department of City Planning. "The Newest New Yorkers: Characteristics of the City's Foreign-born Population." 2013. https:// www.nyc.gov/assets/planning/download/pdf/data-maps/nyc-population /nny2013/nny_2013.pdf.

New York City Department of City Planning. "NYC 2000 Results from the 2000 Census." Spring 2002. https://www.nyc.gov/assets/planning /download/pdf/data-maps/nyc-population/census2000/nyc20002.pdf.

New York State Education Department. "Student Registration Guidance." August 30, 2010. https://www.p12.nysed.gov/sss/documents /studentregistrationguidance082610.pdf.

Ngai, Mae M. *Impossible Subjects: Illegal Aliens and the Making of Modern America.* Princeton, N.J.: Princeton University Press, 2004.

Ochs, Elinor. "Introduction." In *Language Socialization across Cultures,* edited by Bambi B. Schieffelin and Elinor Ochs, 1–14. Cambridge: Cambridge University Press, 1986.

Ochs, Elinor. "Transcription as Theory." In *Developmental Pragmatics,* edited by Bambi B. Schieffelin and Elinor Ochs, 43–72. New York: Academic, 1979.

Ochs, Elinor, and Lisa Capps. *Living Narrative: Creating Lives in Everyday Storytelling.* Cambridge, Mass.: Harvard University Press, 2001.

Ochs, Elinor, and Bambi B. Schieffelin. "Language Socialization: An Historical Overview." In *Encyclopedia of Language Education,* 2nd ed., edited by Patricia A. Duff and Nancy H. Hornberger, 8:3–15. New York: Springer, 2008.

Ochs, Elinor, and Merav Shohet. "The Cultural Structuring of Mealtime Socialization." *New Directions for Child and Adolescent Development* 111 (2006): 35–49. https://doi.org/10.1002/cd.154.

O'Connor, Brendan H. "Language Out of Place: Transgressive Semiotics and the Lived Experience of Race in Borderlands Education." *Journal of Language, Identity and Education* 16, no. 3 (2017): 127–41. https://doi.org /10.1080/15348458.2017.1283991.

Olivas, Michael A. *No Undocumented Child Left Behind: "Plyler v. Doe" and the Education of Undocumented Schoolchildren.* New York: New York University Press, 2012.

Oliveira, Gabrielle. *Motherhood across Borders: Immigrants and Their Children in Mexico and New York.* New York: New York University Press, 2018.

Ong, Aihwa. "Cultural Citizenship as Subject-Making: Immigrants Negotiate Racial and Cultural Boundaries in the United States." *Current Anthropology,* 37, no. 5 (1996): 737–62.

Paik, A. Naomi. *Bans, Walls, Raids, Sanctuary: Understanding U.S. Immigration for the Twenty-First Century.* Berkeley: University of California Press, 2020.

Paris, Django, and H. Samy Alim. "What Are We Seeking to Sustain through Culturally Sustaining Pedagogy? A Loving Critique Forward." *Harvard Educational Review* 84, no. 1 (2014): 85–100. https://doi.org /10.17763/1943-5045-89.2.317.

Parkhouse, Hillary, Virginia R. Massaro, Melissa J. Cuba, and Carolyn N. Waters. "Teachers' Efforts to Support Undocumented Students within Ambiguous Policy Contexts." *Harvard Educational Review* 90, no. 4 (2020): 525–49. https://doi.org/10.17763/1943-5045-90.4.525.

Passel, Jeffrey S., and D'Vera Cohn. "Mexicans Decline to Less than Half the U.S. Unauthorized Immigrant Population for the First Time." Pew Research Center, June 12, 2019. https://www.pewresearch.org/fact -tank/2019/06/12/us-unauthorized-immigrant-population-2017/.

Passel, Jeffrey S., and D'Vera Cohn. "U.S. Unauthorized Immigrant Total Dips to Lowest Level in a Decade." Pew Research Center, November 27, 2018. https://www.pewresearch.org/hispanic/wp-content/uploads /sites/5/2019/03/Pew-Research-Center_2018-11-27_U-S-Unauthorized -Immigrants-Total-Dips_Updated-2019-06-25.pdf.

Patel, Leigh. *Youth Held at the Border: Immigration, Education, and the Politics of Inclusion.* New York: Teachers College Press, 2013.

Pew Hispanic Center. "The Mexican-American Boom: Births Overtake Immigration." July 14, 2011. https://www.pewresearch.org/hispanic /2011/07/14/the-mexican-american-boom-brbirths-overtake -immigration/.

Pew Research Center. "Demographic and Family Characteristics: Gender and Age." April 14, 2009. https://www.pewresearch.org/hispanic/2009 /04/14/iii-demographic-and-family-characteristics/.

Philips, Susan U. "Interactions Structured through Talk and Interaction Structured through 'Silence.'" In *Perspectives on Silence,* edited by Deborah Tannen and Muriel Saville-Troike, 205–14. New York: Ablex, 1985.

Philips, Susan U. *The Invisible Culture: Communication in Classroom and Community on the Warm Springs Indian Reservation.* Long Grove, Ill.: Waveland, 1983.

Philips, Susan U. "Participant Structures and Communicative Competence: Warm Springs Children in Community and Classroom." In *Functions of Language in the Classroom,* edited by Courtney Cazden,

Vera P. John, and Dell Hymes, 370–94. New York: Teachers College Press, 1972.

Plascencia, Luis F. B. *Disenchanting Citizenship: Mexican Migrants and the Boundaries of Belonging.* New Brunswick, N.J.: Rutgers University Press, 2012.

Pon, Gordon, Tara Goldstein, and Sandra R. Schecter. "Interrupted by Silences: The Contemporary Education of Hong Kong–Born Chinese Canadians." In *Language Socialization in Bilingual and Multilingual Societies,* edited by Robert Bayley and Sandra R. Schecter, 114–27. Bristol: Multilingual Matters, 2003.

Pratt-Johnson, Yvonne. "A Collision of Practice and the Law in U.S. Schools and School Districts." *Journal of Civil Rights and Economic Development* 28, no. 2 (2015): 219–26.

Ramanathan, Vaidehi, ed. "Language Policies and (Dis)citizenship: Rights, Access, Pedagogies." In *Language Policies and (Dis)citizenship: Rights, Access, Pedagogies,* 1–18. Bristol: Multilingual Matters, 2013.

Rampton, Ben, and Constadina Charalambous. "Breaking Classroom Silences: A View from Linguistic Ethnography." *Language and Intercultural Communication,* 16, no. 1 (2016): 4–21. https://doi.org/10.1080/14708477.2015.1115053.

Rodriguez, Sophia, and William McCorkle. "On the Educational Rights of Undocumented Students: A Call to Expand Teacher Awareness and Empathy." *Teachers College Record* 122, no. 12 (2020): 1–34.

Rodriguez Vega, Silvia. *Drawing Deportation: Art and Resistance Among Immigrant Children.* New York: New York University Press, 2023.

Rogers, John, Megan Franke, Jung-Eun Ellie Yun, Michael Ishimoto, Claudia Diera, Rebecca Cooper Geller, Anthony Berryman, and Tizoc Brenes. *Teaching and Learning in the Age of Trump: Increasing Stress and Hostility in America's High Schools.* Los Angeles: UCLA's Institute for Democracy, Education, and Access, 2017.

Romero, Mary. "Foreword." In *Living Together, Living Apart: Mixed Families and U.S. Immigration Policy,* edited by April Schueths and Jodie M. Lawston. Seattle: University of Washington Press, 2015.

Rosaldo, Renato. "Social Justice and the Crisis of National Communities." In *Colonial Discourse/Postcolonial Theory,* edited by Francis Barker, Peter Hulme, and Margaret Iverson, 239–52. Manchester: University of Manchester Press, 1996.

Rubin, Beth C. *Making Citizens: Transforming Civic Learning for Diverse Social Studies Classrooms.* New York: Routledge, 2012.

San Pedro, Timothy J. "Silence as Shields: Agency and Resistances among Native American Students in the Urban Southwest." *Research in the Teaching of English* 50, no. 2 (2015): 132–53.

San Pedro, Timothy J. "Silence as Weapons: Transformative Praxis among Native American Students in the urban Southwest." *Equity and Excellence in Education* 48, no. 4 (2015): 511–28. https://doi.org/10.1080/10665684.2015.1083915.

Saavedra, Marco, Claudia Muñoz, Mariela Nuñez-Janes, Stephen Pavey, Fidel Castro Rodriguez, and Pedro Santiago Martinez. *Eclipse of Dreams: The Undocumented-Led Struggle for Freedom.* Chico, Calif.: AK Press, 2020.

Sassen, Saskia. "The Repositioning of Citizenship." In *People of Out Place: Globalization, Human Rights, and the Citizenship Gap,* edited by Alison Brysk and Gershon Shafir, 191–208. New York: Routledge, 2004.

Saville-Troike, Muriel. "The Place of Silence in an Integrated Theory of Communication." In *Perspectives on Silence,* edited by Deborah Tannen and Muriel Saville-Troike, 3–20. New York: Ablex, 1985.

Schegloff, Emanuel A. *Sequence Organization in Interaction: A Primer in Conversation Analysis.* Cambridge: Cambridge University Press, 2012. https://doi.org/10.1017/CBO9780511791208.

Schultz, Katherine. "After the Blackbird Whistles: Listening to Silence in Classrooms." *Teachers College Record* 112, no. 11 (2010): 2833–49. https://doi.org/10.1177/016146811011201101.

Schultz, Katherine. "Interrogating Students' Silences." In *Everyday Antiracism: Getting Real about Race in School,* edited by Mica Pollock, 217–21. New York: New Press, 2008.

Scolon, Ron. "The Machine Stops: Silence in the Metaphor of Malfunction." In *Perspectives on Silence,* edited by Deborah Tannen and Muriel Saville-Troike, 21–30. New York: Ablex, 1985.

Simpson, Audra. "Ethnographic Refusal: Indigeneity, 'Voice,' and Colonial Citizenship." Voice 9 (2007): 67–80.

Shimabukuro, Mira. *Relocating Authority: Japanese Americans Writing to Redress Mass Incarceration.* Boulder: University of Colorado Press, 2015.

Slobin, Dan I., Susan M. Ervin-Tripp, John J. Gumperz, Jan Brukman, Keith Kernan, Claudia Mitchell, and Brian Stross. *A Field Manual for Cross-cultural Study of the Acquisition of Communicative Competence.* University of California, Berkeley, 1967.

Smith, Robert Courtney. *Mexican New York: Transnational Lives of New Immigrants.* Berkeley: University of California Press, 2006.

Solis, Jocelyn. "No Human Being Is Illegal: Counter-identities in a Community of Undocumented Mexican Immigrants." In *The Transformation of Learning: Advances in Cultural-Historical Activity Theory,* edited by Bert van Oers, 182–200. Cambridge: Cambridge University Press, 2008.

Solis, Jocelyn, Jesica Siham Fernández, and Lucia Alcalá. "Mexican Immigrant Children and Youth's Contributions to a Community Centro: Exploring Civic Engagement and Citizen Constructions." *Sociological Studies of Children and Youth* 16 (2013): 177–200. https://doi.org/10.1108/S1537-4661(2013)0000016012.

Suárez-Orozco, Carola, Marcelo M. Suárez-Orozco, and Irina Todorova. *Learning a New Land: Immigrant Students in American Society.* Cambridge, Mass.: Belknap, 2008.

Suárez-Orozco, Carola, and Hirokazu Yoshikawa. "The Shadow of Undocumented Status." In *Transitions: The Development of Children on Immigrants*, edited by Carola Suárez-Orozco, Mona M. Abo-Zena, and Amy K. Marks, 97–118. New York: NYU Press, 2015.

Suárez-Orozco, Carola, Hirokazu Yoshikawa, Robert T. Teranishi, and Marcelo M. Suárez-Orozco. "Growing Up in the Shadows: The Developmental Implications of Unauthorized Status." *Harvard Educational Review* 81, no. 3 (2011): 438–72. https://doi.org/10.17763/haer.81.3 .g23x203763783m75.

Sugarman, Julie, and Courtney Geary. "English Learners in New York State: Demographics, Outcomes, and State Accountability Policies." Migration Policy Institute National Center on Immigrant Integration Policy fact sheet, August 2018. https://www.migrationpolicy.org/sites /default/files/publications/EL-factsheet2018-NewYorkState_FinalWeb .pdf.

Tannen, Deborah. "Silence: Anything But." In *Perspectives on Silence*, edited by Deborah Tannen and Muriel Saville-Troike, 93–112. New York: Ablex, 1985.

Taylor, Paul, Mark Hugo Lopez, Jeffrey S. Passel, and Seth Motel. "Unauthorized Immigrants: Length of Residency, Patterns of Parenthood." Pew Research Center, December 1, 2011. https://www.pewresearch.org /hispanic/2011/12/01/unauthorized-immigrants-length-of-residency -patterns-of-parenthood/.

Thorne, Barrie. *Gender Play: Boys and Girls in School.* New Brunswick, N.J.: Rutgers University Press, 1993.

Tuck, Eve, and Monique Guishard. "Uncollapsing Ethics: Racialized Sciencism, Settler Coloniality, and an Ethical Framework for Decolonial Participatory Action Research." In *Challenging Status Quo Retrenchment: New Directions in Critical Reseacrh*, edited by Tricia M. Kress, Curry Malott, and Brad J. Porfilio, 3–27. Charlotte, N.C.: Information Age, 2013.

Turner, Erica O. "Districts' Responses to Demographic Change: Making Sense of Race, Class, and Immigration in Political and Organizational Context." *American Educational Research Journal* 52, no. 1 (2015): 4–39. https://doi.org/10.3102/0002831214561469.

Turner, Erica O. *Suddenly Diverse: How School Districts Manage Race and Inequality.* Chicago: University of Chicago Press, 2020.

Turner, Erica O., and Ariana Mangual Figueroa. "Immigration Policy and Education: Theorizing Policy in Lived Reality." *Educational Researcher* 48, no. 8 (2019): 549–57. https://doi.org/10.3102/0013189X1987249.

Valdez, Carolina, Edward Curammeng, Farima Pour-Khorshid, Rita Kohli, Thomas Nikundiwe, Bree Picower, Carla Shalaby, and David Stovall. "We Are Victorious: Educator Activism as a Shared Struggle for Human Being." *Educational Forum* 82, no. 3 (2018): 244–58. https:// doi.org/10.1080/00131725.2018.1458932.

Vélez-Ibañez, Carlos G., and James B. Greenberg. "Formation and Transformation of Funds of Knowledge among U.S.-Mexican Households." *Anthropology and Education Quarterly* 23, no. 4 (1992): 313–35. https://doi.org/10.1525/aeq.1992.23.4.05x1582v.

Vieira, Kate. *American by Paper: How Documents Matter in Immigrant Literacy.* Minneapolis: University of Minnesota Press, 2016.

Westheimer, Joel, ed. *Pledging Allegiance: The Politics of Patriotism in America's Schools.* New York: Teachers College Press, 2007.

Westheimer, Joel, and Joseph Kahne. "What Kind of Citizen? The Politics of Educating for Democracy." *American Educational Research Journal* 41, no. 2 (2004): 237–69. https://doi.org/10.3102/00028312041002237.

Wides-Muñoz, Laura. *The Making of a Dream: How a Group of Young Undocumented Immigrants Helped Change What It Means to Be American.* New York: HarperCollins, 2018.

Wood, Chip. *Yardsticks: Child and Adolescent Development, Ages 4–14.* Turners Falls, Mass.: Center for Responsive Schools, 2017.

Woodhead, Martin. "Child Development and the Development of Childhood." In *The Palgrave Handbook of Childhood Studies,* edited by Jens Qvortrup, William A. Corsaro, and Michael-Sebastian Honig, 46–61. Basingstoke, U.K.: Palgrave Macmillan, 2009.

Zavella, Patricia. *I'm Neither Here nor There: Mexicans' Quotidian Struggles with Migration and Poverty.* Durham, N.C.: Duke University Press, 2011.

Zentella, Ana Celia. *Growing Up Bilingual: Puerto Rican Children in New York.* Malden, Mass.: Blackwell, 1997.

Index

A former teacher in New York City public schools, **Ariana Mangual Figueroa** is associate professor of urban education and Latin American, Iberian, and Latino cultures at the Graduate Center of the City University of New York.